KT-166-991

THE FINANCIAL TIMES
GUIDE TO
STRATEGY

Other books by Richard Koch

*Wake Up and Shake Up Your Company** (1993)
The Successful Boss's First 100 Days (1994)
The Investor's Guide to Selecting Shares that Perform (1994)
The Financial Times Guide to Management & Finance (1994, 1995)

*with Andrew Campbell

THE FINANCIAL TIMES GUIDE TO
STRATEGY

Richard Koch

FT
PITMAN
PUBLISHING

PITMAN PUBLISHING
128 Long Acre, London WC2E 9AN

A Division of Pearson Professional Limited

First published in Great Britain 1995

© Richard Koch 1995

British Library Cataloguing in Publication Data
A CIP catalogue record for this book can be obtained
from the British Library.

ISBN 0 273 61308 1

All rights reserved; no part of this publication may be reproduced,
stored in a retrieval system, or transmitted in any form or by any means,
electronic, mechanical, photocopying, recording, or otherwise without either
the prior written permission of the Publishers or a licence permitting restricted
copying in the United Kingdom issued by the Copyright Licensing Agency Ltd,
90 Tottenham Court Road, London W1P 9HE. This book may not be lent,
resold, hired out or otherwise disposed of by way of trade in any form
of binding or cover other than that in which it is published,
without the prior consent of the Publishers.

1 3 5 7 9 10 8 6 4 2

Typeset by PanTek Arts, Maidstone, Kent.
Printed by Bell and Bain Ltd, Glasgow

*The Publishers' policy is to use paper manufactured
from sustainable forests.*

This book is dedicated to Ste

CONTENTS

Part III
AN A–Z OF STRATEGIC THINKERS, TOOLS AND
TECHNIQUES, AND CONCEPTS
AND DEFINITIONS

FOREWORD

We know far more about strategy than we did 5, 10, 20, 30 or 40 years ago, but never has the subject been more baffling and confusing to the practical manager or management student. Knowledge has not bred clarity. Insight has not led to usefulness. The so-called experts in strategy – consultants and academics – have enveloped themselves in controversy, obscurity and proprietary techniques. They have pursued new angles, differentiation and innovation instead of handing on the very real value they possess to those who need it most. The result is that for most managers 'strategy' has come to seem either meaningless or hopelessly academic.

But do not despair. The basic concepts of strategy are clear, accessible, powerful, practical, highly useful and relatively uncontroversial. The 'only' problem is that no-one has yet provided a simple guide to strategy and how to use it profitably.

Having searched in vain for such a guide to hand to friends and clients who are running both large and small companies, or to management students and those in consultancy, I have been reduced to writing it myself.

I have emerged from the process with a simpler, deeper and more crusading faith in the power of strategy. And with enhanced respect for the people, like Bruce Henderson and Michael Porter, who invented the concepts, as well as those Japanese, American and European managers who have created vast amounts of wealth by driving their organisations forward with a simple and clear strategy.

For me, strategy is the super-hero of the past fifty years of commercial experience; it has been vindicated by logic, intuition and experience alike. I hope you will come to see why as you read this book, that you will share my faith in strategy, and profit from it. In doing this I claim no special insight or skill, except the determination to strip away from strategy its dazzling and distracting garments and reveal the raw, naked power underneath.

By far the greatest value of strategy is at the sharp end of business, where operating managers are fighting to create and deliver products and services that customers will like more than those from competing firms. Strategy is most useful when used as a mental discipline by practical managers as they go about their day to day activities. This strategy is very localised, very disaggregated, and very decentralised: it is 'Business Unit Strategy', that is, strategy for individual business units, rather than 'Corporate Strategy', or 'Corporate Centre Strategy', which is the firm's overall strategy co-ordinated by the firm's Centre or Head Office.

Business Unit Strategy, the subject of Part One of this book, is always very powerful when it is sensibly developed and used by operating managers. Few people realise this, and since strategy began to be viewed as a separate business area, it is Corporate Strategy that has hogged the limelight at the expense of Business Unit Strategy. Worse still, Business Unit Strategy has usually been developed by anyone but the people (the operating managers in the trenches) who ought to be developing it: instead, Business Unit Strategy has been the province of clever clogs from the Centre or consulting companies. Strategy has therefore been an alien imposition rather than a liberating and directing experience.

Part One tries to put this right, and show operating managers how they can use and benefit from Business Unit Strategy. There is nothing much which should be controversial in this Part, since the basic principles of Business Unit Strategy are so powerful and persuasive, and are largely common ground between all academics and consultants. This Guide provides an accessible synthesis and the only innovation is my attempt to show operating managers how they can devise their own Business Unit Strategies without any help from the clever clogs.

Part One is the heart of this Guide, and the most useful Part. But for amusement and fireworks Part Two is probably even more stimulating.

Part Two deals controversially with Corporate Strategy, or what I call Corporate Centre Strategy, in an attempt to be quite clear about what it is and who does it. 'Corporate Strategy' could be used simply to mean the aggregation of a firm's business units' strategies, or a firm's general positioning against its main competitors. But what most people mean when they say 'Corporate Strategy' is the strategy for the firm at the corporate level, the strategy set and co-ordinated by the Head Office or Centre. And herein lies a hugely important paradox that few people understand.

The paradox is that whereas Corporate Centre Strategy can sometimes create and sustain a great company, most Corporate Centre Strategy destroys greatly more value than it creates.

The first half of the paradox is perhaps widely understood. There are many examples of great companies where the Centre, and almost always one person, has laid down the overall corporate strategy, often a long time ago, and where the Centre has ensured that it is carried out, with extremely impressive results. Examples include 3M, Apple, Canon, Coca-Cola, Ford, Fujitsu, Hanson, Honda, Johnson & Johnson, Marks & Spencer, Mars, Microsoft, Matsushita, NEC, Procter & Gamble, Toyota, Unilever and Yamaha. All of these companies have grown at rates far exceeding those of most of their competitors, have higher financial returns, high market shares, high customer satisfaction and loyalty, high staff morale, and corporate strategies that most informed observers could describe quickly, succinctly and consistently. For these firms, Corporate Strategy is clearly a good thing.

It would be easy to extrapolate from the winners, and say that Corporate Strategy should generally be a force for good, and that if most companies do not have a good Corporate Strategy, all they need to do is to find one.

Alas, life is not that simple. Let me remind you of the second half of the paradox: most Corporate Strategy destroys, is value-destroying not value-adding.

The blame for this state of affairs does not lie (for once) with the thinkers and consultants who have developed the principles of Corporate Strategy. The gurus of Corporate Strategy have not covered themselves in glory, since they have tried to brand their own narrow concoctions of Corporate Strategy at the expense of allowing the variety and richness of potential forms of it. In general, however, most of what is written about Corporate Strategy is sensible as far as it goes. But it does not recognise one fundamental truth, that explains why Corporate Strategy does more harm than good.

The truth is that Corporate Strategy does damage because it is driven by the Centre of firms, where the firms and the Centre are both too big, and where the Centre has more power than it deserves or ought to have.

Many firms have become too big or diversified, both because the costs of complexity and the demotivating nature of being part of something heterogeneous and remote have not generally been recognised, and because managerial inclinations and rewards have favoured size at the expense of the interests of shareholders, customers and employees. Recently the sheer idiocy of the extremes of this development, and the forces of economics, have created something of a back-lash, and the proportion of GNP taken by the largest firms has gone into reverse. But it is still true that most firms (above a certain size) are too large and too diverse.

This would not matter too much, if the Centre of these firms (that are too large) could be persuaded to sit on their hands and do nothing. But it is not in the nature of highly motivated and paid Head Office executives to do nothing. The things that they do, and the reactions of those running the Business Units, end up subtracting enormous amounts of value.

The basic problem is that those creating wealth, those who actually have businesses to run and customers to please, grow to do one or more of the following: to resent the Centre, to deceive the Centre, to engage in politics to further individual careers based on considerations other than performance, to believe that the Centre will always provide, and/or to try less hard than they would if there was no Centre and it was clear that their destiny was in their own hands, that success or failure in the marketplace depended totally on their efforts.

The Centre has to add an awful lot of value just to counter the negative effects listed above. Most Centres fail to do so. This is the key problem with Corporate Strategy. Corporate Strategy, by definition, has to be carried out by the Centre. The more the Centre does, the more it is likely to destroy value in the operating companies.

There is a political parallel. Society needs government. But most governments try to do too much. It is in their nature, even when they are philosophically conservative or market-oriented. Lady Thatcher increased the power and centralisation of the UK Government and bureaucracy. She preached that government should do less, but she made it do more.

The parallel is not perfect. I believe we must despair of government: it is almost completely beyond redemption. But Corporate Strategy, which is much closer to market disciplines, is not so hopeless a case. Part Two explores six potentially good forms of Corporate Strategy, while pleading for most companies to recognise the currently harmful nature of their Corporate Centre Strategies. If my pleas are disregarded, break-up merchants and the general forces of competition will, either quickly or gradually, do what needs to be done.

The final section of this Guide, Part Three, is completely different. It comprises a lively and opinionated compendium of definitions, ideas,

tools and techniques that are relevant to strategy development and execution. It is divided into three Sections – Thinkers, Tools and Techniques,
Strategic Concepts, and Definitions – each then providing an A–Z glos-
sary. The intention is that any term used in the world of strategy should
be included here, so that Part Three can be used either as a work of reference, or for browsing and relatively effortless learning. Words included in
Part III are shown in the two earlier Parts in SMALL CAPITALS so that the
curious reader can refer to them.

ACKNOWLEDGEMENTS

As I have written this book, my thinking has been powerfully influenced by two groups of people: my colleagues at OC&C Strategy Consultants, and the three directors of the Ashridge Strategic Management Centre.

At OC&C, thanks are due to all the consultants with whom it has been my pleasure to work, but particularly to Ian Godden, for his Calvinistic clarity about what he calls 'pure strategy' (as pure as a good single malt); Chris Outram, for his cheerful tolerance of heresy; and above all to Charles Coates, whose new book *The Total Manager* contains a wealth of practical examples of successful strategies pursued by down-to-earth line managers, and from whom I have stolen ideas shamelessly.

My friends at the Ashridge Strategic Management Centre – Michael Goold, Andrew Campbell and Marcus Alexander – have been responsible for a sea-change in my views on Corporate Centre Strategy (Part Two of this book). I believe that their new book, *Corporate-Level Strategy: Creating Business in the Multibusiness Company*, will prove to be a landmark work, that will change for ever our view about the role of Head Office. They were generous enough to provide me with a pre-publication copy of the book, and its influence can be clearly seen throughout my Part Two. In addition, Andrew Campbell was generous with his time in discussing both the ideas behind his book and the contents of Part Two.

I hesitate to tar Goold, Campbell and Alexander with my own views, which are possibly more extreme (and certainly rather less temperately expressed) than theirs. But many of the points in Part Two, that some readers may think startlingly original, in fact derive from the Goold, Campbell and Alexander research. The errors and the perversions of their thinking are, of course, all my own work. Anyone who finds Part Two stimulating should definitely read their book.

I am, as always, grateful to my club of faithful pre-readers, especially for this book Alex Birch, Robin Field, Anthony Rice and Clive Richardson. I would also like to thank Paul Judge for his insights into the Premier Brands experience.

My sincere thanks, as always, go to the team at Pitman, notably Mark Allin, Rod Bristow, Trish Denoon, Sally Green, Kate Salkilld and Richard Stagg.

No set of acknowledgements would be complete without the name of Marian Clarke, whose enthusiasm and practical help have proved endless, and for which I am deeply grateful.

INTRODUCTION

1. THE USE AND ABUSE OF STRATEGY

Broadly speaking, the best use of Strategy is at the Business Unit level, and the most dangerous is at the Corporate Centre.

Business Unit Strategy

The most valuable use of strategy insights is for managers who are running clearly defined businesses. If you are one of these, strategy can:

- *help you define the different parts of your business, where you need to do different things to be successful*
- *show in detail where you make the most profits and cash, and why*
- *understand the customers' perspective and why they buy from you or from competitors*
- *indicate where you should concentrate most effort and cash*
- *scope the extent of likely profit improvement opportunity, from changing product/customer mix, changing prices, and/or cutting costs*
- *help you to understand why you have been successful or unsuccessful in particular areas and initiatives*
- *show up any missing skills*
- *identify businesses or product lines which should be discontinued or sold*
- *show which customers should be cultivated most and how to build their loyalty*
- *identify whether it is appropriate to make acquisitions, and, if so, of what kind.*
- *indicate the importance and most appropriate way of expanding internationally*
- *develop a firm's culture and competences so that it can be more successful than competitors at meeting the needs of its heartland customers*
- *improve the performance of its business units by close financial control based on a consistent methodology applied through the firm.*

Corporate Centre Strategy

For multi-business companies, the concepts of strategy can also be used to build corporate advantage over and above the competitive advantage built by each business unit's strategy. This is, however, an ambitious and rarely achieved aspiration. A more realistic use of strategy is to avoid the common situation where the Centre inadvertently destroys value through an inappropriate corporate strategy.

It is quite likely that since 1960 in the West the concepts of Corporate Strategy have done more harm than good. They have encouraged the Centre of large organisations to do more than would otherwise have been attempted. Most, though not all, corporate Centres end up destroying much more value than they create.

Corporate Centre Strategy is a dangerous box of tools that needs to be handled with great care, as Part Two of this Guide stresses.

Correctly used, Corporate Centre Strategy can have a number of benefits, though realising the benefits requires a consistent and selective approach. Consequently, it is important to work out the most important benefits sought, and to tailor the Corporate Centre Strategy accordingly. Potential benefits of Corporate Centre Strategy (many of which cannot be obtained together) include:

- *identifying short and long term remedies for firms in financial crisis that provide both short and long term remedies*
- *showing when a firm is at a turning-point, and which way it should turn*
- *finding appropriate acquisitions that will enhance shareholder wealth*
- *a system for successfully integrating acquisitions and improving performance*
- *highlighting which businesses have the greatest value, which should be developed and invested in, and which should be sold or closed.*

Incorrectly used, Corporate Centre Strategy can subtract massive amounts of value, even leading to a firm losing its independence or going bust. The most common disbenefits of Corporate Centre Strategy are:

- *destroying the motivation and sense of personal responsibility for success felt by business unit managers*
- *adding to a firm's costs of complexity, and creating a bureaucratic morass that restricts and slows down customer responsiveness*
- *taking cash from successful core businesses to fund unwise diversifications*

- *paying too much for acquiring good businesses*
- *paying anything for acquiring bad, value-eating businesses*
- *paying absurd amounts for acquiring bad businesses*
- *choosing the wrong businesses in which to invest*
- *encouraging the wrong sorts of investment*
- *restricting funds for investment by paying out too much to shareholders or accumulating cash by having too high a required rate of return on investment*
- *taking too much or too little financial risk.*

Who should develop strategy?

It is no use one set of people drawing up a plan, making recommendations and monitoring their implementation by another set of people. The world does not work like that.

A new strategy has to be adapted to real-life relationships between people (employees, customers, suppliers and so forth), gradually introduced, and crafted and re-crafted as circumstances change and the validity of the underlying assumptions are tested, proved and disproved. This is only likely to work if those pursuing the new strategy not only understand and believe in it, but also have the authority and confidence to develop and/or dump parts of it as commercial life evolves. The sad fact is that strategy development is rarely done by the right people. This book is an attempt to put that right.

Business Unit Strategy should be developed by operating managers in each Strategic Business Unit ('SBU'). Corporate Centre Strategy should be developed by the chairman, chief executive, and a few close colleagues, but should be influenced, checked and approved by a cross-section of the best business unit managers.

The second-best solution, which often does work, is for the firm to have a long term relationship with a strategy consulting firm, and for the firm's consultants to develop strategy alongside those who will implement the new strategy, and for the consultants to be actively involved in the implementation, gradually fading out (oh yes! sometimes very, very gradually!) as the operating managers feel more and more comfortable with their ownership of, and ability to adapt, the new strategy.

This method is very expensive, but can be justified by the consultants because the profit benefits are normally a high multiple of their fees (typically the annual profit increases are 5–20 times the total fee). What the consultants do not say is that all of these benefits, and more, could often be obtained if the operating managers were able to develop the strategy themselves. Almost everyone assumes this is impossible. They are wrong.

2. A BRIEF HISTORY OF STRATEGY

The study of Strategy and the development of the micro-economic intellectual foundations of strategic thinking can be traced back at least to Alfred CHANDLER (b. 1918), who was active and influential from the late 1950s. His 1962 book, *Strategy and Structure*, said that corporations should develop their strategy before deciding their structure. He defined strategy as the setting of long term goals and objectives, the determination of courses of action, and the allocation of resources to achieve the objectives. Arguably, the roots of Strategy go back much further, for example to Alfred SLOAN's reorganisation of General Motors in 1921 (though this was only documented in *My Years with General Motors*, not published until 1963).

A case can also be made that Peter Drucker set the Strategy ball rolling much earlier. His 1946 book, *Concepts of the Corporation*, looked at the General Motors example, as well as General Electric, IBM and Sears Roebuck, and concluded that the most successful companies were centralised and good at goal-setting. Drucker was also the first to see that the purpose of a business was external, that is, in creating and satisfying customer needs.

Whether Strategy began in 1921, 1946 or later, it definitely grew to powerful adolescence in the 1960s. The first half of the decade saw a new focus on Strategy in academic quarters. In 1960 Theodore LEVITT published Marketing Myopia in the *Harvard Business Review*, one of the first attempts to look at corporate strategy from a radical and broad perspective; the article has since sold more than half a million reprinted copies. In 1965 came the Bible of strategic planning, H. Igor ANSOFF's monumental *Corporate Strategy*, a thoughtful and incredibly detailed blueprint for planning a firm's objectives, expansion plan, product-market positions and resource allocation.

But perhaps the most important development in the history of Strategy was the founding in 1964 of the Boston Consulting Group

(BCG) by Bruce HENDERSON. Starting with 'one room, one person, one desk, and no secretary', by the end of the decade Henderson had built a powerful machine combining intellectual innovation and boardroom consulting, and had invented both the EXPERIENCE CURVE and the GROWTH/SHARE MATRIX, probably the two most powerful tools in the history of Strategy. More generally, BCG blended market analysis and research together with financial theory to produce the micro-economic analysis of competitors and their relative costs that is the bedrock of all subsequent Strategy. BCG's period of maximum intellectual creativity and invention can be traced fairly precisely to the years 1967–1973.

In terms of invention, then, the 'golden years' of Strategy were approximately 1960–1973.

Further intellectual development has continued since. In terms of books, the most important in the 1970s were *The Nature of Managerial Work* (1973) by Henry Mintzberg, and *Strategic Management* (1979) by H. Igor Ansoff. The 1980s saw the emergence of two other writers who have influenced and deepened our view of Strategy: Michael PORTER and Kenichi OHMAE. Porter, a Harvard academic, shot to prominence as a result of his very important 1980 book, *Competitive Advantage: Techniques for Analysing Industries and Competitors*. Porter argued that the profitability of corporations was determined not only by a firm's relative competitive position (as Henderson had proved), but also by the structural characteristics of the firm's industry, which could be described in clear, micro-economic terms.

Ohmae, a cosmopolitan Japanese, described quite brilliantly how Japanese companies had benefited by using Strategy (though largely without strategy consultants or Western academics). His 1982 book, *The Mind of the Strategies: The Art of Japanese Business*, is compulsive reading, and still one of the best explanations available of how Strategy is most effective when it combines analysis, intuition and willpower in the pursuit of global dominance.

The best estimate is that the number of strategy consultants employed by the leading, recognised strategy consulting firms grew by an astonishing 15–20 per cent per annum compound between 1965 and 1991, and at a remarkably consistent rate. The strategy consulting industry stopped growing between 1991 and 1993, but is now back on a fast growth tack.

It would have been impossible to sustain this growth, which has few parallels in other professional services, without delivering great value. If the customers are right, the value of Strategy has increased, is increasing, and shows no sign of diminishing.

3. SWINGS IN STRATEGIC THINKING: SIX PHASES

The *first* focus, at the end of the 1950s and in the 1960s, was on the best way to plan the development of large, multi-product firms. This was the province of *classic strategic planning* at the Centre, although the dominant prescription was to decentralise into largely autonomous divisions, and to diversify by making acquisitions in attractive but often unrelated businesses.

The *second* and most fruitful period, roughly from 1965 to 1975, was that dominated by BCG and its concept of *portfolio management*. BCG's micro-economic approach was highly prescriptive, telling firms to:

- *focus on business positions where the firm had, or could realistically obtain, market leadership*
- *divest other businesses*
- *focus on cash rather than profit*
- *aim for cost advantage (lower costs) than competitors*
- *manage competitors so that they withdrew from the firm's key profit segments*
- *use debt aggressively to finance growth, reinforce market leadership and raise returns for stockholders*
- *avoid over-extending the product line or building in too much complexity or overhead*
- *use excess cash flow to diversify and apply the precepts of portfolio management to a new set of businesses.*

BCG's ideas encouraged two already-established and related trends; towards building up large central planning departments in conglomerates, and towards further diversification. Neither of these was central to BCG's view of the world, yet both came back to haunt BCG later.

The *third phase*, the mid to late 1970s, was one of intellectual exhaustion, corporate disillusion, and a retreat into pragmatism on the part of the strategists. By now it was clear that the micro-economic techniques for analysing competitive advantage were very powerful. They were increasingly used, however, not at the level of central, corporate strategy, but for developing *business unit strategy*. This was partly because the earlier promise of central portfolio management became increasingly discredited. After the oil price shock of 1973 and the stock market crash of 1974, which hit go-go conglomerates particularly hard, the virtues of both central planning and conglomerate diversification became seriously tarnished. Further, firms like GE and Siemens that had established huge central strategic planning departments soon found the results from these bureaucratic behemoths profoundly disappointing. Intellectually, the GROWTH/ SHARE MATRIX, the icon of portfolio management, came under sustained attack. The assault was largely misconceived, but BCG chose discretion rather than valour. The BCG MATRIX went largely undefended and became unfairly neglected.

The *fourth* strand in strategic thinking, stretching from 1973 to the present, was a mild dose of heresy, was a wave of reaction to the excessively analytical orientation of the Boston school. It involved a realisation that firms generally did not derive their strategies scientifically and rigorously, and a celebration of the intuitive, adaptive and creative aspects of strategy.

In 1973, Henry Mintzberg challenged accepted thinking about *The Nature of Managerial Work*, pointing out that successful chief executives were intuitive action men, not reflective planners, that they cherished soft information and anecdotes rather than hard facts and figures, and that they read and wrote little, preferring face to face communication and decision-making. Mintzberg has since developed the idea of 'crafting strategy' using the creative, right-hand side of the brain, rather than the logical left side.

The 1980s also brought to prominence Kenichi Ohmae's celebration of successful Japanese strategists: intuitive, creative leaders of Honda, Toyota, Matsushita and other firms, who were totally obsessed with establishing market leadership, beating competitors, and satisfying customers. The period from 1980 to 1994 has further consolidated the ranks of the *soft strategists*, influential writers like Charles HANDY, Rosabeth Moss KANTER, Tom PETERS, Richard SCHONBERGER, and Robert WATERMAN.

The 1980s also saw the *fifth development*: the strengthening of the rigorous micro-economics school of Strategy, with the emergence of the Michael Porter phenomenon. Porter extended the BCG framework of competitive advantage to include structural industry factors like the threat from new entrants, the bargaining power of customers and suppliers, and the threat from substitutes. His message, though based on additional data and analyses, was similar to that of BCG from the start:

the firm should try to find markets and niches where it could dominate and erect barriers against competition, either by low cost or by product/service differentiation. Porter also built on early work by economists and strategy consultants and developed a theory of national competitive advantage to overlay or underpin the micro-economic analysis of individual firms' competitive advantage.

The *sixth trend* has been a new focus on a firm's skills or *competences*, its sense of MISSION, and on the role of the Centre as the *parent* of subsidiaries. The basic idea is that head office strategy should not be about resource allocation, but rather the creation of ambition and skills which can then be applied across several markets. This trend includes several academics, including Gary Hamel, C K Prahalad, Michael GOOLD and Andrew CAMPBELL, as well as shading into the ranks of the fourth school mentioned above.

These trends represent more a progressive enriching of strategic insight than a set of contradictions. At the level of the strategy consultant there have been other influences, notably the renewed integration of strategic analysis and focus with cost reduction (most recently in Business Process Re-engineering); the application of competitive data-gathering and analysis in order to value acquisition candidates; the emphasis on quality and responsiveness to customers; the importance of TIME-BASED COMPETITION, that is, getting the product to the customer as quickly as possible; a renewed focus on limiting the product-line, on outsourcing and on the part of the VALUE CHAIN where the firm can have an advantage, in order to reduce the COSTS OF COMPLEXITY; and a new emphasis on organisation structure as determining the ability of an organisation to get close to the customer and respond appropriately.

At the same time, however, the work of the 1995 strategist is recognisably the same as that of the 1968 strategist. Its core is establishing competitive advantage over competitors by specialising, business focus and segmentation, attaining a low cost position, and having a better product or service. The primitive concepts developed by BCG in the late 1960s are as relevant as ever.

4. TOWARDS A SYNTHESIS

Originality in strategic thinking is of much less importance than synthesising what is already available, being clear about where it is most useful and about the trade-offs between different approaches, and putting the heart of strategy back where it belongs, in the messy entrails of business unit reality.

My charter for making strategy more useful stresses the following five points:

(1) *Business Unit Strategy has greater value than Corporate Centre Strategy.*

(2) *Operating managers are the people to 'do' strategy*, and that as far as possible the well meaning strategy sponsors like consultants and the Centre stay well out of sight.

(3) *Corporate Centres should do less* and if appropriate de-merge or sell large parts of the current corporate portfolio.

(4) *There are different and largely incompatible Corporate Centre Strategies*, so that we have a much more contingent view of what the Centre should be doing, rather than trying to impose one form of Corporate Centre Strategy on all firms, regardless of their circumstances and skills.

(5) *You should be pragmatic about the amount of effort required in formulating strategy.* Be willing to gather insight and improve decision-making, without trying to prove beyond any reasonable doubt that any particular strategy is correct. This method of 'progressive approximation' is discussed immediately below.

5. PROGRESSIVE APPROXIMATION IN DEVELOPING STRATEGY

A great deal of time can be wasted on trying to get precise and definite answers to strategic issues. Very often the worst result is not the waste of time, but exhaustion or impatience on the part of the participants, leading them to throw out strategic thinking as being too academic, wearisome or anti-action. The answer to this syndrome is *Progressive Approximation*.

The basic point is that you should come up with your best initial answer very quickly, and then decide whether it is worth the time and effort to improve on it by data-gathering and analysis. This is actually the way nearly all managers and human beings generally behave as we go about our daily lives, and I see no reason why strategy development should be an exception.

The procedure is:

- *State as clearly and crisply as you can the questions you want to answer: the Critical Issues. The idea is that if you knew the answers to the Critical Issues you would know exactly what to do. Do this on one sheet of paper: you should have no more than seven Critical Issues (ideally between 4 and 6).*
- *Then construct, on another clean, single sheet of paper, your Hypotheses on the Critical Issues. Your hypothesis on each Critical Issue is your best guess at what the answer might be. At this stage it matters not a hoot whether you are right or wrong; the key thing is to imagine the shape of a possible answer, so that you can then reframe the hypothesis later in the light of new information or insight.*
- *Now list on a third sheet the information you would ideally like to help you resolve each Critical Issue. When you have finished, take another sheet of paper and compile two columns, labelled Most Important Data on the left and Easiest-to-Find Data on the right, and rank the information you want under both headings. Decide as a first cut which bits of information you would think about acquiring: in other words, some combination of the most important and most accessible. Circle the data you aim to collect in this first round.*
- *Decide who amongst your fellow-managers to involve in the strategy development process. This should include anyone who will be important in actually carrying out the new strategy. Then ask each of them to go through the steps above.*
- *You and your colleagues should then meet to compare notes and come up with a consensus three pages of Critical Issues, Hypotheses, and Data. Decide how the data are to be acquired, who is to do this, and when you will all meet again to review the results.*
- *Meet again as agreed, review the new data, and see whether it is pretty clear what the new strategy should be. If you are still in serious doubt, or there is lack of consensus, agree what the most important points still at issue are, and decide what data should be gathered in the second round to help settle the issue. Then decide who will collect the data and when you will meet again as a group.*
- *Continue the process until you are agreed either on the answer, or there is a consensus that the answer is likely to be X, and that the cost and delay involved in further investigation is not merited, so that everyone agrees that X should be pursued.*

This process of progressive approximation will give you a quicker, cheaper and probably better answer than conventional methods, but the key benefit is that the new strategy will be implemented more quickly and effectively. On some complex and important issues you may still need to use consultants, but do it under the control of the working managers and do not allow them to usurp the process. You, the operating managers, must remain in charge, and you must do the main thinking.

It is now time to start: with strategy for your own business.

Part I

BUSINESS UNIT STRATEGY

A Do It Yourself Guide

1. OVERVIEW

Business Unit Strategy is the process of developing strategy for a single, largely self-contained business. The business unit could be a whole firm in a small or medium-sized company (or even in a large firm focussed on a single line of business), or a separate, largely autonomous part of a larger firm, comprising a profit centre that has its own set of external customers and competitors (often called an 'SBU', Strategic Business Unit).

This Part will take you through a step-by-step guide to developing strategy for your Business Unit. It assumes you have a real-life business for which you wish to develop or validate strategy. If you don't, it will be easier and more rewarding for you to think of a business you know fairly well – perhaps that of a friend or relative or one you have worked in – and imagine that you are developing its strategy.

The first thing to appreciate is that developing a strategy is not difficult. It is only made to seem difficult by the strategy 'professionals': academics, corporate planners and consultants. Anyone with a reasonable degree of intelligence and knowledge about business can develop a strategy. The first barrier to overcome is the sense of intimidation or fear of stepping over the threshold.

The second barrier is the jargon. The language of strategy is often peculiar. As with most fields of study, the jargon is actually quite useful as a form of shorthand once you have mastered it. I try to explain exactly what I mean by any unfamiliar term, but if you run into difficulties, refer to the A–Z definitions in Part Three. A bit of patience and perseverance should soon make the meaning clear.

Apart from a short conclusion, there are eight sections in this Part, each taking a particular question or topic that will together make up the total picture of Business Unit Strategy. Each section explains the basic idea before providing displays and checklists illustrating the points. Wherever possible you should try to reproduce similar displays for your own business. Do not worry initially if you feel you don't have the information to sketch out your own display: just take your best guess, and then see what insight would follow if your guess were right.

Later you may want to go back and collect whatever data are necessary to compile a more correct display. It is very important, however, to get the total picture of Business Unit Strategy by imagining what it could be in the round. If you stop every time you don't have the answer to a question you will never complete the exercise and will lose interest. If you carry on and see the power of the total process, you will want to go back and make sure your assumptions were probably correct. So the rule is: first time round, if you don't know the answer, *guess!*

To illustrate the voyage of strategy development and discovery I will use the example of one particular American company, which I shall call the United Tea Corporation (UTC). This is a real-life case history but disguised to protect the guilty. We will show how strategy development changed the views of UTC's top executives and see whether its CEO, Randy Mayhew, manages to hang on to his job.

United Tea Corporation
Can Strategy Save Randy?

Randy called me up one warm and sunny November day and asked me to visit UTC's Pasadena head office. UTC is one of America's largest suppliers of branded tea, mainly in tagged bags, and part of a large conglomerate in branded goods generally.

When I arrived Randy, an old friend, came straight to the point. 'I can't figure out what's wrong', he told me. 'We keep growing our sales but our profits hardly go up at all and our ROI [Return on Investment] keeps slipping. We've missed our budgets in the last two quarters and if I can't explain to Chicago [the conglomerate's head office] what's wrong and how I'm gonna fix it, I'm history.'

Randy explained that he was a hands-on manager who'd never had much time for 'all that strategy stuff', but he wanted me to sit down with him (why do Americans always use that expression?) over a weekend and work out what was going wrong, and whether it could be fixed. As Randy had done me a favour in the past I agreed to see if I could help.

I have a list of eight questions to ask both you (as you think about your firm) and Randy. The first question looks easier than it is. It is also the beginning of wisdom and the foundation of all later strategy.

2. WHAT BUSINESSES ARE YOU IN?

Within your total Business Unit, there are almost certainly a lot of different businesses, or BUSINESS SEGMENTS: far more than you realise. The first step is to define what these different Business Segments (or 'segments' for short) are.

Let me explain why this is important. One of the most glorious insights about life, the Universe and everything, is the EIGHTY/TWENTY (80/20) RULE. This states that 80 per cent of the value of any activity is likely to come from 20 per cent of the inputs. Thus, 80 per cent of the value you generate in your work, or come to that, in your home life, is likely to come from the most useful 20 per cent of your time. Similarly, 80 per cent of the profits of a firm are likely to come from 20 per cent of its products. Eighty per cent of the value in a book is likely to come from 20 per cent of its pages (this does not stop publishers churning out long books, because we consumers just won't believe that a short book is worth as much as a longer one!). And so on. Most people could add much more value to the world, and be happier, if they worked out what their most productive 20 per cent of activities were, doubled the amount of time spent on these, and cut out most of the rest.

The 80/20 Rule applies to business, but before you can use it, you need to know (a) what Business Segments you are in (the subject of this section) and (b) what the true profitability of each is (covered by the following section).

What do I mean by a Business Segment? Intuitively, this is anything that a separate product, service or activity; or anything going to one group of customers as opposed to another group; or anything where the main competitor you face is different; or anything that may have different profitability.

Let me illustrate this with some extreme examples. For a publisher, each book published is a separate segment, since its profitability depends on how many copies it sells, and that is largely independent of how many copies of other books are sold (this would not be true, for example, if a certain well-known writer like Dick Francis or Jeffrey Archer *always* sold a given, large and predictable number of books, or if the publishers' cookery books *always* had the same sales, no matter who the author: in this case the segment would be all Dick Francis books or all cookery books).

Another example is provided by a country's postal service. Since Rowland Hill's penny post, most postal authorities charge the same for delivering a letter, whether it goes to the next street or hundreds of miles away. But for the French post office, the letters delivered in Paris comprise a much more profitable segment than the letters going to a remote Pyrenean village near the Spanish border.

Similarly, different customers for the same product are very often different segments. A manufacturer of baked beans will get much less for them from the largest supermarket chains than from smaller chains or independent grocers. A Branded Tea supplier like Typhoo makes far more profit from Typhoo brand tea than for tea going to a retailer to be sold under his own brand.

Any supplier of services to different customers knows that some of them are no trouble, taking the standard product or service with no arguments about price or what is provided, while others haggle, quibble and are difficult to extract payment from. These customers (the easy ones and the difficult ones) constitute different segments.

Different segments can also arise if some customers require a basic product (or COMMODITY) to be adapted to their own requirements (a 'Special' product). This could simply be the requirement to deliver a product to the customer (rather than him or her collect it themselves), or further stages of working on a product to adapt it to the customer's needs, or just an up-market version of the standard product. A higher price will usually be paid for a special product, but the extra price can be significantly more or significantly less than the extra cost (it is usually more), so the special product can be a different segment, with higher (or usually, lower) profitability.

Different segments may be defined by any of the following:

(1) different products or services
(2) different customers receiving the same product or service
(3) different regions receiving the same product, where the cost to serve the different geographical areas is different
(4) different versions or variants of the same product, distinguished by the degree of value added, quality or personal service involved.

Although it is important to identify your separate segments, you should not go overboard on this and come up with a list that is so long as to be unmanageable. Also, potential separate segments may not be actually separate, if it turns out that their characteristics (especially profitability) are so similar to those of other activities that there is no point in singling them out.

Now is the time for you to think about your business and its segments. *Exercise 1* is for you to take a clean piece of paper, write *Potential Business Segments* at the top, and make a list of possible segments defined by the differences in (1) to (4) above. Depending on how big and complex your business is, you should have a list of approximately between 5 and 50 potential segments.

Exercise 2 involves turning this guesswork into a more objective *Definition of Business Segments*. I have compiled two tests that can be used for any of your Potential Business Segments, to see whether they are really separate or not. You need to set up the test by taking two possible segments, that could be separate segments, or that could alternatively just be one bigger segment. For example, let us assume that you are a butcher who has two shops, one in Madrid and the other in Barcelona. You want to know whether you should think of them as separate Business Segments.

The two tests are alternatives: *Test A* is a short, quick-and-dirty test, that will probably give you the right answer. *Test B* is longer and more certain to be correct.

Test A asks two simple questions:

(1) Are your competitors in the two Potential Business Segments different or the same? *If the answer to this question is 'different', then they are probably separate segments, and you do not need to answer Question 2 below.*
(2) If the answer to Question 1 is 'the same', do the competitors (including yourself) have roughly similar market share positions in the two Potential Business Segments? In other words, if Competitor A is the leader in one potential segment, followed by B, followed by C, is this the same ranking in the other potential segment? *If so, the two areas are probably one single segment; if not, they are probably separate segments.*

To go back to our Spanish butcher, let us assume that the butchers in Madrid are different competitors from those in Barcelona, in that case he should think of the two shops as different segments (but if both shops were next door to the same hypermarket chain, they would probably be the same segment).

Or to take another example, a furniture manufacturer in Transylvania has two main product lines: sofas and sofa-beds. His main competitor is Dracula Sofas, who also makes sofa-beds. Question 1 produces the answer 'the same', since both firms make sofas and sofa-beds. But in answer to Question 2, we discover the market shares shown in Illustration 1.1.

Illustration 1.1
Transylvanian sofa and sofa-bed market shares

	Sofas	Sofa-beds
Our firm's market share	30%	50%
Dracula Sofas' market share	60%	10%
Our firm's relative market share	0.5×	5×

Our Firm has only half the market share and sales in sofas that Dracula Sofas has, but has five times the market share of Dracula in sofa-beds, which is clearly our specialty and not theirs. We need to introduce our first piece of jargon here, which is the *Relative Market Share*, usually written as *RMS*. The Relative Market Share is simply your firm's market share divided by the market share of your largest competitor. If you are larger than anyone else in a product, your Relative Market Share will be more than 1.0 (written as 1.0×, or 1×); if you are smaller it will be less than 1, as in the example above in sofas, where our firm is half the size of Dracula, written as 0.5×.

We conclude, therefore, that the relative market share positions in sofas are different from those in sofa-beds, and we should therefore treat them as separate segments. Our firm specialises in sofa-beds, and Dracula specialises in sofas. There must be good reasons for this difference, which are likely to result in different profitability. The chances are that our firm will be much more profitable in sofa-beds than in sofas, and more profitable than Dracula in sofa-beds. Conversely, Dracula is likely to make more money out of sofas than sofa-beds, and to have a higher return on sales in sofas than we do, but a lower return on sales in sofa-beds than us.

Why should it matter whether the competitive positions are the same? The reason is that if they are the same, it says that the way customers vote, and the ability of the two competitors to produce one product rather than another, is not much different in the two areas. The chances are, therefore, that Competitor A will have similar levels of profitability in each area, and that the same will be true for Competitor B (Competitor A is likely to be either more profitable, or less profitable, than Competitor B in both areas). But if one competitor is a specialist in one area, and has a higher market share in that area, there is likely to be something in consumers' preferences, or the firm's own ability to produce efficiently in one area, that means it is likely to be more profitable for him in one segment than in another.

Even if the profitability of two segments is not differential, the fact that a firm is relatively stronger in market share terms in one area than another indicates that this could be the basis of profitable specialisation.

Test B, to see whether segments are separate, takes longer than *Test A* but is even more reliable (though it usually comes up with the same result). We start with the same question – we have two product lines or potential segments, and we want to know whether they are part of the same segment, or comprise two different segments. Illustration 1.2 (see following page) gives the tests for what some irreverent junior consultants of mine once called The Segmentation Mincer:

Illustration 1.2 The segmentation			Column A Score	Column B Score
1	Are the competitors in the two products or areas the same?			
	Yes: Column A	No: Column B	–30	+30
2	Are the Relative Market Shares (RMS) of our firm and the leading competitors roughly the same in the two products or areas?			
	RMS similar: Column A	RMS different: Column B	–50	+50
3	Are the customers the same in the two products or areas?			
	Yes: Column A	No: Column B	–20	+20
4	Are the customers' main purchase criteria and their order of importance roughly the same in the two products or areas?			
	Yes: Column A	No: Column B	–30	+30
5	Are the two products substitutes for each other?			
	Yes: Column A	No: Column B	–10	+10
6	Are the prices of the two products (for equivalent quality) or in the two areas roughly the same?			
	Yes: Column A	No: Column B	–20	+20
7	Is our firm's profitability roughly the same in the two products or areas?			
	Yes: Column A	No: Column B	–40	+40
8	Do the two products or areas have approximately the case need for capital per dollar of sales, i.e., similar capital intensity?			
	Yes: Column A	No: Column B	–10	+10
9	Are the cost structures in the two products or areas similar (that is, roughly the case proportion of cost in raw materials, in manufacturing, in marketing and selling, and so on)?			
	Yes: Column A	No: Column B	–10	+10
10	Do the products or areas share at least half of their costs, that is, the use of common labour, machines, premises and management resources for at least half of their total costs?			
	Yes: Column A	No: Column B	–30	+30
11	Are there logistical, practical or technological barriers between the two products or areas that only some competitors can surmount?			
	No: Column A	Yes: Column B	–20	+20
12	Is it possible to gain an economical advantage by specialising in one of the products/areas by gaining lower costs or higher prices in that product/area as a result of focussing on it?			
	No: Column A	Yes: Column B	–30	+30

You now add the scores together to produce the result. If the result is a positive number, you should treat the two products or areas as separate business segments, and devise strategy for each of them separately. If the result is negative, they are currently the same business segment and should be lumped together, at least initially, in developing their strategy. The further away from zero the answer is, whether positive or negative, the more certain the result.

Let us take the Segmentation Mincer and apply it to our friend, the Spanish butcher. Remember that he has two butchers' shops, one in Madrid and one in Barcelona, and he is trying to find out whether he is in two businesses, two competitive systems if you like, or just one.

Illustration 1.3
The Spanish butcher uses the mincer

		Answer	Score
1	Are the competitors in Madrid and Barcelona the same?	No	+30
2	Are the Relative Market Shares of the competitors the same in Madrid and Barcelona?	No	+50
3	Are the customers the same?	No	+50
4	Are the customers' purchase criteria roughly the same?	Yes	–30
5	Are the two shops substitutes for each other (i.e. would a customer sometimes shop in Barcelona and sometimes in Madrid)?	No	+10
6	Are the prices for the same products roughly the same?	Yes	–20
7	Is the butcher's profitability in the two locations similar?	Yes	–20
8	Do the two shops have the same capital intensity (need for capital per peseta of sales)?	Yes	–10
9	Are the cost structures similar?	Yes	–10
10	Do the two locations share at least half their costs?	No	+30
11	Are there barriers between competitors participating in both areas?	Yes	+20
12	Can you gain an economic advantage by just competing in one area?	Yes	+30
TOTAL SCORE >>			+110

The result is +110, indicating that the two shops are different business segments and that the butcher should therefore develop a strategy for each shop, as well as a strategy for the business overall.

Now it's time to return to Pasadena, California, and see how Randy Mayhew and I are dealing with our first strategy question: defining United Tea Corporation's business segments.

Randy Defines UTC's Business Segments

As you've probably gathered, Randy is a no-nonsense guy. When I told him we were going to define his business segments, he sighed. 'Aw shucks,' he started, 'that's typical consultantese. Lemme tell you a few simple facts about my business.'

'We have three businesses, or maybe four. Our biggest business by far, with over $700m of sales, is the Mainstream Tea business under the '5 Unicorns' brand. You know, we buy tea from plantations around the world, we put it into tea-bags, we put tags on the ends of the bags, we box them up with pretty packaging and we sell them to the grocery trade, especially to the big supermarkets.'

'You can split this business into two if you want. The US business stinks. We have nearly $600m of sales revenue, but we make almost nothing out of it. We used to make a fair return, nothing great, but now the supermarket chains have tightened up on us and squeezed our nuts. Fortunately, the export business keeps us alive: we make $8.5m pre-tax out of revenues of just $115m, $120m, something like that.'

'Then we have two smaller businesses, but growing fast. One is Herb Tea (he pronounced it 'erb', something I had still not grown accustomed to despite years in America). That's just $65m in revenues, but we make even more at the bottom line out of that than the Mainstream Tea exports. Finally there's the latest craze, Fruit Tea, and we make $3m profit out of just under $30m revenue. We bought these two businesses a couple of years ago and they're still separate. If I hadn't a done those two deals, I'dda been on welfare by now.'

Knowing that businessmen often misquote numbers, I asked to see last year's management accounts. But in this case, they proved that Randy was right (see Illustration 1.4).

Illustration 1.4
Universal Tea's previous profit report

Organisational Unit	Sales $m	Profit ($000)	ROS%
Mainstream Tea US	599.6	233	0.0
Mainstream Tea Exports	117.2	8,510	7.3
Herb Tea Corporation	66.5	8.870	13.3
Fruit Tea Corporation	27.9	3,249	11.6
Total	801.2	20,862	2.6

'It's difficult to make money out of tea in America. We've put all our development effort into growing our export sales and profits. The exports deliver, but our advances here are overturned by the slide in domestic margins. Herb and fruit teas are very profitable and growing, and we have been successful in growing exports, which must also be the most profitable bit of the business.'

Randy was convinced that he had just four business segments, as shown in the accounts above. But I was not sure.

'Let's start with the Mainstream domestic [US] business,' I probed. 'Are there any chunks of the business where you face different competition, or have higher or lower margins, than the rest?'

'Nah, not really. Not unless you count the private label stuff we do for two of the supermarkets. It's true we're up against specialist players there, you know, commodity firms with no brands and no marketing overheads. Our biggest headache there is a guy we call Cheapco, cos he always under-cuts us for the Big Boy Supermarket contract, or so Big Boy tells us.'

'Doesn't that make the private label business less profitable than the branded business?' Randy had to pause before answering, a rare event. 'Well, mebbe. But the branded business is no great shakes anyway. We're dealing with the supermarkets in both cases, and they're real SOBs.'

Despite Randy's reservations, I was convinced that private label business was a separate segment, because the main competitor was different. To cut a a long story short, I then pressed my advantage, and discovered that there was another private label contract, for Small Fry Retailers, a contract that Cheapco did not try to win, because it was too small. The main competitor here was another commodity player, and I marked the Small Fry business down as another potential segment.

I was also unhappy at the way Randy lumped all the exports for the Mainstream Tea business together. Didn't he face different competitors in Canada, in Europe and in the Rest of the World [ROW]? 'Half right,' he conceded. 'In Europe and ROW the main competitor is the same as here, United Foods, but in Canada it's a local outfit, Canadian Tea.' I wrote down 'Canada' as a separate segment, but was not yet willing to give up on having Europe and the Rest of the World as separate too. 'How big are you relative to United,' I asked, 'here, in Europe, and in the Rest of the World?' 'Well, we're the biggest at home, but much smaller than they are in Europe, hell, United Foods is based in Switzerland. In ROW, though, we're several times their size, which is stronger even than in America, they're probably about three quarters our size here in Branded Tea, though they don't do private label.'

I then asked similar questions about competitors in herb tea and fruit tea. I established that in both markets there were different foreign competitors, though one firm (Auntie Dot's) was the main competitor in the export markets for both herb and fruit teas.

I could see that Randy was getting itchy, and sure enough, he suggested it was time for lunch. While he visited the men's room I wrote down my idea of UTC's segments on a paper napkin. Instead of his 3 or 4 segments, I thought there were at least 10:

(1) Branded (5 Unicorns) Tea: US
(2) Branded (5 Unicorns) Tea: Canada
(3) Branded (5 Unicorns) Tea: Europe
(4) Branded (5 Unicorns) Tea: ROW
(5) Big Boy Supermarkets private label
(6) Small Fry Retailers private label

> (7) Herb Tea: US
> (8) Herb Tea: Exports
> (9) Fruit Tea: US
> (10) Fruit Tea: Exports
>
> When he came back, Randy rapidly agreed that we could take these ten segments, and got down to the serious business of ordering lunch.

You probably already have the idea, but in case you are in any doubt let's give one more example (skip this if you are confident you know how to 'mince'). Two firms, who we shall call Heinz and Imperial Foods, are manufacturers of sauces. They both make tomato ketchup (catsup) and thick brown sauce. One of the firms wishes to know whether they are separate business segments for strategy purposes. At first sight it appears obvious that they are the same segment, because the main competitors are the same and because there is very high cost sharing between the two types of sauce: they are made in the same factories, using the same machines, by the same workforce; they are marketed to the same consumers and sold to the same customers (the supermarkets and other grocers) by the same salesforce. Nevertheless, it is useful to put these two potential segments through the Mincer (Illustration 1.5).

Illustration 1.5
Heinz versus Imperial Foods

Is Tomato Ketchup the same segment as Thick Brown Sauce?		
Test	Answer	Score
1. Are the competitors the same in the two sauces?	Yes	−30
2. Are the Relative Market Shares of the competitors roughly the same in the two sauces?	No	+50
3. Are the customers the same?	Yes	−20
4. Are the customers' purchase criteria roughly the same?	Yes	−30
5. Are the two sauces substitutes for each other?	No	+10
6. Are the prices for the two products roughly the same between the two competitors, with no brand premium?	No	+20
7. Is Imperial Foods' (or Heinz') profitability in the two sauces similar?	No	+40
8. Do the two products have similar capital intensity?	Yes	−10
9. Are the cost structures similar?	Yes	−10
10. Do the two sauces share at least half their costs?	Yes	−30
11. Are there barriers stopping one firm or the other from competing as effectively in one sauce as in the other?	Yes	+20
12 Can you gain an economic advantage by competing in just one sauce?	Yes	+30
TOTAL SCORE >>>	+40	

The result is +40, indicating that, contrary to first impressions, the two sauces, are separate business segments.

We need to explain why the questions were answered as they were. Heinz is the market leader in tomato ketchup, several times larger than the nearest competitor. But in thick brown sauces (under several brands, including Daddies') Imperial Foods is the market leader, where it is several times larger than anyone else. There is no particularly good reason for this difference, except (and it is a big 'except') that consumers are attached to the brands, Heinz in tomato ketchup and Daddies in brown sauce. The consumers obstinately and persistently vote massive majorities for the two brands in each of their areas. This has the result that Heinz commands a high brand price premium in tomato ketchup, and Daddies enjoys the same higher price in brown sauce because of the strength of the brand. Consequently, Heinz is very profitable in tomato ketchup (but not in brown sauce), whereas Imperial Foods is very profitable in brown sauce and not in tomato ketchup. Each area therefore deserves a separate strategy, with separate pricing and differential degrees of brand support. It would be wrong for either firm to treat both products as part of one sauce business and have the same strategy in each area.

The Segmentation Mincer does not always say businesses are separate segments! If red sauce is a separate segment, what about red cars? Clearly no-one can command a price premium or have lower costs by specialising in producing red cars today (though Henry Ford did once have lower costs by painting all Model T automobiles black), so the Mincer would produce a high negative score (actually the maximum possible negative score, −290).

To come back to your business, apply the segmentation mincer to your list of *Potential Business Segments* to arrive at your list of 'real' business segments. You may now want to rank these in order of sales revenues, or, if you know it, absolute amount of profit produced by each segment. Now you should attempt to answer each of the questions below for each segment, either doing it one segment at a time (starting with the most important segment at the top of your list) or doing all segments at once.

3. WHERE DO YOU MAKE THE MONEY?

Now that you have defined your business in a new way, by its real business segments, the most important thing to know is which of these segments generate most of your profits, both in terms of absolute amounts of money and in terms of profitability (measured by return on sales, or, preferably, return on capital employed).

It is possible that your accounting systems already provide this information, or that they can be easily tweaked to do so. If so, great. It is much more likely, however, that profit by segment, the way we have just defined them, is not readily available.

What usually happens at this stage is that your accountant, or your systems analyst, tells you that to restate the accounts in the way you want is a major job that will take several months. Should you give up, or wait?

Neither! You must find out your segment profitability – I can tell you in advance that it will be full of valuable surprises. And you are just getting into the game of developing your strategy, and to stop now would be defeatist. The answer is to estimate your segment profitability as best you can.

First, start with what accounting information you do have. You will certainly be able to discover your sales per segment, and probably also the gross margin (sales less cost of goods). You will also know the total costs for all the segments. It is quite likely that you will also know the profitability of certain segments on an aggregated basis: all sauces, for example, even if you can't yet split tomato ketchup from brown sauce. Now all that you need to do, to arrive at the return on sales for each segment, is to allocate the costs to each segment on some reasonable basis.

The crudest way of allocating costs is on a percentage of turnover basis, and it might be a good idea to start just by doing this. A moment's reflection, however, will convince you that this is not terribly accurate, since some products take a lot more of some costs than other products: more advertising, for example, or more time selling, or more time in the factory because the production runs are shorter.

What you therefore need to do is to take each major category of cost, however arranged in your accounting system, and make a rough allocation of costs to each segment. You might want to start with the simplest, easiest-to-make-and-sell product, and say that it should have a cost of y per product in the particular department you are looking at. Then ask how much more difficult it is to make the next product, and allocate an appropriate cost: 1.5y for example, or 2y, or 10y. Do the same for each other product, then multiply by the factor (1.5y or whatever) by the volume of that product. Go through the same procedure for all other products, add up the total number of ys, and then allocate the departmental cost on the basis of each product's ys divided into the total number of ys.

Before long you will have arrived at a rough-and-ready estimate of the product's return on sales. If you want to take this to the stage of return on capital, you clearly have to follow a similar procedure to allocate the capital used by each product or segment. If this is going to be time-consuming, or if it seems unlikely it will yield any extra insight, stop for the moment at the return on sales.

Meanwhile, back in Pasadena, Randy's accountant and I spent Saturday afternoon beavering away to turn his previous profit numbers for 4 businesses (see page 25) into profits split by the new 10 segments, while Randy went off on a long-standing golfing obligation. Shortly after ten at night, we were satisfied that we had it about right (see Illustration 1.6).

The following morning, I went through the numbers with Randy. He was stunned. 'You mean to say that we really do make good money out of the domestic branded business, but lose it all on the private label contracts? And that the US brand is more profitable than Canada or Europe? That's amazing! Perhaps we can do things to get even more branded sales here. But I don't know what to do about the private label contracts. You may tell me to cut them out, but they're too big a part of our business and they still make a contribution to my overheads.' We agreed not to jump to conclusions until we had gone through my other questions.

Illustration 1.6
Randy's profit numbers after proper segmentation

Universal Tea Corporation segment profitability			
Segment	Sales ($m)	Profit ($000)	ROS%
5 Unicorns Brand: US	200.1	17,800	8.9
5 Unicorns Brand: Canada	23.7	1,232	5.2
5 Unicorns Brand: Europe	45.0	1,215	2.7
5 Unicorns Brand: ROW	48.5	6,063	12.5
Private label for Big Boy Supermarkets	353.6	(18,034)	(5.1)
Private label for Small Fry Retailers	35.9	467	1.3
Herb Tea US	55.5	7,715	13.9
Herb Tea Exports	11.0	1,155	10.5
Fruit Tea US	23.2	2,784	12.0
Fruit Tea Exports	4.7	465	9.9
Total	801.2	20,862	2.6

This is, of course, only one example. But let me assure you that compiling segment profit data nearly always stands some received wisdom on its head, and provokes thought about the direction of your strategy. You generally discover that some business is *much* more profitable than you thought before, and that some business you thought worth having is in fact very unprofitable. It is wrong to jump to conclusions, however, before you have completed the strategic diagnosis. Our next port of call for more strategic insight is to look at our competitive position by segment.

4. HOW GOOD ARE YOUR COMPETITIVE POSITIONS?

For each of your business segments, we now want to find out how strong they are in competitive terms, because our strategy will be different depending on this. Assessing competitive strength is not as difficult as it sounds. Most of the insight available here can be gathered just by knowing three facts for each segment:

(1) the business's *Relative Market Share* (RMS) in the segment,
(2) the *trend* in RMS,
(3) the expected annual future growth rate of the segment's market, and
(4) the ROCE (Return on Capital Employed) of each segment business.

Remember that the *Relative Market Share* is the market share or sales that your firm has in the segment divided by the market share or sales of your largest competitor in the segment. Work this out now. If you are not exactly sure of your largest's competitor's sales in the segment, make a note to find out later, but for the time being put down your best estimate. Now calculate the RMS. As an example, let's revisit Pasadena.

Randy Defines His Relative Market Shares

After Randy's astonishment about his segment profitability (see Illustration 1.6 on page 29), we spent the rest of Sunday morning with his marketing director, establishing how large United Tea was to its major competitors in our newly-defined segments. By noon we had the answers (Illustration 1. 7).

Illustration 1.7
Randy defines his segment Relative Market Shares (RMS)

Segment	UTC Sales	Largest Competitor	His Sales	UTC RMS
Branded tea: US	$200m	United Foods	$150m	1.33×
Branded tea: Canada	$23.7m	Canadian Tea	$25m	0.95×
Branded tea: Europe	$45m	United Foods	$200m	0.22×
Branded tea: ROW	$48.5m	United Foods	$15m	3.2×
Big Boy PL	$355m	Cheapco	$490m	0.72×
Small Fry PL	$36m	George's Contracts	$45m	0.8×
Herb tea: US	$55.5m	Herbal Health	$20m	2.8×
Herb tea: Exports	$11.0m	Auntie Dot's	$20m	0.55×
Fruit tea: US	$23.2m	Fruit-Tea Fun	$8.5m	2.7×
Fruit tea: Exports	$4.7m	Auntie Dot's	$10m	0.47×

How good are these Relative Market Share (RMS) positions? First I explained to Randy and his marketing director some rules of thumb about these (see Illustration 1. 8).

Illustration 1.8
Rules of thumb concerning Relative Market Share (RMS) positions

RMS Position	Name	Rule of Thumb
4.0× or greater	Dominance	Extremely strong position
1.5× to 3.9×	Clear leadership	Very strong position
1.0× to 1.49×	Narrow leadership	Strong position
0.7× to 0.99×	Strong follower	Fairly strong position
0.3× to 0.69×	Follower	Moderate position
Less than 0.3×	Marginal player	Weak position

I then went on to tentatively classify UTC's segment position portfolio (Illustration 1. 9).

This looked, on the face of it, pretty good. But before coming to any judgments, I wanted to look at the **trend** in RMS.

This requires going through the estimates of RMS again (as in Illustration 1.7), but this time for the position in RMS as it was in the past, 3 years ago. Since then, have you gained or lost in terms of Relative Market Share? The results for Universal Tea Corporation's segments are shown in Illustration 1.10.

This looked like a deteriorating picture, although Randy's first reaction is that this is OK, since in the attractive export markets, the ones with the highest profitability, UTC was gaining share. I was not so optimistic, but before I could make any comments Randy had stood up to march us off to lunch.

Illustration 1. 9
Strength of UTC segment positions

Segment Category	Segments	Total % of UTC Sales
Dominance	None	0
Clear Leadership	Branded tea; US Branded tea: ROW Herb tea: US Fruit tea: US	41
Narrow Leadership	None	0
Strong Follower	Branded tea: Canada US Private Label	52
Follower	Herb Tea: Exports Fruit Tea: Exports	2

Illustration 1.10
Trend in RMS of Universal Tea Corporation

Gaining Share	Holding Share	Losing Share
Branded tea: Canada Branded tea: Europe Branded tea: ROW Herb tea: Exports Fruit Tea: Exports	US Private Label	US branded Tea US Herb Tea US Fruit Tea
17% of Sales	**48% of Sales**	**35% of Sales**

How does this picture compare to the trend in your segment positions?

It's time to introduce you to a new display, the GROWTH/GROWTH MATRIX (Illustration 1.11), which compares the growth in the market to the growth in your own business.

We can now superimpose on this bubbles representing your own segment businesses. By definition, where your businesses have grown faster than the market over the past few years, they will be bubbles (circles) below and to the right of the diagonal line (shown in

Illustration 1.11
Growth/growth matrix

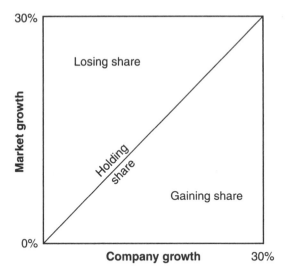

Illustration 1.12 in grey), where you have grown at exactly the market rate the bubbles will be centred on the diagonal line (shown as clear circles), and where your business has grown slower than the market, the circles (shown in black) will be above and to the left of the diagonal.

Note that the size (area) of the circles is proportional to revenues (they can also be drawn with the area proportional to profits or to capital employed in the segments).

Randy Looks at Growth/Growth Bubbles

I thought that after lunch Randy, the marketing director and I should mock up some rough charts showing the growth in the market and in their sales for the ten segments. After asking them a few questions, the chart we generated looked like this (see Illustration 1.13).

Partly this was just a graphic way of showing the information from Illustration 1.10 (page 32), but it also made us realise that there was an interesting pattern here. As we noted before, there is more area in the circles to the left of the diagonal (where Randy was losing market share) than to the right (where he was gaining share). But we could also note 2 other interesting facts:

Illustration 1.12
Growth/growth matrix with illustrative segment positions

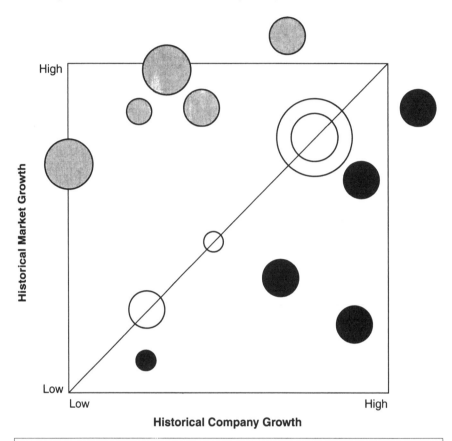

(1) The markets for herb tea and fruit tea were both growing very fast everywhere, at roughly the same rates (between 15 per cent and 20 per cent each year). Yet our growth rate was very different, averaging 5 per cent in the US and more than 20 per cent in the export markets. This was because more marketing effort was going into the smaller export markets, in the mistaken belief that these were more profitable. In fact we were losing market share in the profitable and high growth US markets. UTC was cutting itself off from most of the growth in the largest and most profitable segments: US herb and fruit teas. Surely Randy could do something about this!

(2) The branded Mainstream markets were low growth everywhere, while the private label market in the US was growing fast. This was bad news for UTC, because we made lower returns (in fact lost money overall) in

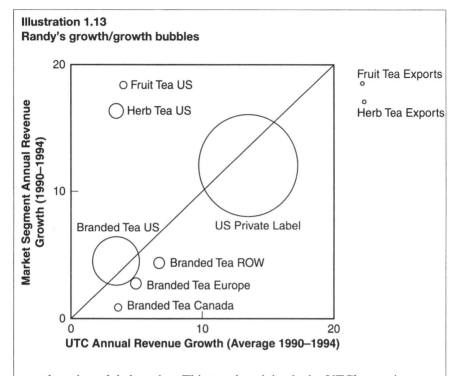

Illustration 1.13
Randy's growth/growth bubbles

the private label market. This trend explained why UTC's margins were sliding overall. But it also raised the intriguing question of whether private label was growing in some of the export markets, and whether we could profitably enter any of these.

Before leaving this section on competitive positioning, I want to introduce you to three other charts on which to display your segment data. The first of these is perhaps the most famous strategic tool of all, the celebrated (and derided) GROWTH/SHARE MATRIX. We do not need to be detained by a lengthy explanation of the theory behind it (those who are interested should consult Part Three, pages 166–74); all we need to know is how to use it and how it helped Randy.

The Growth/Share Matrix uses the dimension of market growth that we've just looked at, except that you should plot your best estimate of the expected *future* annual market growth (this should also be in terms of units of volume of the product or service; if you find this more difficult to estimate than the value of the market in money terms, it is OK to use this although you should take real value growth and not include inflation).

The other dimension is Relative Market Share (RMS) that we referred to earlier (page 20), though we did not then put it on a chart. Now just go ahead and plot your segment positions on the matrix (see Illustration 1.14), again making the area of the circles correspond to your sales in each segment.

Although many writers are sceptical about the Growth/Share Matrix or regard it as old hat and discredited, my experience is that sensibly used, based on the real business segments we have already discovered, the Matrix is still a powerful diagnostic tool. The significance arises from the prescriptions accorded to each of the four quadrants of the Matrix. First we need to give names to each of these (see Illustration 1.15):

I will now give my own comments (adapted from the original BCG prescriptions) on each of the quadrants. Your job is to see if this gives you insight into any of your businesses.

(1) The most interesting businesses and insight comes if you have any businesses in the top left, the *star* quadrant. Star businesses are where you are the market leader in a high growth business. Most of you will have few or no star businesses. For those of you

Illustration 1.14
Growth/share matrix

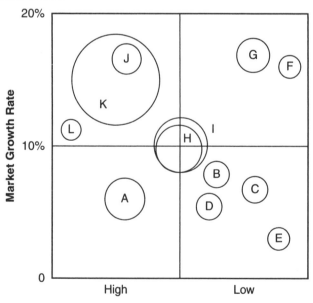

Illustration 1.15
The growth/share matrix quadrants named

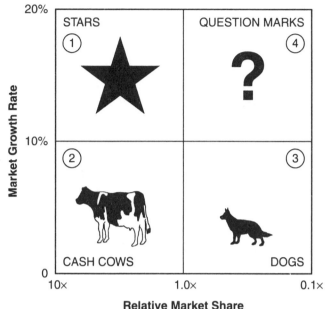

who have them, realise first of all how valuable such a business is. If you manage to remain the segment leader, your profits from the segment should be very high and growing all the time. When the market growth cools off, you will have a large, valuable business which should still be very profitable and will now begin to throw off very large amounts of cash (it will be in box 2 and now be a cash cow).

The rule for star businesses is to invest, invest and invest. *Do whatever is necessary to hold, or if possible, gain market share.* You will never regret doing so.

(2) Box 2 contains the *cash cows*, business segments where you are the leader but where the growth is not particularly high. These businesses will generally comprise a minority of your sales, but a majority of your profits and cash generation. They are a classic illustration of the EIGHTY/TWENTY RULE: 20 per cent of the sales generating 80 per cent of the profits and cash (in fact, sometimes more than 100 per cent of the profits and cash). They are great businesses to have.

The rule for cash cows is to make sure that they have the highest grade grass, that they are well protected, and that they grow even bigger and stronger. Cash cows are generally quite easy to keep happy, since their appetites are nowhere near as voracious as those of stars, but remember: contented cows make bigger and better dollops of cash.

(3) The bottom right box, labelled here 3, is the *dog* kennel. Forget all you have been told about dogs. They are a motley crew, but some of these businesses are quite valuable.

If they are towards the centre of the chart, that is, if they are towards the left of the box (although still on the right of the middle of the page), they are MARKET CHALLENGERS or strong followers, and likely to generate nice profits and cash. Try to gain segment leadership if this can be done without too high a cost. Otherwise look after these businesses well.

For businesses towards the right edge of the box, the really doggy dogs, not too much should be expected. Find out if any of them are losing money and are a cash drain. Sell these, and if they can't be sold, close them.

(4) Box 4 is in many ways the most intriguing one, the *question-mark* businesses. They pose the greatest strategy dilemmas. On the one hand, it is nice to be in a high growth business, but on the other hand it's bad news to be in a weak market share position. If you could be confident about becoming the market leader (driving the business to the star position) this would be a great move. But this will cost you. And if you don't make it, you will never get your money back.

The answer with question-marks is to be very selective. Only back those you know can become number one in the segment. Otherwise, think about selling the business if it is not too closely connected with your other businesses. You could get a very nice price (people always pay a lot for growth businesses, even those in weak competitive positions) and you won't risk pumping cash into a black hole.

Randy Draws a Growth/Share Matrix

Randy had liked his Growth/Growth bubble-chart, which was just as well, because he couldn't believe I was suggesting making a Growth/Share Matrix. 'Jeez, Richard', he bleated, 'that stuff went out with the Ark.' I told him to shut up and trust me, and drew a blank Growth/Share Matrix on the flip-chart.

With only nine businesses to plot (we agreed to combine the two private label contracts) we did it fast. This is what we came up with (Illustration 1.16).

'So what do you make of that?' Randy asked me, not bothering to hide his scepticism. Brushing that aside, I made five comments.

'First, that's a portfolio many managers would kill for. You have leadership in four segments and a lot of growth. Most portfolios are much weaker than this. So we ought to able to find a way round the present difficulties.'

'Second, look at the US Herb Tea and US Fruit Tea businesses. The Matrix says they are enormously valuable, but you haven't been treating

Illustration 1.16
Randy's growth/growth bubbles

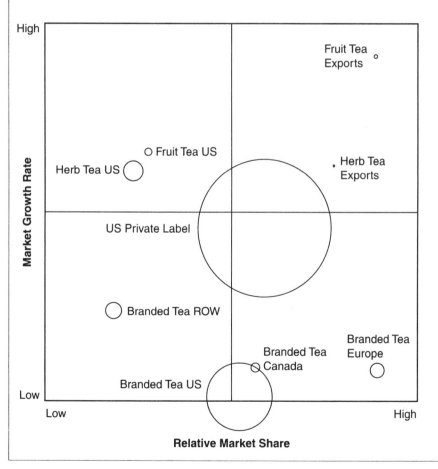

them that way. If you carried on losing share they would drift over to the question-mark box and end up as dogs. But it's probably not too late. You should be investing whatever it takes to hold share and even regain share in these two businesses.'

'Third, US Branded Tea is interesting. You're a leader, but not by a wide margin. And you're losing share, so this too could end up as a dog. You should probably aim to regain market share. But there's a question the Growth/Share Matrix can't answer about whether this is a good business to be in. It's under attack and losing to private label. You think it's a bad business. I don't know. A final view on this will have to wait.'

'Fourth, Herb Tea Exports and Fruit Tea Exports are question-marks. We're gaining share but we're still in very weak positions. We have to reach a view on whether we can gain leadership. That will have to wait until after we've studied competitors and talked to customers.'

'Fifth, we have very different positions in Branded Tea in Europe, Canada and the Rest of the World. Europe is very weak and not very profitable. Canada is fairly strong and has OK profits. Rest of the world is very strong and profitable. I'd try to consolidate even further here. I'd want to know how much it would take to become clear leader in Canada. On the face of it, Europe looks a lower priority unless we could think of something dramatic to do there.'

By the end of my monologue Randy was looking more thoughtful.

You may want to draw two other charts for your business before leaving this section on competitive advantage. The first, called an RMS/ROS Chart, simply displays the data we already have on your segments' Relative Market Shares and Return on Sales. As before, I'll provide you with a blank chart on which to draw in bubbles showing your segments' positions (see Illustration 1.17).

The reason this is interesting is that there is often, but not always, a positive relationship between high Relative Market Share and high Return on Sales. If this does apply, it shows you the value of Relative Market Share, and should reinforce your desire to increase RMS wherever possible.

But if there is no pattern like this, this is also interesting. It may indicate opportunities or vulnerabilities for your business. I think you'll see why if we return to Pasadena.

Illustration 1.17
Your segments' RMS/ROS chart

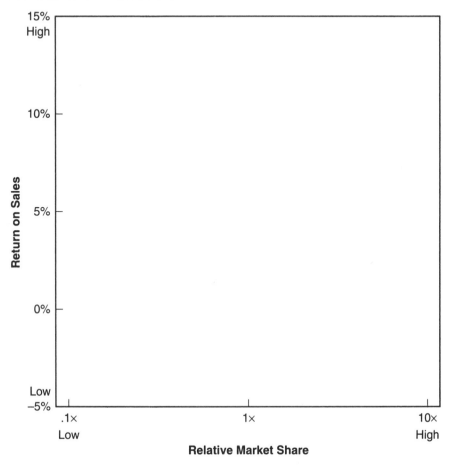

Randy Gets the Message from his RMS/ROS Chart

After the insight from the Growth/Share Matrix, Randy was subdued and patient as I sketched out UTC's RMS/ROS Chart (Illustration 1.18). He even asked me politely what I made of it.

'Well', I began, 'There is clearly a relationship: you tend to make the most money where you have the leading competitive positions. This should lead you to want to gain market share wherever possible, which we've just talked about. But the most fascinating thing is this big US Private Label blob, where the Relative Market Share is not bad at all, but you're losing money.'

'Can't do anything about it', Randy interjected. 'Cheapco can always undercut us. We've got higher overheads, what with marketing and all.'

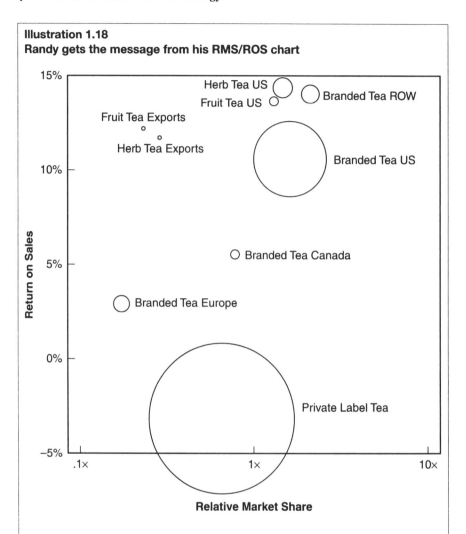

Illustration 1.18
Randy gets the message from his RMS/ROS chart

He shot a glance at the marketing director, who started looking uncomfortable.

'We'll come to that later', I retaliated. 'First I want us to draw up the final chart, which will end this afternoon's session. It's very similar to this one, except it looks at ROI or Return on Capital Employed, instead of Return on Sales. The bottom axis of the chart remains Relative Market Share, though I'm going to switch around the axes to keep you on your toes. In this chart (like the Growth/Share Matrix) the best, highest, RMS positions are on the left. We call this chart the Opportunity/Vulnerability Matrix, or Bananagram. You'll soon see why.' Then I sketched it out (Illustration 1.19):

Once I had drawn it, I took a yellow marker pen and coloured in the band in the middle (marked Normal Zone). 'This', I asserted, 'is the

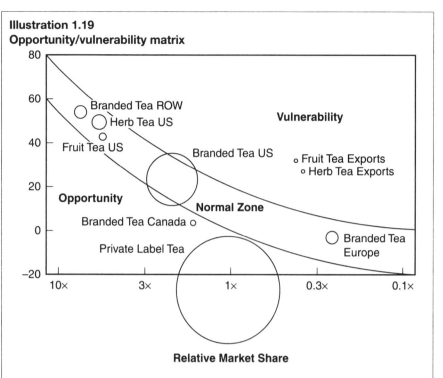

Illustration 1.19
Opportunity/vulnerability matrix

Relative Market Share

Banana, more formally known as the Normal Zone or the Normative Curve. Experience and the collection of lots of boring data has shown that most business positions fall inside this band, because Relative Market Share does correlate with Profitability (in this case with Return on Capital). Roughly three quarters of all businesses I have looked at fall within this band, after proper segmentation and product line profitability. In a way this just shows the RMS/ROS relationship in another way. You got that Randy?'

He grunted, which I took as agreement. 'But of your nine positions, only five of them fall in the banana. The exceptions are worth looking at carefully. This chart says, first of all, that you may need to be worried about anything above and to the right of the band. We call this the Vulnerability Zone, because you have high profits without the high market share we would expect to back them up. The theory says that either these businesses must improve their relative market shares a lot, or you'd expect the profits to fall a lot.' I took a red marker and drew a circle around the two dots for exports of Herb Tea and Fruit Tea, and drew an arrow taking them down to the middle of the banana. 'The chart doesn't say that this will happen, just that it may.'

'But there's potential good news as well. Any business that is to the left and the bottom of the banana may be an Opportunity. That business has high market share but low profits. And if you could take this private label business...', I circled it in green, 'and take it up to the line', I drew an arrow up, 'you'd make several million dollars more profit.'

'Can't be done', Randy returned to his refrain. 'Maybe not, but maybe yes,' I replied, 'I haven't given up hope yet. The same applies in a much smaller way to the Canadian Branded Tea business: you may be able to improve its profitability a bit.'

'To see if we can do anything about these businesses, we need to look at them in much more detail, understand their economics, whether they are bad businesses, and know what the customers think about you and their other suppliers, your competitors. We need a bit more investigation for that, which I'll do next week, and we'll fix a time to meet again next weekend.'

'Good. Time for cocktails, guys', Randy concluded. He looked much more cheerful now, though whether that was due to the news about his business or the thought of a drink, I couldn't tell. Anyway, it was warm on the sidewalk, and Randy was already ordering.

We've taken a long time exploring your competitive positions, but I hope you've found it rewarding. Segmentation, profitability, and relative market share are all related and looking at these three together is the fastest way to generate insight about a business. But competitive position alone doesn't explain everything. We next need to understand the economics of your business and how attractive it is, whatever your competitive position.

5. IS THIS A GOOD INDUSTRY TO BE IN?

Competitive position is one thing; the attractiveness of an industry something different again. One determines whether you win the race; the other how much the race is worth. There have been long and boring disputes about the relative importance of the two factors, but we need not bother with these. At the extreme, a business where no-one makes money and never will is of no interest, and a leadership position here is worthless; and there are some businesses (but very few) where almost everyone makes very high returns, regardless of competitive position. My own experience, for what it is worth, is that industry attractiveness on average explains about 30 per cent of the difference in firms' profitability, and competitive position within the industry (including the skill of the individual firm's management and the firm's culture) about 70 per cent. That is why I started with competitive position of the segments. But industry attractiveness is unquestionably important.

A good industry will have the following characteristics:

- *high returns on capital for players accounting for most of the market*
- *a stable or rising average industry return on capital*
- *clear barriers to entry keeping out many new entrants*
- *capacity at or below the level of demand, and low exit barriers*
- *reasonable or high market growth*
- *little or no threat from substitutes (competing industries)*
- *low bargaining power of suppliers relative to the industry*
- *low bargaining power of customers relative to the industry.*

It is worth commenting briefly on each of these.

The best empirical measure of industry attractiveness is the *return on capital* for the industry, weighted by sales. Not everyone has to earn a high return, but the players supplying the bulk of the market should have a high average, well above the cost of capital. Many cute theories about particular industries' attractiveness or lack thereof can be quickly disproved by looking at the weighted average returns on capital in them. Many professional service businesses, for example, are alleged to be fiercely competitive and unattractive, but you wouldn't know this if you looked at the returns. Similarly, people often disparage 'commodity' businesses, without realising that many of these can be highly profitable.

The *trend in ROCE* is also important. If it is falling, from whatever level, this is often a warning signal. On the other hand, some industries invest very heavily at the outset but show steadily increasing returns on capital as volume builds.

Barriers to entry include investment scale, branding, service, cost to switch, a lock on distribution channels or sources of raw material, property/location, corporate expertise or access to the highly skilled people, patents, ability to produce at low cost, corporate aggression vis-à-vis newcomers, and secrecy. Part Three, page 196, discusses each of these.

The industry *demand/supply balance* and *barriers to exit* are also clearly important. Barriers to exit include costs of firing employees, investment write-offs, disengagement costs, costs shared with other parts of a business, customer requirements for a 'package' of goods and services, and non-economic reasons like pride or desire to keep a large empire (these are elaborated in Part Three, page 196).

Market growth, especially the recent trend, shows how healthy demand currently is, and how well the industry is coping against competing products.

The *threat from substitutes* can arise from competing technologies (gas, electricity and nuclear power versus coal, or airlines versus railways), or simply from products that consumers tend over time to prefer (wine versus spirits, healthier versus less healthy foods, convenience versus labour intensive products, green versus non-green products, etc.). A threat from substitutes may exist and be very serious, but not yet show up in the statistics, as was the case with the threat to cross-channel ferries from the Anglo-French Channel Tunnel.

The *relative bargaining power of the industry vis-à-vis its suppliers and its customers* is pivotal. Broadly speaking, if an industry has a more concentrated structure (fewer suppliers accounting for, say, 75 per cent of total output) than its suppliers or customers, it will tend to have greater bargaining power.

In the 1950s and 1960s, most grocery and fast moving consumer goods manufacturers had more concentrated industries than either their suppliers or their customers (the retailers). Since then, they have generally maintained the advantage vis-à-vis suppliers, but in most countries the emergence of a few large supermarket chains has wiped out the manufacturers' advantage against the retailers. Both groups are now highly concentrated. Both still have high returns on capital, but that of retailers has gone up while that of most grocery manufacturers has stabilised, indicating that the advantages from greater industry efficiency have tended to go to the retailers rather than the manufacturers.

The relative power of suppliers includes that of individual employees. In some industries (notably entertainment and investment banking) the power of the individual star can redirect profits from corporations to individuals. George Michael can take on Sony. Bond or foreign exchange traders can try to double their pay, or threaten to go down the road for a multi-million dollar golden hello. Over the next decades, we will see a serious redistribution of corporate super-profits in 'knowledge industries' from shareholders to the most highly valued employees.

So you can see that industry attractiveness is a many-headed monster. One of the problems of such a long list of attributes is that it is difficult to provide an objective quantification, so that industry attractiveness is very much in the eye of the beholder. Talk to ten people in an industry in different firms, and you often get ten different opinions. In an effort to reduce the subjective element, I have distilled my *Industry Attractiveness Checklist* below, which you can now apply to your own business or businesses. If you find that you want to give different answers for different groups of your segments, you should go through the checklist separately for these. If you have ten segments, it is likely that you will have between one and three groups for assessing industry attractiveness purposes.

Industry attractiveness checklist

(1) What is the weighted average ROCE (Return on Capital Employed) in your industry over the past 5 years?

Score: whatever the average ROCE is, with a minimum of 0 and up to a maximum of 40.

(2) What is the trend in ROCE over the past 5 years?

Score: (a) falling – no points; (b) erratic and no trend – 3 points; (c) stable – 7 points; (d) rising – 10 points.

(3) How substantial are the barriers stopping new entrants to the industry?

Score: (a) few barriers – no points; (b) low barriers – 3 points; (c) fairly high barriers – 7 points; (d) very high barriers – 10 points.

(4) What is your best estimate of the next 5 years' average annual market growth?

Score: (a) negative – no points; (b) 0-5 per cent p.a – 3 points; (c) 5-10 per cent – 7 points; (d) over 10 per cent – 10 points.

(5) What is the current balance in the industry between customer demand, and the total industry capacity?

Score: (a) there is serious industry overcapacity, and no plans to remove it – minus 20 points; (b) there is serious overcapacity, but plans are in place to remove the excess – minus 10 points; (c) there is minor excess capacity – minus 5 points; (d) supply is in line with demand, or lower than demand – no points.

(6) What is the threat from substituting products, services, or technologies?

Score: (a) serious threat – minus 20 points; (b) may be a serious threat, but uncertain – minus 10 points; (c) only minor threats expected – minus 3 points; (d) threats do not appear to exist and unlikely – no points.

(7) What relative bargaining power do the industry's suppliers have?

Score: (a) the suppliers are more concentrated and can dictate terms to the industry – no points; (b) the suppliers are slightly more powerful and concentrated than the industry – 3 points; (b) the suppliers are slightly less powerful than the industry – 7 points; (d) the industry is more concentrated and more powerful than suppliers and can dictate terms to them – 10 points.

8) What relative bargaining power do the industry's customers have?

Score: (a) the customers are more concentrated and powerful – no points; (b) the customers are slightly more powerful than the industry – 7 points; (c) there is a rough balance between the power and concentration of customers and the industry – 12 points; (d) the industry is more concentrated than the customers and has more collective bargaining power because there are few suppliers and little choice – 20 points.

INTERPRETING THE SCORES

The scores will range between minus 40 and plus 100. Industry attractiveness can be interpreted as follows:

Negative score [minus 1 to minus 40]: try to get out of the industry. If you are still reporting profits or anyone is foolish enough to buy the business, sell.

Score of 0 to 25: this is an unattractive industry. If you are not the market leader, sell the business.

Score of 26 to 50: the industry is not very attractive, but it is possible for segment leaders and very well run firms to make a living.

Score of 51 to 60: the industry is neither attractive nor unattractive. Competitive position is all.

Score of 61 to 75: the industry is attractive. If you are in it, consolidate your position and gain or maintain leadership. If not, consider entry if it is adjacent to your business and you have the expertise or can share costs with your existing business.

Score of over 75: the industry is unusually attractive. If you are in it, invest heavily for leadership. If you are not in it, you may find it difficult to enter without acquisition, but if there is a suitable way in, take it with both hands.

Randy Tests Industry Attractiveness

The week after I saw Randy, I was busy on other assignments. But I did ask an assistant to check the ROCE for firms in the tea business, both branded suppliers and firms like Costco that just manufacture for retailers own labels. Next weekend, armed with my Industry Attractiveness Checklist and these data, I returned to Pasadena.

Randy rapidly agreed that we should do the Checklist separately for his Branded and Unbranded tea businesses. 'That's what you persuaded me last time: unbranded stinks!' he said emphatically. He was therefore surprised to find that Costco and the other unbranded specialists had an average ROCE of 20 per cent, exactly the same as the average for the branded suppliers. He found that difficult to reconcile with his heavy losses in the unbranded segment. Still, he knew that barriers to entry were lower without a brand, and so was confident that unbranded would turn out to be a bad business. He wasn't sure that Branded Tea manufacture would score very well either.

When we went through the test, there were a number of surprises for Randy. Not only was the Unbranded Tea ROCE as high as Branded Tea, but it was also rising over time, whereas the Branded Tea average was stable. Branded scored higher on barriers to entry, but worse on market growth. And when we came to the last question, we realised that whereas the degree of concentration and power was roughly the same for Branded Tea manufacturers and the retailers, the latter actually had less choice when it came to unbranded suppliers. There were very few of these, since the manufacturing scale required acted as a barrier to most firms, and since none of the other branded manufacturers apart from Universal Tea would supply private label, as a matter of policy.

The scores were as shown in Illustration 1.20.

Illustration 1.20
Randy's industry attractiveness scores

Test		Branded Tea		Unbranded Tea	
		Result	Score	Result	Score
1.	Industry ROCE average	20%	20	20%	20
2.	Trend in ROCE	(c)	7	(d)	10
3.	Barriers to entry	(d)	10	(c)	7
4.	Future market growth	(b)	3	(d)	10
5.	Capacity/demand balance	(d)	0	(d)	0
6.	Threat from substitutes	(c)	-3	(c)	-3
7.	Suppliers' power	(d)	10	(d)	10
8.	Customers' power	(c)	12	(d)	20
	Total Score		**59**		**74**
	VERDICT	**ATTRACTIVE**		**UNUSUALLY ATTRACTIVE**	

As you can imagine, Randy and I had to battle to keep his prejudices in check. At the end, when he had finally accepted the scores, he restated his puzzlement: 'If Unbranded Tea supply is very attractive, how come I lose money in it?'

'I don't know for sure', I replied. 'But Costco must be doing things differently. Perhaps they get a higher price than you do. Almost certainly they have lower costs. But if you did what they do, you could get costs as low as well. What we have realised is that the retailers are not as much in the driving seat as we thought beforehand. It's time to talk to them, the customers, and to look more closely at the competitors, especially Costco.'

'And another thing,' I added, 'cheer up, Randy. Your branded business is attractive too. And your segment competitive positions are not at all bad on average. So we should be able to find a way to make more money for you, so you can keep your job and keep buying me lunch.'

He was slow to take the hint. Randy was still scratching his head, and I surprised us both by being the first to suggest that lunchtime was now.

6. WHAT DO THE CUSTOMERS THINK?

While we were lunching, I told Randy that afterwards I would show him the result of my customer interviews. Characteristically, he volunteered to guess what the results would be.

'They'll all say that we are lousy on price and pretty good on everything else. So the only way we could improve our market share is to buy it, to cut into our profits. As you know, lower prices would mean lower profits, a lower share price, and an enforced vacation for Randy Mayhew. But I suppose we might as well see the interview results,' he yawned.

If I had chosen to show Randy the average results of all the interviews, Randy would not have been too wrong, and he would have remained bored. But I knew better than that. I showed him the results by segment, using a simple but very effective technique called Comb Analysis.

First I showed him the results from the US Branded Mainstream Tea business. You will recall that this was a large, important and profitable segment for Universal Tea, but one in which UTC had been losing market share. Would the customer interviews explain this?

Comb analysis asks the customers first of all to score what is important to them in deciding which supplier to use – their purchase criteria – on a scale of one (unimportant) to five (essential). We can then display the results on a chart like that in Illustration 1.21, which shows what was important to the supermarket buyers of Branded Tea:

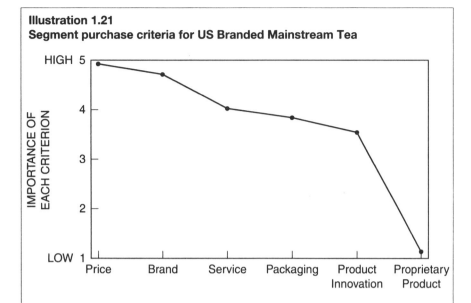

Illustration 1.21
Segment purchase criteria for US Branded Mainstream Tea

It can be seen that Price is the most important criterion, scoring a very high 4.9, followed by Brand, also very important (4.7), Service (which meant responsiveness to the customer and things like delivery efficiency), which was also important (4.0), with Packaging (3.8) also quite important, and Product Innovation (3.5) moderately important. Not surprisingly, the ability to supply proprietary product was almost completely unimportant (1.1) in the branded segment.

'Nothing new there,' commented Randy. I told him that the next stage in Comb Analysis was to ask the customers to score the client, in this case Universal Tea, on each of the purchase criteria, again on a one (terrible) to five (excellent) scale, and to overlay these scores on the previous chart, as in Illustration 1.22.

'Still no surprises,' Randy injected. I had to agree: UTC was very close to meeting all the performance criteria of the segment, with the single exception of price.

The third and final stage of Comb Analysis is to ask the customers to score the client's competitors on a similar one to five scale on each of the criteria, and to further overlay these results, as in Illustration 1.23.

'We can see from this,' I told Randy, 'that the only real selling point for the competition in this segment is price. Unfortunately that is also the most important criterion. We at UTC appear to have significant advantages in terms of brand and service, which are also important.'

Illustration 1.22
Rating of Universal Tea's performance relative to purchase criteria for US Branded Mainstream Tea

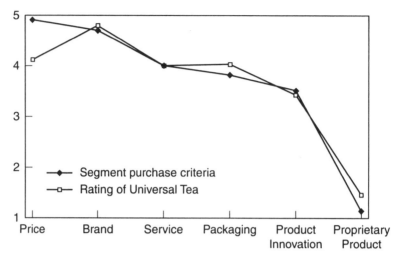

Illustration 1.23
Rating of competitors overlaid for US branded Mainstream Tea

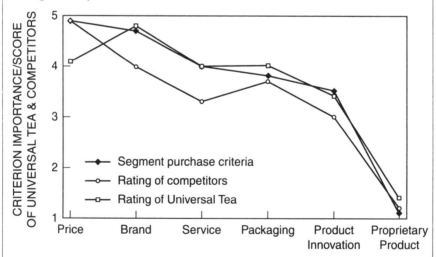

'Now remember,' I went on, 'that this segment is large and important for us, but that we have been losing market share. But I conclude from these data that we should be able to do something about that. The gap between our rating and that of the competitor on price is not enormous, and we are at least as good on everything else. My guess is that if we showed a bit more flexibility on price we could get a lot more of the business. We should also stress the fact that our brand and our service are superior to the competition's, so perhaps we do not absolutely have to match their price to win more business.'

'But that would mean lower profits,' objected Randy, 'and what if they cut price still further? Only the customer would win.'

'Profits would not necessarily be lower,' I retorted. 'I think that if we did the sums, given the costs in the business that would not increase with more volume, costs like advertising and all the corporate overheads, not to mention the factory fixed costs, so that we could afford to cut price if we could be fairly sure it would give us more market share. Even if our return on sales dipped a bit, we'd make a much higher return on capital, and a lot more absolute profit, which is what concerns the shareholders.'

'But as you say,' I went on, 'the key thing is the reaction of the competition. We shouldn't make any final decision until after looking at their position and likely behaviour. But bear in mind that our leading competitor, United Foods, has only $150m of sales here compared to our $200m. There is no reason, therefore, why they should have lower costs than us, if we were equally efficient.'

'So, Randy, there are really only two alternatives. Either they are more efficient than us, or they are not. If they are, we should be able to become as efficient at them by lowering costs. If that is true, we can compensate for lower prices by lowering costs. If they are not more efficient, they must be accepting considerably lower profit margins than we are, and a further reduction in price to stop us getting more business could cut their profit margins to an unacceptable level, or even push them into making losses. We need to understand what United Foods characteristically does when faced with these sort of decisions, so we can predict what they might do. But either way, we can probably get more volume and also increase our profits simultaneously.'

Without stopping to debate this further, I moved on to report on the second important segment, US Private Label. Here I saved time by displaying straight away all three sets of results: the segment purchase criteria, the rating of Randy's UTC, and the rating of his key competitor, Cheapco. In this case, the results had Randy jumping out of his chair, demanding to know if I had drawn the lines wrong on Illustration 1.24!

Illustration 1.24
Comb analysis of US private label tea

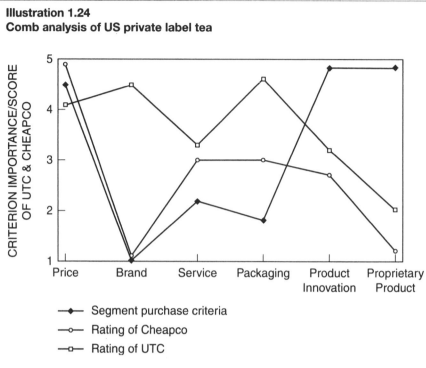

'That can't be right', exclaimed Randy. 'The chart says that the buyers of private label for the supermarkets value product innovation and proprietary products most of all, even more than price. Our people tell me that the only thing these buyers, especially Big Boy Supermarkets, want is a cheap price. And you've seen for yourself how much money we lose in supplying them, because of the ridiculously low price they demand.'

'I agree that the data are surprising', I countered, 'but I've double-checked the results of the interviews, and I think there are a number of things here that are interesting and potentially helpful for us.'

'First, just concentrate on the segment purchase criteria compared to their rating of us. It's interesting that they give us a higher rating on price than their purchase criteria, suggesting that they are surprised at how flexible we are on price. Look particularly, though, at the rating for our packaging, which at 4.6 is far higher than their purchase criteria at 1.8. This suggests that we might potentially give them cheaper packaging and save ourselves money, without in any way causing them concern. Now look at the surprising importance that they attach to product innovation and proprietary products. What the Big Boy buyer was saying was that they wanted to be able to offer a distinctive product under their own private label, where they would be selling a high quality product at a reasonably high price. This is a change in strategy for them, and they admitted that it is a recent development, but they're very keen on it.'

'Now the interesting thing is, if we look at the rating of Cheapco, the Big Boy buyer is really saying that he couldn't see Cheapco coming up with a proprietary product for them, and although we haven't been at all responsive so far, he sees us as the logical supplier of this.'

By now I had Randy's interest, though not his agreement. 'So', he queried sarcastically, 'you want me to do more unprofitable business with Big Boy, do you?'

'No, but I think it is possible that if you did supply Big Boy with a proprietary product, perhaps a different shape of bag, or product for different regions depending on the water quality, that you could negotiate a profitable contract with much higher prices than on the commodity business. It's also just possible that you could do this in exchange for negotiating slightly higher prices, maybe 5 per cent higher, on the commodity business. They want this proprietary product and you are virtually the only possible supplier. Also, given that Big Boy are very happy with the prices they are getting from you and Cheapco, it's likely that their margins on tea are above average and that prices could be edged up a bit. That depends upon the line that Cheapco take, so we can't be confident yet, but it's possible.'

Randy grunted, but I could see the cogs in his brain going round. I decided to move on to the results for the US Herb and Fruit Tea segments, which were so similar that I put them together (Illustration 1.25).

Illustration 1.25
Comb analysis of US Herb and Fruit Tea segments

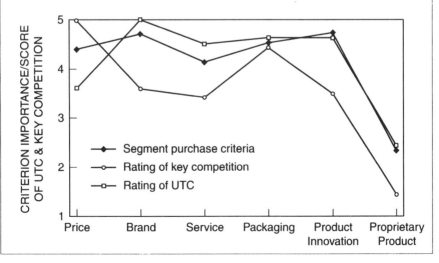

'Now, this is different picture, but also a very interesting one', I lectured. 'We see that with the notable exception of price, UTC is meeting the segment's purchase criteria very well. In contrast, our main competitor is rated a 5 on price, but under-performs the segment's purchase criteria on almost all other dimensions, especially brand strength and product innovation, both of which are very important to the buyers. Note that this segment values product innovation, just the same as the private label segment did, but in contrast to the latter, the buyers of fruit and herb teas don't really want proprietary product – they want to sell it under the name of the known brand, which is us.'

'Remember', I went on, 'the data we showed earlier about these segments. They are extremely profitable for us, fast growing, and we are clear leaders, nearly three times bigger than Herbal Health in herb tea and Fruit-Tea Fun in fruit teas. Out of our $21m profits, we make half in these two segments. But we are losing market share in them. And why do you think, Randy, that that is?'

'Well', he replied, 'it must be down to price, since we're far better than the competitors on everything else.'

'Right', I said, 'if we matched the competitors on price, there would be no reason for anyone to buy from them. Of course, they might undercut us again, and we could get dragged into a price war, so we'd need to understand their likely reactions. But the fact is that we could afford to cut price a bit. Another consideration is that we probably have some bargaining power with our buyers, since they need us for our brand strength and product innovation in particular. It's entirely plausible that we could negotiate higher quantities, and regain market share, if we were to shave our price just a bit. The other thing we could do is to speed up the pace of product innovation, and make more of the market new products, where our competitors would find it harder to respond.'

I decided to draw the session to a close. 'I think you'll agree, Randy', I stared hard at him, 'that we've learnt a lot from talking to the customers. But before drawing any definite conclusions, we need to take a closer look at the competitors and their freedom of manoeuvre. I'll see you back here in a week.'

7. WHAT ABOUT THE COMPETITORS?

Modern management thought presents two opposite views on how important it is to analyse competitors. One view is that understanding competitors and how to beat them is at the heart of competitive advantage and strategy. The other is that the key thing is to get on with your own life, learn how to serve customers best and reduce costs, and not worry too much about what anyone else is doing.

My view is poised nicely between the two extremes. I would never start doing business unit strategy by looking at the competitors, except to help define the segments. The key things to understand, to start with, are what your own firm is good at, where it makes the most money, and what your customers think of you. I also agree that it is more important to serve customers and make high returns than it is to 'beat' competitors, and that co-existence and implicit co-operation between competitors (especially if this involves tacit admission of each others' turf and avoidance of head-to-head competition by focussing on separate segments) is often a better route to sustainably high returns than a determination to do down the opposition.

My final concession to the 'worry about customers, not competitors' school of thought is to agree that strategy consultants often want to study competitors because they think this is a good thing to do rather than because they have very sharp and particular questions to answer. Such 'fishing expeditions' are usually a huge waste of time and money.

But in my experience, there is scarcely a business around that could not benefit terrifically from asking a few very specific questions about its competitors.

Randy's business was no exception. For each of the three major business segments we were looking at, there were one or two questions about competitors that needed answering before we could work out a strategy to boost profits. The questions I wanted to answer are shown below.

A Few Things That Randy Really Needed to Know About His Competitors

A. US Branded Tea Segment

A1. Is United Foods much more efficient and lower cost in Branded Tea than Randy's UTC? If so, why and how?

A2. How would United Foods react if UTC lowered its prices and started to regain market share in Branded Tea?

B. US Private Label Tea Segment

B1. Is Cheapco much more efficient and lower cost in private label tea than UTC? If so, why and how?

B2. What would be Cheapco's reaction if UTC raised its prices and attempted to move the general level of prices up?

C. US Herbal and Fruit Tea Segments

C1. What is the profitability and relative cost position of Herbal Health and Fruit-Tea Fun, each compared to UTC?

C2. What would be the reaction of each of Herbal Health and Fruit Tea Fun if UTC moved closer to them on price by cutting its currently high prices?

Note that the questions I wanted to answer for Randy were very focussed. Most of the answers, as it happened, came from a relatively straightforward look at the financial documents filed by the competitors, combined with a press search and a few phone interviews with industry observers, brokers and some people within the competitor companies. My report back to Randy a week later is summarised below.

What I Told Randy about his Competitors

A. US Branded Tea Segment

A1. United Foods is making a return on sales of just over 7 per cent in the US Branded Tea business. Its prices in the supermarkets are on average some 5 per cent below those of UTC. The supermarkets are thought to be earning about 2 per cent higher margin on United Foods tea than on UTC tea. Therefore it seems reasonable to conclude that if United Foods had the same prices as UTC in tea, United Foods return on sales would be 14 per cent (7 per cent + 5 per cent + 2 per cent). We know that UTC makes roughly 9 per cent return on sales in Branded Tea. We can therefore conclude, roughly, that United Foods has costs about 5 per cent below those of UTC.

Note, however, that United Foods has Branded Tea sales of only $150m in the US, compared to $200m for UTC. Normally, you would expect this to give UTC a cost advantage because of economies of scale, especially in marketing, that would be worth about 2 per cent return on sales.

It follows that the potential for UTC to reduce costs is in excess of 5 per cent of sales, with a rough target of 7 per cent.

UTC is losing market share to United Foods. We can conclude from the customer analysis that this is solely due to price: the lower prices being offered by United Foods to both consumers and to the supermarkets. Because UTC's brand, 5 Unicorns, is superior to that of United Foods, and because UTC's service to the supermarkets is better, it follows that market share loss could be arrested without completely matching United Foods' price.

If United Foods did not react to UTC lowering prices, it seems reasonable to conclude that a 4 per cent price cut (split between the consumer and the supermarkets) would stabilise market shares, that is, stop the loss of market share from UTC to United Foods. A 7 per cent price cut should lead to UTC regaining market share from United Foods, again in the absence of the latter also cutting price.

A2. United Foods is a well-run company, but it has publicly declared that it will seek to increase its earnings per share and stockholder dividends by a minimum of 10 per cent per annum. Analysts expect that to be difficult for United Foods to achieve this year, because of problems in the banana market. Tea is expected to comprise 25 per cent of United Foods' profits this year. It appears vital for United Foods to maintain its tea profits this year, and price-cutting would make a severe dent in these.

It seems reasonable to think, therefore, that unless UTC began to take large amounts of volume away from United Foods, the latter would be unlikely to cut prices.

B. US Private Label Tea Segment

B1. By the same process of analysis as in A1, we conclude that Cheapco is a staggering 10 per cent lower cost than UTC in private label tea. A lot of this difference, perhaps up to 3 per cent, is due to the cheaper packaging used by Cheapco. As we have seen from the Comb Analysis, the buyers place zero value on UTC's more expensive packaging. UTC could therefore raise its margins, or cut its prices, by about 3 per cent almost overnight by a change in its packaging purchasing policy.

There is no discernible difference in prices between Cheapco and UTC in this segment.

There is the opportunity for UTC to lower its costs by up to 10 per cent. This could turn a business losing 5 per cent on sales into one making 5 per cent on sales, within say two years.

Cheapco currently makes 6 per cent return on sales on private label tea.

B2. From sources I cannot attribute, I am fairly confident that a 2 per cent price rise by UTC would be followed by Cheapco.

C. US Herbal and Fruit Tea Segments

C1. Herbal Health has a return on sales of 9 per cent (UTC: 14 per cent in herb tea), and Fruit-Tea Fun a return on sales of 8 per cent (UTC: 12 per cent in fruit tea). Both companies price about 5 per cent below UTC.

It is likely, therefore, that each competitor's costs are roughly the same as those of UTC.

UTC has a scale advantage, being nearly three times larger than either Herbal Health or Fruit-Tea Fun. This advantage should be worth about 4 per cent return on sales.

There may well, therefore, be the opportunity to reduce UTC costs by up to 4 per cent.

C2. Moving closer to the competitors in price would probably reverse the loss of market share, unless they followed us down in price. Neither company can afford to do that. Herbal Health has just floated on the stock market by means of an IPO (Initial Public Offering), and Fruit-Tea Fun plans to do the same in 1996. For the next two years, both companies need to show steadily increasing profits, and they have no other businesses.

8. HOW DO YOU RAISE PROFITS QUICKLY?

This section should interest all readers. The way I will deal with it is to continue with the Randy/UTC example, before providing a more general checklist relevant to all businesses.

I had now reached the point where I felt sure of Randy's full attention. 'I'm going to summarise what we have learnt so far, and then outline how I feel you can increase profits', I told him. I used an overhead projector and put up a slide, reproduced below.

Summary of Findings for UTC

(1) UTC is in ten different segments, each of which requires a different strategy.

(2) UTC currently makes 85 per cent of its profits in the US Branded Tea business. UTC is the market leader, a third larger than United Foods. The segment is low growth, and UTC is losing share to United Foods. It is an attractive business to be in.

(3) The supermarkets' most important purchase criteria are price and brand strength, with service and packaging also important. UTC scores better than United Foods on all criteria, with the important exception of price. United Foods prices its tea to consumers 5 per cent below UTC's prices, and also gives the supermarkets an extra 2 per cent margin more than UTC. Price is the only reason why United Foods is gaining market share from UTC.

(4) United Foods has 5 per cent lower costs in producing and selling its tea than UTC. Given UTC's greater scale, equal efficiency would lead to UTC having costs 7 per cent lower than today.

(5) US Herb Tea comprises less than 7 per cent of UTC's sales but is responsible for 37 per cent of its profits (the reason that US Branded Tea and US Herb tea provide over 100 per cent of current UTC profits is because of losses in private label). This is a highly attractive market, with 15 per cent market growth annually. UTC is a clear market leader, and enjoys a return on sales in this business of a staggering 14 per cent, but is losing market share quite fast to Herbal Health.

(6) The most important purchase criteria in herb tea are brand and product innovation, closely followed by packaging, price and service. UTC performs better than Herbal Health on all criteria except price, where it is significantly less competitive, since Herbal Health prices 5 per cent lower.

(7) Herbal Health has roughly equal costs to UTC, which, taking into account UTC's advantage from being nearly three times larger, suggests there is an opportunity to lower UTC costs by 4 per cent.

(8) Herb tea is a 'star' business, where market share must be defended for the sake of long term profits and cashflow. If UTC priced 4–5 per cent lower than today, to roughly match Herbal Health prices, it is unlikely that Herbal Health would reduce its prices. If this is correct, UTC could reverse the loss of market share and consolidate its leadership position.

(9) The US Fruit Tea business constitutes under 3 per cent of UTC revenues but provides over 13 per cent of profits. Its characteristics are almost identical to those of Herb Tea, though the leading competitor (Fruit-Tea Fun) is different. This is another star business where UTC is losing valuable market share through pricing too high.

(10) The export markets for Branded Tea together comprise 15 per cent of revenues but 40 per cent of profits. UTC is gaining market share in all major export markets, but is only the leader in 'Rest of the World' (that is, markets other than Canada and Europe), which mainly means positions of strength in Asia. The 'Rest of the World' Branded Tea business is highly profitable and well run.

(11) The herb and fruit tea exports markets are very small, but profitable and fast growing. UTC is in weak but improving market share positions. Profits may be vulnerable if market prices fall, but it is worth while trying to attain leadership positions, particularly if this can be done by acquisition.

(12) By far the biggest UTC problem, and by far the biggest opportunity, lies in the US private label tea business. The losses on the contract with Big Boy supermarkets come to $18m, or 86 per cent of the net level of profits. Yet this is an attractive business to be in, with few suppliers and a high average level of profitability (UTC is the only player losing money in it). UTC has a reasonable market share position.

(13) The unbranded market has surprising purchase criteria, with the most important being product innovation and being willing to provide new and unique products under the supermarkets' brands. Price is also important. Packaging is not. UTC is rated well on price (as is Cheapco, the largest competitor), but performs poorly on product innovation and offering proprietary products to the supermarkets. It is important to note, however, that Cheapco performs even worse, and significantly worse, than UTC on these two most important criteria.

(14) Cheapco has costs 10 per cent lower than UTC in Unbranded Tea, of which 3 per cent relates to cheaper packaging. There appears to be an opportunity to move the general level of prices up.

(15) The most important opportunity for UTC in Unbranded Tea, besides lowering costs, lies in providing proprietary product to the chains. This could lead to large and profitable new business, since price sensitivity on unique product is lower and the volumes could be very large, without any need for expensive advertising.

As I went through the slide, Randy was uncharacteristically silent and attentive. At the end, he asked simply, 'But what do I do?'. This was the perfect lead into my next slide, shown below.

Five Key Recommendations to Randy

(1) In US Branded Tea, cut list prices by 2 per cent and offer another 2 per cent additional margin to the supermarkets, in order to stop market share loss.

(2) Cut costs in US Branded Tea by 7 per cent within two years.

(3) In US herb and fruit teas, cut prices by 4–5 per cent to reverse the market share loss. Reduce costs by 4 per cent within 18 months.

(4) In the US Unbranded Tea market, raise prices by 2 per cent immediately, and cut costs by a total of 10 per cent over two years, 3 per cent of which (relating to packaging) can be done immediately.

(5) Mount a campaign to provide leading retailers (especially Big Boy) with unique new products to be sold under their own house brands. Target revenues of $100m by the end of year 1 and $250m by the end of year 2.

I then moved on to a final slide, shown as Illustration 1.26 summarising the potential profit impact if the recommendations could be successfully implemented.

Note that the implied return on sales is calculated as a reality check. In this type of business, the successful competitors make 10 per cent return on

Illustration 1.26
Potential profit impact of recommendations to UTC: Effect on operating profit ($m)

	Year 1	Year 2	Year 3
1. US branded tea 4% price cut	(8.0)	(8.0)	(8.0)
2. US branded tea new volume	0.8	2.0	4.4
3. US branded tea cost cutting	3.7	7.3	12.8
4. US fruit and herb tea 4–5% price cut	(3.5)	(4.1)	(4.7)
5. US fruit and herb tea new volume	0.9	2.1	3.5
6. US fruit and herb tea cost cutting	1.1	2.4	2.7
7. US private label tea 2% price rise	7.8	7.8	7.8
8. US private label tea cost cutting	12.0	24.1	40.2
9. US private label tea new unique products	1.5	8.8	12.5
Net change	16.3	42.4	71.2
Previous budget	22.0	24.2	26.6
Total Profit	38.3	66.6	97.8
Total Revenues after new initiatives	950	1265	1370
Implied Return on Sales	4.0%	5.3%	7.1%

sales, but anything above that over a business as a whole is not generally sustainable. It can be seen that although I estimated that Randy had the potential to increase his operating profits to over 450 per cent of today's level, the third year return on sales, at just over 7 per cent, still looks reasonable.

So much for Randy's business, which is a disguised example of a real-life business that did make similar (actually slightly larger) profit increases with these sort of actions. Illustration 1.27 provides a diagnosis of profit improvement opportunities that can be used for any business.

Some of these themes will be expanded in the next section, which covers the development of secure, high-quality long term profits, and expansion into related and new businesses.

9. HOW DO YOU BUILD LONG TERM VALUE?

Short term profit improvement is almost always possible as a result of cost reduction and a refocus of the business on fewer segments, where your firm has a clear competitive advantage. It may also be possible to push through some tactical price increases, particularly if the product or service can be improved. But the sources of long term profit improvement are generally different. Paradoxically, because they are long term, they need to be worked on now, immediately after you have worked out how to raise short term profits.

Illustration 1.27
General diagnosis of profit improvement opportunities

Profit Improvement Type	Diagnosis
A. Cost reduction	1. The business is unprofitable
	2. Competitors have higher return on sales
	3. Customers do not value some part of your product offering
	4. Unit costs have been rising historically
	5. Some competitors outsource large parts of the process that you produce yourself
B. Price increases	6. Competitors would probably follow a rise
	7. Segment profitability is low
	8. You are gaining market share
	9. Customers rate you highly
	10. You have lower prices than competitors
C. Price decreases	11. Competitors are lower price
	12. You are losing market share due to price
	13. Competitors are unlikely to match your cut
	14. Profits are above the 'normal zone' on the bananagram
	15. Customers say price is the most important criterion
D. Changes in business mix	16. You have wide differences in your segment profitability
	17. ... and in your relative market share positions
	18. ... and in customers' rating of you in different segments
	19. You have the opportunity to seize leadership in a segment, provided you focus on it
E. Changes in activity focus	20 You are clearly best at just one part of the 'value added chain' (such as R&D, manufacturing, marketing, etc.) and should just concentrate on that and outsource everything else
	21. You can 'lock up' a channel or business by integrating forward or backward
F. Expansion in existing segments	22. You have the knack of growing faster than the market
	23. You can mop up competitors by acquisition without paying a fancy price
	24. You can attain higher prices and/or lower costs than any competitor in your chosen segment
G. Expansion into adjacent segments	25. There are business segments which can use your skills or cost base well that you are not currently
	26. No competitor in those adjacent segments is bigger or better financed than you
	27. The adjacent segments are at least as profitable as existing segments
H. Invention and innovation	28. You are good at it
	29. The industry has not historically been very innovative
	30. Suppliers have been innovating
	31. New customers can be created by innovation
	32. You can copy new trends from other industries, that have not yet been applied in your industry
	33. You spot innovation in your industry currently only applied in other countries

Long term profit improvement almost always rests on one or more of the following five sets of actions:

(1) actions to increase market share in existing segments

(2) actions to 're-compete', that is, to change the basis of competition in your key segments, nearly always involving a transformation of the cost base

(3) actions to enter new segments that your firm is not currently serving

(4) actions to transform the firm's total cost base

(5) actions to increase the firm's competences and ability to learn.

Now let's discuss each of these, with a checklist for you to review what may be relevant to your firm.

Checklist: How to raise long term profits

A. Actions to increase market share in existing segments

Note: you should only aim to increase market share if the segment is a core segment for you and the market is attractive. In certain segments you should actively aim to 'sell' market share, to pay for market share expansion in your key segments. Be selective.

(1) Cut prices. Price should be cut if (i) the market or an important and profitable part of it is price sensitive, and (ii) you can be fairly confident that competitors will not match your price cuts for long, *or*, in any case, if you are lower cost than your competitors in serving the segment. In the latter case it will not matter much if the competitors cut price, because sooner or later they will be forced to raise prices again or exit the segment (unless the segment is so important to them that they will lose money in order to hold market share).

Price sensitivity varies enormously between markets, but few segments can resist the allure of higher value for money over the long haul.

Cutting price is not a very popular tactic, but is nearly always effective in increasing market share. The payback may not be quick: cutting price usually leads to substantially lower profits for the first 3–5 years. But there are very few examples of price cutting, which, consistently followed, have not worked and led to a much more valuable business long term.

Price cutting should lead to a virtuous circle: increases in market share, immediate pressure on internal costs because of lower profits, higher volume leading before long to lower unit costs, still greater market share gains, pressure on competitors to leave the business or retreat to higher price segments alone, further increases in market share, further reductions in unit costs, and so on.

The only cases where price cutting has hurt the initiator and everyone else is when there is serious excess capacity in the business and there are also non-economic barriers to exit. Otherwise, it is a very good bet.

(2) Build in extra features, value, service and quality. This tactic should accompany cost reduction, not be seen as an alternative. Having said that, it is a much more popular tactic than price cutting, and one that succeeds much less often. This is not because it is inferior, but simply because it is much more difficult to do. Firms that are successful in the long run, however, almost always constantly strive to deliver more to their customers – more than they did the year before, and more than the competitors.

(3) Remove a competitor, either by buying it or forcing it to exit from the segment. In one sense, all profitable business activity involves establishing a very high relative market share of a segment, or, to use emotive words, setting up a monopoly or at least an oligopoly. In general, the best way to achieve this aim is to provide a better and cheaper service to your customers.

But there is also no doubt that 'taking out' competitors helps enormously. Fortunately, anti-trust/anti-monopoly constraints do not operate with sufficient precision or pervasiveness to stop this happening in most cases.

Almost the only case where removing an important competitor does not help is when the barriers to entry are low and removing one firm may simply lead to another one entering the market, so you will need to assess the chances of this happening. If the chances are low, buying a competitor or pricing so that he or she has to leave the market will nearly always pay off handsomely in the long run, whatever your cost/benefit analysis shows today.

(4) Invest more, and more intelligently, than competitors. Market share goes in the end to the competitors who are most committed, who invest the most. Traditionally, investment meant laying down physical capacity, in terms of plants, distribution networks, service centres, retail outlets and/or computer systems. These are still important in some industries, but increasingly the most effective investments are in software, research and development, training, brand-building, getting close to customers, design and innovation.

But investments are not investments unless they are costly. By definition, investments do not have an instant payback, and usually not a short one. Make a checklist of all possible investments you could make. Then assess the potential benefit in terms of market share in ten years' time. Force yourself to guess these on a consistent basis for each possible investment. The numbers will be wrong, but still helpful. Then guestimate the cost of each investment, and rank them according to cost-effectiveness. Then make all the investments you can possibly afford.

The second way to raise the quality and quantity of long term profits is to change the rules of the game in a key segment. In stratspeak, this is often called *'re-competing'*. Examples include Kwik-fit in the UK, which set up specialised exhaust and tyre fitting services with a very quick and low cost formula, completely outwitting the traditional suppliers, the broad-line garage repairers/service stations. Another example is Ikea, the Swedish furniture retailer, which engaged the customer in providing much of the labour (such as selection and assembly of the product) traditionally taken on by the retailer, making it possible to provide high design at a low price, combined with instant availability.

Or take the example of First Direct in banking or Direct Line in insurance, where customers can obtain superior and faster service by using the phone, without needing to visit a bank branch or insurance agency, rendering existing competitors' cost bases (expensive retail networks) unnecessary. Home delivery of pizza and other fast food provides another example of successful re-competing.

Some hints about possible ways to re-compete are provided below.

Checklist: How to raise long term profits

B. Actions to re-compete

Note: Re-competing is a terrifically powerful weapon, but may not be possible, or may not be appropriate for a particular firm. But it is always worth engaging in the most creative thinking you can regarding re-competing, if only to be aware of potential dangers to your traditional business. And you may just hit the jackpot ...

(1) **Think of radical ways to cut costs in any activity,** to below half of their current level. This will not be possible without doing something radically different. Brainstorm possible ways, however bizarre.

(2) **Think specifically of where less might be better,** for example, self-service in supermarkets and petrol retailing, where, simultaneously, cost can be removed and the customer might prefer to be more actively involved.

(3) **Think of the most expensive part of the existing industry's operations,** and brainstorm how it might be removed.

(4) **Imagine what information technology,** creatively applied, could do the industry. What might it look like in a generation's time?

(5) **Put yourself in the position of the customer.** What irks him or her today about the way they are currently served. How could it be done better? Could the customer be engaged in providing some of the service?

(6) **Roll back history and pretend the product/service does not exist today.** How would you set up the industry from scratch today, if you could not simply replicate how it developed historically? You are not allowed to use the existing systems in answering this question.

(7) **What would a 'greener' industry look like? A more socially responsible one? One more in tune with social changes? One that is more fun, for both operator and customer?**

(8) **Steal ideas from other industries where re-competing has taken place.**

(9) **Steal ideas from other countries, where they do it differently or cheaper.**

The third way to raise long term profits is to enter new segments, particularly those which are 'adjacent' to your existing profitable segments. Some ideas are given below.

Checklist: How to raise long term profits

C. Entering new segments

(1) **Think of ways in which you could use your existing cost base** in a new segment...

(2) **... or use your existing skills,** where you believe these are better than competitors'.

(3) **Imagine products/services that your existing good customers might want to buy from you.**

(4) **Dream up other uses for technologies you have.**

(5) **Make a list of all the segments your competitors are in. Why aren't you?** (But beware: there may be good reasons.)

(6) **Look at the range of services provided by your counterparts in other countries and/or similar industries.**

(7) **Are there any competitors who are leaders in a segment adjacent to your own? Could it make sense to acquire them or form a joint venture?**

More detail is provided in the entries in Part Three (B) on the ANSOFF MATRIX and in Part Three (C) on ADJACENT SEGMENTS.

The fourth route to long term profit improvement is to transform the firm's total cost base, via a customer-focussed '*re-engineering*' exercise.

This is much more than finding short term cost reduction opportunities. It is concerned with the whole way that a firm should operate.

Peter DRUCKER is right again: 'So much of what we call management consists of making it difficult for people to work.' Re-engineering, often called BUSINESS PROCESS RE-ENGINEERING or BPR, attempts to remove the obstacles placed in the way of satisfying customer needs by traditional, hierarchical management.

BPR is a huge subject well beyond the scope of this book, but let me do two things here: first, to explain the basic principles and why BPR is important; and second, to explain the linkage between strategy and BPR, and why strategy for any business should be arrived at before undertaking BPR. If you wish to, you can then look up the entry on BPR in Part Three.

Most people, when asked to describe a business, fall back on a *structural* view: so many employees, this and that factory, here's the organisation chart, the places where different functions are located, the sales offices are there, and so on. This is the old-fashioned mentality from which BPR seeks to liberate us.

In contrast, BPR takes a *process* view and a *skills* view.

The *process* view is how the firm's people interact in order to produce something that customers want: for example, how marketing and R&D jointly develop new products, or how customers' orders are fulfilled, or how a product is made in the factory by a sequence of process steps.

The *skills* view looks at how effective the firm's people are at doing what customers want, or finding new customers: how pleased customers are with how they are treated and what they receive, how quickly and efficiently are goods made and delivered, how good the firm is at developing new products or finding distributors, and so on.

This leads to the second point. Conducting BPR using a process and skills view can lead to dramatic cuts in cost, and even more importantly, increases in sales through greater customer satisfaction and loyalty. But BPR is an expensive and time-consuming one-off exercise. It should be undertaken after, rather than before, a strategic review. If a business is competitively weak or worth more to another firm, a decision may be made to sell it, for example, so that time spent on a BPR exercise might be wasted if BPR were to be undertaken before looking at strategy.

In thinking about both processes and skills, time is a critical dimension. Here the old adage that 'time is money' really comes alive. If something can be done quicker, it can kill two birds with one stone – both please customers, and also do things at lower cost.

The process view therefore aims to streamline operations to reduce throughput time: how long it takes to manufacture a product, how long it takes to deliver it to customers (from the time the order is taken to the time the customer has it in his hands), how long it takes to bring a new product to market (from having the original idea to having it in the shops), and so on.

The process view looks at flows: of money (cash flows), of physical product, and of information. Compression of cycle times in delivering product to cutomers is the key to reducing the costs and increasing customer satisfaction, and therefore the firm's market share.

Through looking at processes, it is possible to work out better and cheaper ways of doing what the firm already does. Through looking at skills, it is possible to work out which skills customers value the highest, which skills are possible areas where the firm can be better than its competitors, and how these core skills can be enhanced and made 'world class'. Since this is easier if fewer things are attempted, the skill-based view usually ends in the firm deciding to use outside contractors for some of its activities (those where it does not currently have, and would find it difficult to build, skills superior to those of its competitors).

The relationship between BPR and strategy is summarised in Illustration 1.28. BPR should be conducted only after a strategic review, for core businesses that are to be retained. It should not be conducted for weak businesses with poor competitive positions, except as a last resort.

The fifth way to raise sustainable profits is to *deepen and enrich the company's distinctive culture, its competences and its ability to learn.* This is true at the operating company or divisional level as well as at the overall corporate level.

Very often, a company's success derives not so much from its products, technology, strategic positions or other 'hard', structural reasons, but from 'softer' influences: operational excellence; high service to customers; employees' ability and energy levels and the way that they co-operate with each other; and the company's whole personality, culture and way of doing business.

Illustration 1.28
When is BPR appropriate?

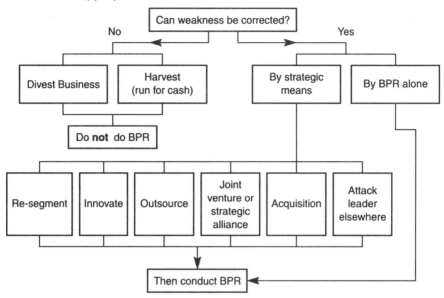

Different firms in the same industry (and sometimes different divisions or operating companies within the same corporation) frequently have different average levels of employee ability and commitment. Some companies attract the best people; others repel them. Some companies get the most out of all their people; others systematically get the worst out of their people. Some companies exhibit teamwork; most do not. It is not surprising that these differences lead to greater or lesser efficiency and customer satisfaction.

Ultimately, a company will only be successful if it has people who are above average in their skills and in their commitment to the company. Such commitment will only be forthcoming if they believe in what the company does and feel that they are a key part of it.

As with **BPR**, further elaboration on this subject lies well beyond the scope of this book. Some hints are provided in the entries in Part Three on COMPETENCES, corporate religion, CULTURE, LEARNING ORGANISATION and KNOWLEDGE MANAGEMENT STRUCTURE. A practical guide on how to change corporate culture is provided in *Wake Up and Shake Up Your Company* by Koch and Campbell.

You can make a start on thinking about these issues, however, by asking yourself the following three questions:

(1) Is our company above-average in terms of the way that we execute what we do, in terms of operational excellence and service to customers?
(2) Do we find it easy to attract and keep above-average staff? Do they enjoy their work and feel personally committed to the company?
(3) What, specifically and in very concrete terms, are we particularly good at doing, in the eyes of our customers and in terms of making the highest profits?

Unless you can honestly answer *yes* to questions (1) and (2), you should think seriously about the company's culture and how to change it.

Question (3) is not easy to answer, but if you persevere you may gain a very useful insight into how to develop the firm. To illustrate, answers that certain firms have arrived at include the following:

'We are good at supplying high margin, branded stationery items in Europe, delivering high quality product quickly. We cannot be efficient or low enough in cost for lower margin or unbranded product, and we are not operationally effective in America or the Far East.'

'We are excellent at product invention and innovation. We are poor marketeers and inefficient at manufacturing.'

'We are good at churning out high volume, standard products at low cost. When we go up-market or try to meet special requirements we fall flat on our face.'

'We are good at pleasing customers who have rigorous engineering requirements. We are bored and slow when it comes to satisfying standard needs.'

'We are good at project management on complex, high value projects.'

'We have no advantage in terms of product, brand or geography. But our people love meeting customers and delivering exactly what they want, fast. We prosper because our customers, in turn, love us.'

Once you have discovered the specific source of your company's success, or where it is most successful, there are three things that you could, in theory, do, only two of which are generally sensible:

(1) Most people's first instinct is to *correct* their *weaknesses*. For instance, we are good in Europe but not in America, *ergo*, let's sort out America.

This usually ends in tears. There are generally good, deep-rooted reasons for failure in America (or whatever). It normally requires a lot of time, energy, skill, money and luck to turn bad into good. Most of the time it is not worth the effort and the risk.

Far more productive, in most circumstances, are the following two approaches:

(2) *Further enhance your areas of strength.* Take what is very good and make it excellent. Take what is better than competitors can do, and make it so much better that they give up entirely. Take something that is excellent by local standards, and make it world-beating. Take something that is excellent but brittle, and dependent on a few people, and make it broader-based and so deeply rooted in the company's mentality and way of doing business that it could survive the departure of the current experts and leaders.

(3) *Focus on the functions, parts of the value chain, products and/or markets that really play to your strengths*, gain market share and sales in these areas, and migrate out of other areas. It may be that only 20 per cent of your sales are in the areas of real strength, though these generate 60 per cent of your contribution and 90 per cent of your fully costed profits. In that case, aim to migrate, over time, out of the 80 per cent of sales that do not play to your strengths. Plan so that in 5–10 years, your 20 per cent of profitable sales have been tripled, the 80 per cent of unprofitable sales eliminated, and the surplus cost associated with the latter also eliminated. You will have a smaller, simpler, more focussed business, and profits nearly three times as great as today's.

Some of you may feel that I have strayed well beyond the province of strategy, to talk about operational excellence, culture and competences. This accusation may even be correct, if 'strategy' is thought to be confined to hard, analytical issues. Yet 'strategy' should mean thinking about how to improve a company's worth and competitive positioning, and such thinking should not ignore non-analytical issues.

A firm's competitive strategy cannot be confined to purely structural issues. Operational issues and strategic position are all of a piece. Awareness of structural strengths and weaknesses, and operational strengths and weaknesses, are simultaneously necessary. Only then can the company focus on what it does best, and make excellence permanent and deeply engrained. Only then can customers be delighted, won and retained. Only then can competitors be outpaced. And only then can short term profits and long term shareholder value be raised.

10. CONCLUSION

We have now reached the end of the section on business unit strategy, for those running real businesses with customers and competitors. This is where the greatest value of strategy lies: in detail, at the sharp end, with those who are in the thick of the battle. I hope that, if you have read this far, you are now convinced of the value of strategy to operating line managers.

But for thirty years the conventional wisdom has been different. The accepted view or assumption of strategists throughout this period has been that the main value of strategy is at the overall corporate level, at the Head Office. In the process, more value has been subtracted than added.

To understand why this is the case, and what are possible antidotes to value destruction at the central level, we need to turn to Part Two: Corporate Centre Strategy.

Part II

CORPORATE CENTRE
STRATEGY

1. THE GREAT MYTH OF CORPORATE STRATEGY

When I was a child, there was a great song by Danny Kaye called *The King's New Clothes*, which I recall started, 'The King is in the Altogether, the Altogether, the Altogether'. It featured the old myth of a king who had been conned into buying a non-existent suit, which everyone, out of flattery or embarrassment, pretended to see and admire. Only a small and naive boy was prepared to point out that the king was actually naked.

So it is with corporate centre strategy. For years businessmen and academics have believed that there is something called corporate strategy, distinct from business unit strategy, involving the head office or Centre of a company adding value by making astute moves, buying and selling companies within the corporate portfolio, divining great new strategies for individual businesses, extracting superior performance from the latter, and generally providing valuable leadership.

A whole industry has grown up to advise on corporate strategy, involving tens of thousands of highly paid strategy consultants and academics, and hundreds of millions of pounds of annual revenues. Millions have been made from single books on corporate strategy, such as Porter's '*Competitive Strategy*'.

Investment banks have made literally billions of dollars out of advising on and sponsoring major changes in corporate strategy, involving huge acquisitions and divestments. With each acquisition comes the promise of better corporate strategy, and were this not believed in, the funds would not be forthcoming.

Yet it is time to find a small boy, and blow the whistle. The King is in the Altogether, the Altogether, the Altogether.

Corporate centre strategy is, in general, and in aggregate, a snare and a delusion. Let me be precise about this. What I mean is that the efforts of those at the head of multi-business companies to add value to their subsidiary businesses fail. The Centre of such companies usually destroys far more value than it creates. It would be far better for everyone (except the managers at the Centre) if the Centre did not exist, or, if this is impossible, if the Centre was minuscule and did as little as possible.

This is not just because most corporate strategy is flawed or poorly implemented. The problem is far deeper than that. It is rooted in the very nature of corporate reality. Managers at the Centre, however competent, are natural value destroyers.

When you think about it, the whole idea of a corporate Centre is pretty curious. A Centre does not have businesses, revenues or customers, independent of the operating companies underneath. Nearly all multi-business companies are organised so that the operating companies are stand-alone entities that could survive perfectly happily were the Centre to be blown up and everyone in it killed. The Centre is just an intermediary between the businesses that create wealth, and the bankers and investors who provide funds.

Anything other than a minimal Centre can only be justified if the Centre adds more value than it costs and subtracts from the businesses. Yet it should be clear that three things are true, both about the majority of corporate Centres and about the corporate Centres in aggregate:

(1) Few corporate Centres are small. Most are very expensive to run and consume a lot of the profit generated by the operating businesses they own.

(2) Most corporate Centres do not add enough value to the businesses to justify their cost.

(3) Independent of their cost, most corporate Centres destroy more value than they add. In other words, even if the people at the Centre worked for free, the businesses would be better off without it.

These may seem extreme conclusions. They are certainly, if true, revolutionary in their implications. In case you are not yet convinced, I will call in support three types of evidence: academic, empirical financial data, and the experience of those who work in business.

First the academic evidence. The most exhaustive review of corporate strategy in practice has just been published in North America and the UK. Called '*Corporate Level Strategy*', and subtitled, '*Creating Value in the Multi-Business Company*', this landmark book is by Michael Goold, Andrew Campbell and Marcus Alexander of the Ashridge Strategic Management Centre. Based on 11 years of research, it is one of the most important books on strategy ever published.

These sober academics do not mince their words. The first paragraph ends, 'The conclusion we reach is that, while a few successful parents create value in multi-business companies, the large majority are value destroyers.'

Value destruction operates when the Centre makes mistakes, such as the wrong acquisition, appointing the wrong chief executive, or imposing inappropriate controls. But the most pervasive reason for Centres destroying value is the subtle but negative influence that the Centre has on the operating companies. Put simply, just by existing, the Centre takes responsibility away from those running the businesses. Those who should be excited by the prospect of making or losing money, who should feel themselves in charge of their own destiny, do not – simply because there is a central owner. Consequently they behave like managers, not like owners; like bureaucrats, not like entrepreneurs.

The second set of evidence for the proposition that corporate Centres, and most corporate strategies, are inherently value-destroying, is empirical. Empirical evidence can never be totally conclusive, but two different sorts of such evidence, one relating to buy-outs and de-mergers, and the other to 'value gaps', is quite convincing.

There are many well documented examples of companies that have performed significantly better after the Centre (in the Ashridge academics' term, the 'parent') has been removed, after either a buy-out or a de-merger. One example of which I have first-hand experience, also quoted by Goold, Campbell and Alexander, is that of Premier Brands. It is an instructive tale.

Premier Brands was, until 1986, the Food Division of Cadbury Schweppes, a well managed company with a respected Centre. The products included Typhoo tea, Hartley's jams, Cadbury drinking chocolate, and a variety of other canned foods, coffee, biscuits, mashed potato and dried milk. The interesting thing about Premier Brands is that the management team after the buy-out was exactly the same as it was before the buy-out, with the sole exception of Paul Judge, the new CEO, who had worked at the corporate centre.

But after the buy-out, the team could perform without the Centre, and for themselves. The results were astounding. Trading margins went from 2.1 per cent in 1985 to over 8 per cent. Profits rose from £6.6m in 1985 to £31m in 1988. Market share also went up. The business, sold for £97m to the managers, realised £310m when it was sold on to Hillsdown Holdings in June 1989.

Paul Judge and his team at Premier increased the value of the business, not by 10 per cent or 20 per cent, but by over 300 per cent. They did this because there was a new sense of ownership, of urgency, of challenge, of being at the frontier rather than being in the boondocks. Put another way, the Centre did not just add cost to Food Division; it had subtracted a majority of the value from the business.

Premier Brands is not just an isolated example. Most management buy-outs have improved operating profits dramatically, and where they have failed, it has been because of the capital structure, with too high debt and rising interest charges, rather than because of what was happening in the business.

We may also point to what happens when de-mergers occur. In the UK, the two most important de-mergers in recent years have been Courtaulds, and the split of ICI into the new ICI (commodity chemicals) and Zeneca (pharmaceuticals and speciality chemicals). Both have been clear successes, resulting in clearly distinct cultures in each business and a new sense of enthusiasm, energy and commitment to results.

Stockbrokers in the UK and US often calculate 'value gaps', where it is apparent that large, diversified companies are worth more dead than alive: that the value of the parts exceeds the value of the whole, and that the Centre is subtracting value. Despite the cost of mounting bids against the entrenched interests of the managers running such companies, and the need to pay a 30–50 per cent premium to market value, many corporate break-ups have taken place. Though not all of these worked for the backers of leveraged bids, the evidence we should be interested in is what happened to operating profits in the old businesses in aggregate, under their new, Centre-less, existences. In the majority of cases aggregate operating profits improved either considerably or dramatically.

In 1979, the Fortune 500 comprised almost 60 per cent of US GNP. By 1991, this share had dropped to 40 per cent, a fall of nearly a third. Corporate giganticism is clearly on the retreat. There are good economic reasons why.

The third set of evidence for the dead hand of corporate strategy is the experience of those who work in companies.

Anyone who has worked in a business with a separate Centre know the jokes about Head Office, the stress created by central controls even in decentralised corporations, the bungled efforts of Head Office to find out what is happening, the lies passed up to Head Office, the cynicism about central initiatives, the competition for resources between different divisions, the time wasted on internal politics at the expense of giving customers what they want, and, above all, the demotivation created by excessive corporate layers and insulation from business responsibility. Given the near universality of such experience, it is remarkable that the value-destroying nature of corporate Centres has been so well concealed.

Once the value-destroying nature of most corporate centres, and corporate strategy, has been recognised, we can advance the first two *New Tenets of Corporate Strategy*:

- **Tenet One.** *Most multi-business companies should be smaller, and have fewer businesses in them. This is for two reasons: first, so that more businesses can be, to the greatest extent possible, freed from the dead hand of the Centre. And second, so that the remaining company can be more compact and homogeneous, with a more common culture, less politics, and a greater focus on external business opportunities.*
- **Tenet Two.** *Most corporate Centres should be very small, be very selective, and play a much smaller role than they currently do. Again, there are two reasons why. The first and most obvious is that a smaller Centre will destroy less value. The second reason is that a small Centre, with a limited but clear and focussed role, may actually add some net value. This is discussed further in the rest of Part Two, especially in sections 2 and 3 immediately following.*

Note that the Tenets start with the word 'most'. There are exceptions, where corporate strategy conducted by the Centre adds more value than it subtracts. These are discussed later in this part. There are examples where enormous value has been added by corporate level strategy. These examples involve some of the greatest and most successful corporations in the world. But remember to bear in mind that the conditions for good, value-adding corporate centre strategy are stringent and that most companies would be far better off having as little corporate strategy as possible.

2. SIX LEGITIMATE ROLES FOR THE CORPORATE CENTRE

We have stressed so far that most corporate strategy, conducted by the Centre, is harmful. Yet not all corporate strategy is bad, or even avoidable.

There are many examples of consistently successful corporate strategies orchestrated and led by the Centre. Companies as diverse as 3M, ABB, Apple, BancOne, Body Shop, BTR, Canon, Coca-Cola, Cooper Industries, Courtaulds, Dover, Emerson, Glaxo, Grand Metropolitan, Guinness, Hanson, Hewlett-Packard, Honda, Ikea, Johnson & Johnson, McDonalds, Marks & Spencer, Marriott, Mars, Mazda,

Matsushita, Merck, Microsoft, NEC, Nike, Nordstrom, PepsiCo, Procter & Gamble, Reuters, Sony, Tate & Lyle, TI (UK), Toshiba, Toyota, and Virgin have all exemplified successful corporate strategies, where the Centre has, over long periods of time, clearly added more value than it has subtracted. Each company has followed one or more of the long term, activist corporate strategies listed below as routes 3–6 to legitimate corporate strategy.

Moreover, many companies find that they cannot ignore pressing issues of corporate strategy, because of the way that they or their industries have evolved and are developing. In many cases diversification is unnecessary, and focus in small units beneficial, and this can be attained by de-merger, sale of misfitting divisions, and severe retrenchment of the size and role of the Centre. But this is not always true. There are many forces of history and economics that work the other way, that mean that companies may be forced to become larger or more complex in order to compete effectively in particular parts of their business.

These forces include regional or global economies of scale, brand benefits, the ability of some competitors to find a cost-effective and/or popular formula that can cross national boundaries, the convergence of consumer tastes, the uneven but clear trend towards the enlargement of markets and reduction of import barriers, and the applicability of expensive technology and know-how across different product areas and regions.

All of these forces require clever strategies that it is difficult or impossible for individual business units to mastermind, so that a central corporate strategy may be required in order to exploit potential advantages on the proper scale, or even to survive in the face of a competitor's mastery of the forces.

For example, a regional pharmaceutical company, one perhaps strong just in Europe, cannot afford to ignore forces in its industry that are rendering a regional strategy increasingly untenable. What is happening in pharmaceuticals is that a few, aggressive companies are expanding, organically or by acquisition, into very large, global corporations that are dominant in certain product categories everywhere around the world. These large, global concerns have great advantages, both because they are able to afford the escalating cost of research and development, and spread the R&D cost over high volumes of product derived from all national markets, and because they have marketing and selling muscle everywhere.

A regional company has lower volume over which to spread its R&D costs, and either has to build up expensive and under-used salesforces in markets outside its regional heartland, or do licensing or distributing deals with the big companies (where the latter will capture most of the profits).

It follows that regional pharmaceutical companies require a new corporate strategy. They cannot stay as they are. They cannot remain one business unit or a loose confederation of independent business units. Marketing presence needs to be built up in different countries, and these marketing companies must be co-ordinated with each other and with the product divisions and with R&D. Even in a decentralised company, the Centre will be forced to develop and implement a new corporate strategy, because it is beyond the ability and vision of the individual parts of the company to see what is happening and react effectively to it.

So, although corporate strategy should be approached with great scepticism and caution, and the natural value destroying tendencies of corporate Centres should always be remembered, corporate strategy should still be approached!

There are six legitimate roles for central corporate strategy, one that is temporary, for emergencies only, and five that are for normal circumstances. Of the five, one is essentially a minimalist central role, and the last four are 'activist' central corporate strategies. The six roles are:

(1) Emergency Corporate Strategy
(2) Olympian Corporate Strategy
(3) Acquisition Driven Corporate Strategy
(4) Market Expansion Corporate Strategy
(5) Competence and Culture Building Corporate Strategy
(6) Performance Control Corporate Strategy.

The six corporate strategies are shown graphically in Illustration 2.1, with examples of firms successfully pursuing each corporate strategy in Illustration 2.2.

The first, Emergency Corporate Strategy, will naturally require elements of C–F strategies, but because of the time pressure is worth describing separately. It may then be followed by any of the B–F strategies.

Strategy B, the Olympian approach, is self-contained and limited, and excludes the possibility of following one of the C–F strategies.

Strategies C–F may involve substantial elements of one or more of the other strategies in this group, but for the strategy to work there must be one clear, dominant strain that can largely be described as one of C, D, E or F.

Illustration 2.1
The six Corporate Strategy options

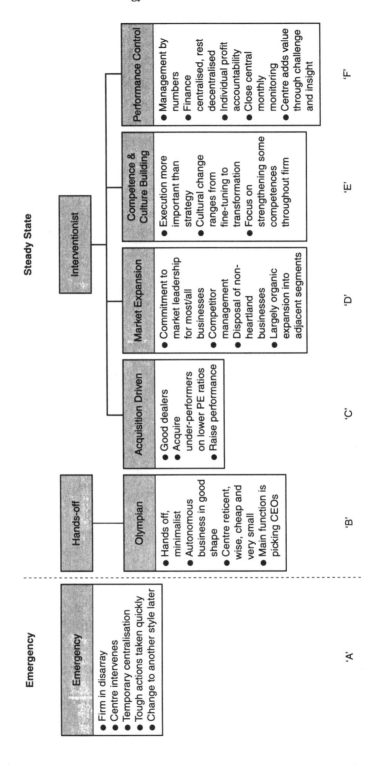

Emergency

Emergency
- Firm in disarray
- Centre intervenes
- Temporary centralisation
- Tough actions taken quickly
- Change to another style later

'A'

Hands-off

Olympian
- Hands off, minimalist
- Autonomous business in good shape
- Centre reticent, wise, cheap and very small
- Main function is picking CEOs

'B'

Steady State

Interventionist

Acquisition Driven
- Good dealers
- Acquire under-performers on lower PE ratios
- Raise performance

'C'

Market Expansion
- Commitment to market leadership for most/all businesses
- Competitor management
- Disposal of non-heartland businesses
- Largely organic expansion into adjacent segments

'D'

Competence & Culture Building
- Execution more important than strategy
- Cultural change ranges from fine-tuning to transformation
- Focus on strengthening some competences throughout firm

'E'

Performance Control
- Management by numbers
- Finance centralised, rest decentralised
- Individual profit accountability
- Close central monthly monitoring
- Centre adds value through challenge and insight

'F'

Illustration 2.2
Examples of Corporate Strategies

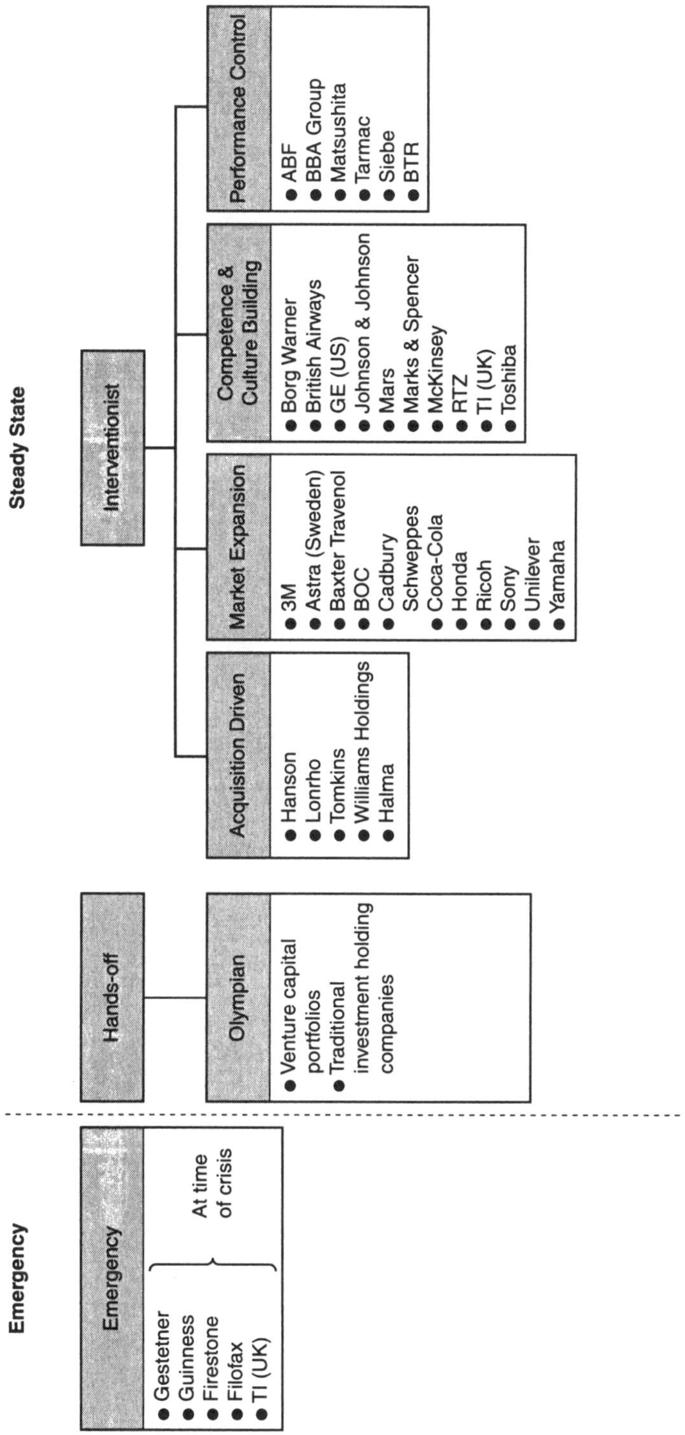

Emergency

Emergency

At time of crisis

- Gestetner
- Guinness
- Firestone
- Filofax
- TI (UK)

Hands-off

Olympian

- Venture capital portfolios
- Traditional investment holding companies

Steady State

Interventionist

Acquisition Driven

- Hanson
- Lonrho
- Tomkins
- Williams Holdings
- Halma

Market Expansion

- 3M
- Astra (Sweden)
- Baxter Travenol
- BOC
- Cadbury Schweppes
- Coca-Cola
- Honda
- Ricoh
- Sony
- Unilever
- Yamaha

Competence & Culture Building

- Borg Warner
- British Airways
- GE (US)
- Johnson & Johnson
- Mars
- Marks & Spencer
- McKinsey
- RTZ
- TI (UK)
- Toshiba

Performance Control

- ABF
- BBA Group
- Matsushita
- Tarmac
- Siebe
- BTR

Sections 3–8 below describe, in turn, each of these legitimate types of corporate strategy, with examples of successful implementation of the strategy. Very importantly, the sections also describe when each of the strategies is appropriate *and inappropriate*. Grand corporate strategy is always seductive, particularly when we admire great companies of the world that have succeeded through each strategy, but it is essential to be realistic about whether your company should or can attempt the strategy. Keep in mind that the more attractive the strategy appears, it is likely to be more difficult to execute and more dangerous for the majority who will fail to do so.

3. EMERGENCY CORPORATE STRATEGY

Sometimes a company is in such disarray that the Centre must intervene forcefully to sort things out. Such disarray could arise from many causes: a collapse in the market in one or more important areas; a dramatic drop in profits or surge in losses; market share losses to competitors, especially of one or a few customers on which the firm is dependent; lawsuits exposing hidden or under-estimated liabilities; an unexpected shortage of cash; damaging squabbles between divisions or senior managers within divisions; or any other sudden change threatening the stability and well-being of the corporation. Occasionally, it is hard to detect the moment when slow and genteel decline turns into a full-scale rout by sharper competitors, but the need for an emergency corporate strategy will normally be obvious.

Should you have an Emergency Corporate Strategy?

(1) Has there been a significant decline in profits and cash generation?

(2) Has financial forecasting been inaccurate and over-optimistic?

(3) Has market share been lost in some of the firm's important markets?

(4) Have there been major disagreements within the boardroom and/or between senior operating managers?

(5) Has the firm's share price, relative to the market, declined by at least 25 per cent over the past year?

(6) Is there disagreement about the cause of the firm's problems?

(7) Are managers blaming each other?

(8) Do the firm's non-executives, and/or other impartial observers, believe that senior management is not fully on top of things?

(9) Are there powerful barons within the firm who insist on doing things their way, within their areas?

(10) Have any important customers been lost (without corresponding gains of new customers buying equivalent amounts)?

Scoring

If you answered yes to four or more of the questions above, an emergency corporate strategy is clearly appropriate. If you answered yes *either* to question 8, *or* to any six questions, the chief executive must be replaced immediately. If you answered yes to eight or more questions, the emergency may be terminal, and action must be extremely swift, radical and ruthless.

A summary of when the Emergency Corporate Strategy is appropriate is provided in Illustration 2.3.

Emergency corporate strategy should follow three broad stages:

- *Diagnosis: identifying the root causes of the malaise*
- *Thinking: what to do about the problem, developing the solution*
- *Action: ruthless intervention to implement the solution.*

Illustration 2.3
When is Emergency Corporate Strategy appropriate?

Business Conditions	• Firm in disarray • Financial crisis – and/or expectations gap • Divisions cannot/will not take appropriate action • Threat of takeover/dismemberment
Skill Within Firm	• Centre must be willing to suspend normal relations with businesses and intervene • Centre must be able to establish 'the facts' • Centre must be decisive and ruthless

Diagnosis requires pinpointing the reasons for decline, distinguishing between the symptoms and the causes. For example, Gestetner in the early 1980s saw its profits and market value slump dramatically, and its cash needs escalating, and many conflicting reasons were advanced as to the root cause. The answer, however, was simple: high cost manufacturing, and the inability to compete against the Japanese in developing and making photocopiers.

Similarly, Firestone in the mid 1980s had one fundamental problem, that management were reluctant and slow to recognise: that the firm was higher cost and lower volume than its main global competitors, and could not afford to compete any longer in the mass tyre business.

Or take Guinness at the start of the 1980s, before Ernest Saunders took over. The company suffered from weak management and lack of information, but the main cause of decline was inappropriate and cash-draining diversifications. The basis stout business was still cash positive and its competitive position, though being eroded, was still strong.

More recently, Filofax experienced a life-threatening crisis in 1990, when sales slumped, high profits turned into ever mounting losses, and the cash ran out. The then management believed that the death of the Yuppie and market decline were to blame. These were in fact false alibis. The real reason was loss of market share to lower cost and lower price competitors.

Successful diagnosis depends on ignoring the excuses and conventional wisdom of those who have failed, and looking clearly at the main segments of the business, their profitability and cash characteristics, and their competitive positions. The only way to do this properly is to look at business unit strategy as described in Part One, though clear thinking may give you the answer without the need for much detailed fact gathering and analysis.

The second phase is *thinking* about the solution. The thinking will not be useful if the diagnosis is not correct. But even a correct diagnosis will not give you most of the answer. To be useful, the solution must include careful thought about *how* to reverse the decline. Such thought must be both practical and radical, and will require the Centre to exert itself to an unusual degree.

For Gestetner, the real answer was not just to exit from making photocopiers, importing Japanese models instead. The management and culture needed to be changed from top to bottom, to eliminate high cost manufacturing and the dominance of manufacturing in the company's thinking. This took many years to do, and only began to happen on a serious enough scale when the firm's ownership and top management changed.

Firestone had to leave its base business of manufacturing tyres, that then comprised 80 per cent of its operations, and concentrate on sales and service.

Guinness had to sell a huge number of non-core businesses, and rebuild market share for stout.

Filofax had to develop new products, dramatically lower its costs and prices, and regain market share in all important markets. This did not begin to happen until existing top management had been retired and a strong-minded outsider installed as chief executive.

In all cases, *action* required not just a change in strategy, but a change in the way the firms in crisis did business. In all cases, appropriate action only happened as a result of vigorous new chief executives, who had to change some key managers underneath them and change the behaviour of those who remained.

Successful emergency corporate strategy nearly always requires the Centre to appoint and support a tough, uncompromising, new chief executive, from outside the firm. The Centre must ride roughshod over vested interests within the firm, must knock heads off or together, must make it clear what new standards of performance are acceptable, and must take hard actions quickly. The Centre must, temporarily, centralise. It must demand full access to the facts, full loyalty to the new cause, full support for the new top management team, full co-operation to achieve short term profit and cash improvement targets and to close loss-making activities.

Emergency corporate strategy is never pleasant. To succeed it needs to be extremely forceful.

Equally, however, emergency corporate strategy is not the way to run any company once the crisis has been averted. One of the following five permanent approaches must then be selected. The first of these is minimalist, in contrast to the other four, that are activist. But the first approach, though rarely followed, is normally the most appropriate.

4. OLYMPIAN CORPORATE STRATEGY

This is my term for a hands-off, minimalist approach, consistent with the recognition that most central strategy destroys value. The Olympian

Centre will be extremely small, usually comprising a part-time non-executive chairman, a chief executive who spends most of his or her time on non-central activities (see below), and one or two accountants to add the score, consolidate the accounts and comply with statutory reporting requirements.

The Olympian strategy requires that the chief executive does not interfere with the smooth running of the individual business units, the latter being genuinely autonomous. The chief executive should, therefore, do very little of a central nature. Unless the chief executive plays a lot of golf, or goes to the races most days, this corporate strategy requires that he or she has one or more useful non-central roles. It is best if he or she doubles up by running one of the main divisions within the firm. The central role is thus a part-time additional job, almost honorific in nature, and conferring no special power over and above that enjoyed by the other division heads.

Another way is to for the chief executive to take a number of project roles within the firm, either within particular divisions, or in terms of non-directive cross-business roles, perhaps concentrating on liaison with and support of important customers that buy from several of the firm's units. This solution is more tricky, since it requires someone who can be flexible and effective in project roles, who neither needs, nor will be tempted to use, seniority of rank to achieve the project objectives. This rules out most senior executives for such a role.

A third way is to abolish the position of chief executive altogether, and have the business heads report directly to the part-time chairman. In many ways this is the best, though the rarest, solution.

The Olympian Centre should therefore be very low cost, and, because it is essentially inactive, should avoid subtracting very much value from the businesses. But it would be wrong to regard the Olympian Centre as a necessary but very small evil. There is a positive and valuable, though selective, role for the Olympian Centre.

It is called Olympian after Mount Olympus, the place where the Greek gods resided and looked down on humanity from a great height. The Greek gods were a pretty rum bunch, mainly keeping themselves to themselves (and each other), but occasionally intervening in the affairs of men. These interventions were sometimes (though not always) benign and successful.

To fulfil the Olympian role for today's businesses, the Centre should be reticent but wise, unobtrusive but respected, selective but effective. It should understand the businesses underneath and have the measure of the people running them. It should be able to spot a sea-change, or discontinuity, in the market or climate surrounding the businesses. It should have the self-confidence to intervene every few years, if and when this is for the good of the firm.

Should you have an Olympian Corporate Strategy?

(1) Is it generally accepted by the operating businesses that Head Office/the Centre adds much more value than it costs and subtracts?

(2) Does the Centre have special and valuable expertise related to all or most of the group's businesses?

(3) Is the Centre currently unobtrusive?

(4) Are the different operating companies different in character from each other, or different in their key success factors?

(5) Is the group's business, or are important parts of it, currently in a crisis?

(6) Is the firm very much in the public eye?

(7) Is there a general perception that the quality of management in the operating businesses is poor?

(8) Do the individual business units' strategies appear to need major revision in the face of important changes in the market or competitive environment?

(9) Is internationalisation a major and pressing issue for the group?

(10) Is there substantial controversy about how the group should be organised, and, in particular, how the different businesses should relate to each other?

Scoring

Score ten points for every NO. Add the total score. The higher the score, the more likely it is that the Olympian strategy is appropriate, but you cannot decide definitely until you have completed the checklists on pages 99, 108, 122 and 127, one for each of the other permanent strategies. The highest score of the five strategies (B–F) from all five checklists will indicate the corporate strategy most likely to be appropriate.

Illustration 2.4 displays when the Olympian Corporate Strategy is appropriate.

The most important task of the Olympian Centre is to appoint, and if necessary remove, the heads of the autonomous businesses. Appointing the right top people should not be necessary very often, but it is clearly of paramount importance. It is also a black art. Some people are very good at it; most are not.

Illustration 2.4
When is Olympian Corporate Strategy appropriate?

Business Conditions	● Stable market and competitive environment ● Attractive market ● Similar key success factors in all businesses ● Internationalisation is not major issue
Skill Within Firm	● Centre not respected ● Centre's costs exceed benefit ● Good operating management

The Olympian Centre must know when to remove a failing business head. It should be apparent to the wise Olympian chairman when this is necessary, both from the results achieved and from discussion with the business head and his or her top team. The discussion should be discreet, perhaps mainly social, non-threatening, and continuous. Nevertheless, the chairman must know when to act. Some do; most let things drift too long.

The only other important task of the Olympian Centre is to keep a weather eye out for discontinuous change. The chairman of a property company must have an instinct for when the cycle is about to change. In a high tech firm, the chairman must be able to sense when a new technology may leave existing approaches high and dry. In consumer products, the chairman must know when the value of a brand is about to plummet or when it could suddenly flower. In a professional service business, the chairman must detect when the quality of staff or new recruits is beginning to crumble. The Olympian Centre need not, indeed, should not, be very frequent in offering its advice. One insight, of genuine importance and value, every five years, is the rough target.

Aside from appointing and removing the business heads, and having the occasional, fundamental insight, the Olympian Centre should do next to nothing. It should not come up with ideas for acquisitions or disposals: these should come up from the businesses. It should not think about grand (or petty) strategy for the businesses; this is not its job. It should not aim to change corporate culture, to develop important customers, to negotiate with government, to meet with the great and good, to change the City's perception of the firm, to initiate joint ventures or strategic alliances, to tell the businesses what to do, or to add value in any other regular way. If it tries to do any of these things, it ceases to be an Olympian Centre. In seeking to add value, it will probably subtract it.

It is important to realise that the Olympian Centre does not exercise financial control over its operating divisions, beyond doing what is statutorily required to ensure the integrity of the accounts in an auditing role. The Olympian Centre does not absorb cash from the divisions, hand it back according to corporate priorities or make investment decisions.

This means that the operating businesses are essentially self-contained financially, in exactly the same way that the invested companies are in a venture capital portfolio. Venture capitalists provide the initial funds to start or develop an enterprise, but they do not then hold reviews annually (or at any other frequency) to reallocate cash between businesses in their portfolio. Each must fend for itself, and if further cash is required, make its own case on its own merits, without any comparison with the rest of the venture capital portfolio (about which it will have no knowledge).

Similarly, the divisions within an Olympian firm must work out their own salvation. If they need extra funds, they will approach the Centre, but only as a necessary intermediary (really a post-box) before reaching the real funders, the bankers and investors who have cash. The Olympian Centre has no hidden (or open) funds for investment, no special financial expertise, no investment appraisal role, and no ability to frustrate or assist the divisions in their search for funds.

It is hard for the Centre to do little. It is against its nature. But it is worth striving to do little. That way lies avoidance of major value destruction. It sounds a modest goal, but in fact it is an ambitious target. Most multi-business firms would be much better off if they had an Olympian Centre.

The next four sections discuss non-Olympian, activist, corporate strategies. Each strategy can work brilliantly well, though the odds are against any of them working. Remain fully sober while you read the following pages.

5. ACQUISITION DRIVEN CORPORATE STRATEGY

Perhaps the most popular form of corporate strategy in Anglo-Saxon business is that based on making frequent acquisitions. Academics are puzzled by this, since a large number of studies have indicated that acquisition strategy often fails, and that the only people certain to gain are the shareholders in the acquired companies. The balance of evidence is that, in aggregate, acquisitions are of no net benefit to the acquiring companies. Yet businessmen continue to make acquisitions, including hostile ones, with great determination.

Our distinctive perspective on corporate strategy throws this paradox into a new light. For if most corporate strategy ends in tears, and is in aggregate harmful, it is perfectly logical for ambitious corporate level managers to go after the only form of activist corporate strategy that is in aggregate neutral in its impact on shareholder wealth. For note that the academics do not claim that acquisitions harm the acquiring companies, only that they do not in aggregate benefit them.

From our viewpoint this is a remarkable achievement. It is like going into a casino where you ought to lose money if you stay long enough, and emerging many hours later with exactly your original stake. In the casino a skilled player can manage to break even at blackjack; it is the only game where this is true over the long haul. Similarly, most players at corporate strategy will harm their shareholders' wealth, but those who go for an acquisition driven strategy will on balance break even. Since managers like to play at corporate strategy, diverting them all to play at acquisitions would be good for shareholders.

But it is possible to do better than break even. There are certain players who consistently win at the acquisition game. Interestingly, most of them are of British extraction, running UK PLCs. The Americans and Australians usually over-reach themselves at some stage. But diversified companies like BTR, Hanson, Lonrho, Tomkins (at least until RHM), and Williams Holdings have a long term record of outstanding success at making acquisitions and building earnings per share growth and shareholder wealth as a result.

There is also a category of British companies where they are largely focussed on a particular broad industry but are aggressive acquirors within that industry. Examples of generally successful 'focussed' (as opposed to diversified) acquirors include AAH, BBA Group, Guinness,

Halma, Pearson, Siebe, Smiths Industries, Tate & Lyle, TI Group, United Newspapers and Wolseley.

This is a selective list of those who have a generally successful track record, but it is interesting to note a recent study by OC&C Strategy Consultants divided large British companies into those that made a number of acquisitions (dubbed the 'acquisitive') and those that did not ('the organics'). The OC&C study found that in aggregate, between 1984 and 1992, the 'acquisitive' grew sales, profits and earnings per share much faster than the 'organics', with the 'acquisitive' also having a higher average return on equity (21 per cent, versus 15 per cent for the 'organics').

The objective OC&C study is consistent with our view of corporate strategy, namely, that an acquisitive Centre will, on average, create no value but not destroy it either, whereas an activist but non-acquisitive Centre will, again on average, end up destroying much value.

What is of interest to corporate Centre managers (rather than shareholders), however, is how to improve the odds so that value can actually be added. Here we can be quite definitive, because the list of successful aquirers above, especially the first list of 'diversified' acquirors, shows a clear pattern common to most of the acquirors and most individual acquisitions made by them. The lessons are clear and unambiguous, and are summarised in the checklist below.

How Successful Acquirors Do It

(1) *They acquire companies that have under-performed* the stock market and their industry average performance significantly. The target companies generally have excess overhead and often management that is weak and complacent. Next time you meet an unimpressive chief executive at a cocktail party, add his company to your long list of possible targets.

(2) They look for *profit improvement potential* of a specific nature. For example, if the industry return on sales averages 10 per cent, and the target bumps along at 3 per cent, the predator becomes interested. He then looks to see if there is any reason (such as a weak market share position) that could explain the discrepancy. If not, he looks further, talking to people in the industry to see how far return on sales could be raised.

Some 'focussed' acquirors go further and identify 'synergy' potential from specific actions, such as 'concertina-ing' two salesforces into one, closing factories and putting the business through existing facilities, raising prices where the combined market share is very high, cutting out one set of administration costs, and so on. A number of observers are cynical about whether such synergy benefits actually happen, but my experience as a consultant over 18 years, involving over 100 deals, is that when careful studies of synergy potential have been carried out, the acquiror nearly always realises the planned savings, and sometimes much more besides.

(3) *They acquire companies that are on a lower price earnings (PE) ratio than they themselves enjoy.* The importance of this rule has been generally overlooked by most commentators. Let me explain.

Most successful acquirors have a good record of increasing their earnings per share (EPS). It is logical, therefore, for them to have a high PE ratio, that is, for the stock market to value the company's earnings (which tend to increase) higher than the earnings of more pedestrian companies that are not so good at raising their earnings per share over time. Thus, if the stock market average PE ratio is 15, a successful acquiror might be on a PE of 20.

But a prospective target company, that has under-performed its peers, and has a poor record of increasing earnings per share, is likely to be on a below-average PE. Let us imagine that the PE of the target is 10.

Now, the acquiror can afford to pay a 30 per cent premium to the pre-bid share price of target, when it was on a PE of 10, and still acquire the company on a PE of 13. If we assume that the acquisition does not change the PE of the acquiror, we have a company on a PE of 20 acquiring a company on a PE (after the bid) of 13.

The interesting point is that, *even if the acquiring company does nothing at all to improve the performance of the acquired company*, the acquiror is bound to improve its earnings per share. The acquiror has paid 13 times earnings for profits that are now valued at 20 times earnings.

Barring a stock market crash, or running out of big enough acquisition candidates, this game can be played indefinitely. A virtuous circle has been created that is difficult to break. Each time an acquisition is made on a lower PE than the acquiror, the latter's earnings per share are automatically enhanced. Given that the acquiror constantly increases earnings per share, it is logical for investors to continue to pay a PE premium for access to those earnings. Given the high PE, the acquiror can continue to buy other companies on lower PEs. And so, *ad infinitum*.

One way that smaller companies, like Halma, play this game is to buy private companies that do not command the same sort of PE ratio. At the time of writing, Halma is on a PE of 26.6, because of impressive earnings growth. Halma can buy private companies on a PE of, say, 10, and hence enhance its earnings per share. To be fair, Halma also improves the performance of its acquisitions, and so gets a 'double whammy' that further justifies the high PE ratio. Since 1991, Halma has been a terrific performer. There is no reason to expect this cycle to be broken.

(4) They have their own small but *experienced in-house corporate finance teams* for identifying, screening, and doing deals with potential targets. They are astute and hard negotiators. They are prepared to walk away from deals on which they have laboured greatly, if the price is not right. They are patient, resourceful and remorseless, sharp of brain and hard of heart. They tend to use consultants only in a secondary role, if at all, and they treat investment bankers as fund raisers rather than idea generators or financial engineers.

(5) They have a *systematic post-acquisition process* for the first 12–18 months through which they put the acquired companies. Companies like Hanson and BTR have fast, cheap and efficient ways of deciding which businesses to keep, who should run them, and of making clear what financial results are to be attained. They fire managers if they are incompetent or not fully committed to themselves.

(6) *They always integrate* the acquired companies into their financial control systems with the maximum despatch, rigour and ruthlessness. They insist on the same high quality of financial information as in their existing businesses.

(7) They *squeeze* out excess *working capital*.

(8) *They sell* any businesses which are more valuable to third parties than to themselves, where the imputed PE of the sale price exceeds their own PE.

(9) They pay particular attention to any cyclical businesses in their portfolio. They try to *spot* when *the cycle* is about to turn, and then sell any business that they suspect is near the top of its cycle.

(10) They have highly *sophisticated tax management*, and in many cases lower the effective rate of tax of acquired businesses.

Before summarising, we need to consider one further aspect of acquisition driven corporate strategy: the scope of the financial control that it does and should exercise.

In practice, most acquisition driven firms have a hybrid strategy, incorporating large parts of what we have called the *Performance Control Corporate Strategy* (Strategy F: see pages 124–8 below). This means that although they are generally highly decentralised, the Centre does exert close, vigilant and detailed financial control, usually by an elaborate system of budgetary accounting controls. Experience suggests that the two strategies (Acquisition Driven and Performance Control) work well together, though the Performance Control strategy does not in any way require acquisitions. Nearly all of the successful, diversified, acquisition-led companies mentioned above (BTR, Hanson, Lonrho, Tomkins, Williams Holdings, etc.) use the techniques of performance control.

It is not necessary, however, for an Acquisition Driven Corporate Strategy to require close financial control along the Performance Control model. Some 'focussed' acquirors, like Guinness and Halma, have a more decentralised approach to financial control. It would even be possible (though I am not aware of any current real-life examples) to combine an Acquisition Driven Corporate Strategy with the complete absence of financial re-distribution that is part of the Olympian model. This is, after all, how venture capital portfolios are already run, on the whole with considerable success.

We conclude, therefore, that close financial control is not a require-ment of Acquisition Driven strategy. The vast majority of companies following such a strategy will incorporate Performance Control into their central functions (including tight financial control via budget setting and monitoring), but it is possible for an Acquisition Driven strategy to have a totally hands-off, Olympian approach to financial management.

Acquisition driven corporate strategy is an art as well as a science. Aside from quantitative skills, it also requires intuition, flair, daring, parsimony, negotiating skills, a good sense of timing, judgment about businesses and those who run them, lateral thinking and also plain common sense. Few individuals or teams combine these dis-parate and often mutually exclusive attributes. For those who do, it is easy to outperform.

Like all successful corporate strategies, the acquisition-led approach is seductive, and it is easy for the wannabee acquiror to think that all that is necessary for success are a few ideas and the phone numbers of good firms of consultants and investment bankers. In these circum-stances, everyone will want to do a deal, be it good, bad or indifferent, and at any price that can be funded. Remember that the road to hell is paved with good advisers. Sometimes the wrong acquisition can end a company's independence or even its existence: take Letraset's acquisi-tion of Stanley Gibbons, or British & Commonwealth's purchase of Atlantic Computers.

It is almost always true that you should not make major acquisitions unless you have a track record of making them successfully already. Novices should beware.

Should you follow an Acquisition Driven Corporate Strategy?

(1) Does your company have a good record of earnings per share growth over the past few years?

(2) Is your firm on an above-average PE ratio?

(3) Does the chief executive have experience of making takeovers and making them work?

(4) Is the Finance Director experienced in making takeovers and a good negotiator?

(5) Could you generate a list of at least 3 possible targets right now, together with the rationale for how you could improve their profits?

(6) Are your own financial controls excellent?

(7) Do you have highly sophisticated tax management, resulting in lower tax payments than are normal in your industry?

(8) Are at least some of your businesses in areas that allow high synergy potential with potential acquisitions?

(9) Do you have experienced and confident operating management that is capable of running a much larger business?

(10)If you made an acquisition, would you immediately begin to integrate it with your own firm and insist that things be done your way?

Scoring

Score ten points for every YES. Compare the total score to that for the other strategies (B, D, E, F) from pages 91, 108, 122 and 127.

Illustration 2.5 shows the appropriate conditions for the Acquisition Driven Corporate Strategy.

Illustration 2.5
When is Acquisition Driven strategy appropriate?

Business Conditions	● Industry with wide range of profitability ● Targets exist where it is clear performance could be greatly improved
Skill Within Firm	● Good EPS record ● On high PE ● CEO & FD very experienced in takeovers ● Excellent financial controls and systems ● In-house corporate finance team ● Operating management good and could run bigger firm

6. MARKET EXPANSION CORPORATE STRATEGY

The Market Expansion Corporate Strategy is the direct descendent of the 'portfolio planning' strategy pioneered by BCG. The keynotes of the Market Expansion approach are a determination to gain market share in existing markets and to then expand into 'adjacent segments', markets close to the firm's existing operations, that can share costs, skills or customers.

Although the BCG portfolio planning ideology has been popularly discredited, it has much more enduring value and influence than is commonly thought, and it lies at the root of the Market Expansion strategy. It is therefore worth a substantial apparent detour to examine 'portfolio planning' carefully.

Portfolio planning started in the late 1960s, when the Boston Consulting Group (BCG) discovered the GROWTH/SHARE MATRIX (see Part Three, page 165), complete with its menagerie of dogs, cash cows, question marks and stars. It came very much into vogue in the 1970s, supplying a role for the Centre as the overseer of the corporate portfolio, deciding which businesses to channel cash into and which to take it from, and generally setting corporate development priorities based on an understanding of each product line's relative market share, market growth and cash characteristics.

The BCG ideology was enormously attractive to chief executives. It justified them looking into each business and finding out what was happening there, so it could be used by a chief executive to clip the wings on his (almost always his, rather than her) barons who were running divisions or countries. It also provided the first integrated framework for bringing together market and financial issues, giving the chief executive a rationale, language and unifying theme for talking to both the chief financial officer and the marketing director, and for getting the latter two to talk to each other. As such, arguably, the process was even more important than the content.

But content there was, also, in abundance. Although nobody today pays much attention to the Growth/Share Matrix, and BCG, its originators, appear happy to consign it to the dustbin of history, it was, and is, full of useful insight. For a full explanation, see Part Three, pages 165–74. Suffice it here to summarise the most important useful points emerging from the Matrix and portfolio planning generally:

(1) The market share that a business segment has, relative to the share that competitors have, is important. In general, high share leads to high profitability. If it does not, the business is unusual, competitors are behaving irrationally, or the business (if low profit in a high relative share position) is being badly managed.

(2) Most of the cash and profit that businesses have are generated by their high relative market share positions. If this is not realised, this is likely to be due to poor segment definition or poor analysis of segment profitability. In general, the firm would do well to concentrate on these high share, high profit segments and concentrate most investment and management talent on these.

(3) The most valuable businesses, and those that must be invested in most, are the 'star' businesses with high relative market share and high market growth.

(4) If you cannot be number one (preferably), number two, or (sometimes) number three in a segment, you should probably sell the business or close it down.

(5) Gaining a leadership position from a weak follower position is difficult. The best chance of this happening is in a high growth market. But even here, it is a difficult, risky and expensive business to displace the market leader. It will always cost more cash investment than estimated. It is worth while, but only if you succeed in becoming market leader. You should therefore be very selective in which of these 'question mark' (high market growth, low relative market share) businesses you try to drive to leadership. It will always be lower risk, and often higher return, to sell these businesses for a fancy price.

All of these observations are true. They were true in 1970 and they are true today. They were neglected in 1970 and they are neglected today. Following these precepts is a route to business success – not a surefire route, because that depends upon the operational skill in implementing the precepts – but nevertheless, the best simple road map that anyone has ever devised. These precepts ought to be graven on the heart of anyone involved in business, especially in complex businesses with several segments and product lines.

BCG had a wonderful set of insights and a great consulting product. But they made two mistakes, one theoretical and one practical, that led to the downfall of both the insights and the consulting product.

The theoretical mistake was to assert that the product portfolio ought to be 'balanced' for cash purposes. In other words, that the Centre ought to take in all surplus cash and then re-distribute it to the businesses according to the principles of portfolio planning. Cash within the corporation was viewed as a closed system, with the Centre holding the purse-strings.

The theoretical error related to the closed system. At times BCG seemed to be saying that corporations should never need to raise cash from shareholders (via rights issues and the like), nor give cash back to shareholders (except via small dividends), since it should use whatever cash is available from the businesses (but no more) to invest in the places that would yield the most long term cash.

This was not logical, and not in accordance with theories of shareholder value that began to evolve in the late 1970s (and are still fashionable today). The shareholder value camp advances the perfectly sensible argument that if there are opportunities to create shareholder value, over and above the rate of capital return required by shareholders, then firms should make those investments, even if to do so requires going to the shareholders to ask for more money.

Conversely, shareholder value analysis asserts, again quite rationally, that if a firm just has a collection of cash cows, and no sensible opportunities for creating shareholder wealth elsewhere, the excess cash should be returned to the shareholders via a special dividend or in some other way. The shareholder value school objected forcibly, and successfully, to the idea that the Centre of a corporation should be an intermediate 'bank', blocking the free flow of funds between investors and business opportunities.

The hoo-ha over this objection obscured the fact that this modification to the BCG theory could easily be accommodated within it, and did not in any way challenge its most useful insights. BCG portfolio analysis can quite happily calculate what cash is required by all the businesses, and available from them, in a way quite consistent with the principles of shareholder value analysis. The Centre could then either obtain any cash deficit from shareholders, or distribute excess cash to them. This was not a fundamental objection, nor should it have been allowed to cripple the basic principles of portfolio analysis.

But what really led to the baby of portfolio analysis being thrown out with its bath water was a practical rather than theoretical point. The practical point was that portfolio analysis was conceived of, and used as, a tool of the Centre. As such, it was inherently centralising. The centralising process was associated with a whole apparatus of strategic planning at the Centre that turned out to be stifling, harmful and resented by the operating companies in multi-business firms.

In short, portfolio planning led to strategic planning, with armies of analytical planners (supported by other armies of consultants) at Head Office, and an attempt at down-grading the responsibilities of those actually running the businesses in the field.

As such, portfolio planning really did more harm than good. The backlash from operating divisions against portfolio planning and centrally-led corporate strategy succeeded, not just because of the vested interests of those in the field, but because it deserved to succeed. Decentralising multi-business firms, including responsibility for strategy, is a more effective way to run them than the reverse. Eventually this was realised, the market cleared, and corporate strategy (together with its main ideology, portfolio planning) became devalued.

No-one who has read Part Two this far can be in any doubt that, in aggregate, centrally driven, portfolio-based corporate strategy, has destroyed more value than it has created.

Yet there are two paradoxes that deserve our attention.

The first paradox is that the principles of portfolio planning, or at least of the BCG Growth/Share Matrix, are essentially correct and highly useful today. The second paradox is that many of the world's most successful firms have a centrally driven corporate strategy based around these principles. Let's examine each of these paradoxes in turn.

How can the principles of portfolio planning be right, and the implementation of them by the Centre be so wrong? The answer is desperately simple. *The principles of portfolio planning are at least as applicable at the business unit level, and the segment level within business units, as they are at the corporate level. There is no need whatsoever for the principles of the*

Growth/Share Matrix to be tainted with centralisation, or for them to require any central planning resource.

Any business unit is itself an agglomeration of a number, usually a large number, of individual business segments. The greatest potential value from portfolio planning is at the business unit, not the central, level. In fact, combining portfolio planning with shareholder value analysis at the business unit level is the best way to devise strategy. These principles have been incorporated and fully explained in Part One, where great stress was laid on portfolio planning (without actually using the phrase).

Justifying portfolio theory at the business unit level does not, in itself, legitimate any new model of Market Expansion Corporate Strategy. For this we have to turn to the second of our two paradoxes: that many successful firms follow the strategy. That many of these firms are Japanese will lead us on, in due course, to yet a third paradox, which in turn will pave the way for a new model (at least for the West) of Market Expansion Corporate Strategy. But I am getting ahead of myself. First we need a definition of what it means to follow the Market Expansion Corporate Strategy.

My definition is simple. Market Expansion Corporate Strategy involves the following:

(1) a commitment to market leadership for most of the businesses in the portfolio
(2) active awareness and management of competitors, to try to gain market share against them in priority markets
(3) avoidance of businesses outside the priority heartland of businesses sharing common characteristics (in terms of industry, customers, technology and the way of doing business); and, if such businesses already comprise a substantial part of the portfolio, their gradual disposal
(4) corporate expansion via gaining share in existing heartland businesses, and/or entering 'adjacent segments' where existing skills and resources (e.g. factories, salesforces, brand names, technologies, customer relationships) can be used to give competitive advantage.

Market Expansion Corporate Strategy usually involves some historical or current impetus from the Centre in laying down this approach, but it does not necessarily imply any substantial central planning resource. Indeed, both logic and experience suggest that the strategy is likely to be most successful when the latter is either very small or non-existent, that is, when the portfolio strategy is built into the firm's culture and comes naturally to all its operating units.

The principles of Market Expansion Corporate Strategy do not exclude acquisitions, including periodic very large acquisitions, but the strategy is largely an organic one, and quite distinct from the Acquisition Driven Corporate Strategy.

Firms successfully practising Market Expansion Corporate Strategy over long periods of time include 3M, Astra (the Swedish pharmaceutical firm), Baxter Travenol, BOC, Cadbury Schweppes, Canon, Casio, Coca-Cola, Courtaulds, Dun & Bradstreet, Ford, Fujitsu, GE (US), Honda, Mars, Matsushita, Mazda, J Menzies, Nippon Electric (NEC), Nike, Nikon, Nissan, Omron, Panasonic, Pentax, Procter & Gamble, Ricoh, Sanyo, Seiko, Sharp, W H Smith, Sony, Tokyo Electric, Toshiba, Toyota, Unilever, UB and Yamaha.

Market Expansion Corporate Strategy, with its emphasis on market leadership, lends itself naturally to international, and often truly global, outreach. Sometimes it has turned whole industries upside down and led to seemingly irreversible shifts in global market share, for example with the Japanese firms' secure world leadership in motorcycles, semiconductors, televisions and most other consumer electronics products, photocopiers, lap-top computers, and certain segments of the car industry.

There is no great magic to Market Expansion Corporate Strategy. Those firms that have succeeded with it have manifested six clear characteristics. The implied rules of thumb themselves are not profound, but the passionate commitment to implementing them and producing results are what have set the winners apart from the rest of the pack:

(1) Obsessive determination to gain market leadership: a win or die mentality.

(2) Relentless pursuit of leadership within certain segments, often initially quite small segments, which are then used as a beachhead to reach out to larger segments. Examples include the way that Honda and Yamaha first took world leadership in low powered motorcycles, before moving on to conquer the mid-cc range and then the high-cc and superbikes; similar, later strategies in cameras, watches and stereo equipment; and, currently, the way that Honda, Toyota and Nissan are launching up-scale car lines and creating second-dealer networks (especially in the US) through which to beat the German car makers.

(3) A long term orientation, focussing more on market share gains than margin gains or short term profit enhancement. Contrary to popu-

lar myth, this does not mean profits have to be ignored or that earnings enhancement will not follow. Most of the companies that have been serious about pursuing Portfolio Corporate Strategy have seen increases in their share price well ahead of their market index sustained over long periods. But share price, earnings per share and next year's profit progression do not have the major influence in these firm's investment decisions or strategies.

(4) A company-wide culture stressing market share gain. This is not sometimes imposed from the Centre, or the top of divisions, but something in the ethic of the firm, built into the way that its people at all levels think.

(5) Expansionist thinking, that expresses itself not just in seeking to gain share within existing businesses, but in seeking to branch out wherever possible into nearby markets. Again, successful followers of the Portfolio Corporate Strategy manifest a company-wide culture in this respect, cutting across functional, divisional and geographical boundaries. Technologies, ways of doing business and customer contacts are shared between established and emerging product lines.

In this way, Honda was able to use the piston engine design, originally developed for its motorcycle business, to exploit opportunities in lawnmowers, small generators and cars. Similarly, Sony's original core business of transistor radios depended on skills in product innovation that were successfully deployed later on in consumer electronics, televisions, cameras and computer components. NEC's key skills in semiconductor technology, originally confined to semiconductors and PABXs, were later used to establish segment leadership in mobile phones, faxes, and certain office automation segments.

All of these new markets were entered organically, without risky and expensive acquisitions, because there were no internal barriers to the use of corporate skills and because there was an underlying ethic of organic expansionism.

(6) A search for continuous improvement in the way that things are done, in order to lower cost, increase customer satisfaction, or increase the speed of delivery to the customer (which in turn both lowers cost and increases customer satisfaction).

It is easy to get carried away with the impressive success stories of those firms that have used the principles of Portfolio Corporate Strategy to good effect. We should not forget that this is one of the activist corporate strategies that have, in aggregate, destroyed much more value than they have created. There are many examples of companies that have tried this approach, only to fail to varying degrees. The failures or relative failures over the past decades include, in the UK, Boots, BP, the Imperial Group, Plessey, Ferranti, Sears, Ratners, Coloroll, Harris Queensway and Lowndes Queensway, Hillsdown Holdings, and Chloride. In the US, relatively poor performers like Exxon, ITT, Sears Roebuck, Textron and TRW; and in Continental Europe, companies like Philips, Vendex and VNU all provide instructive caution. Companies that fail at this strategy appear to demonstrate some or all of the following unlucky 13 characteristics:

(1) A top-down or *Head Office driven approach* that does not capture the hearts and minds of the operating companies
(2) A focus on *bureaucratic planning* rather than creative exploration of market opportunities
(3) A *large central planning staff*, and/or excessive use of consultants
(4) *Competition between divisions* for resources, resulting in obfuscation, baronial behaviour, lack of co-operation and a culture of inter-divisional, inter-country and inter-functional sniping and scapegoating
(5) *Inconsistent* emphasis on market share gain, tempered from time to time by cost reduction or margin enhancement blitzes, in order to meet short term earnings expectations
(6) Too much *reliance on external, acquired growth*, so that organic expansion becomes an optional extra rather than the basic engine of growth
(7) Too wide a business focus, so that there is *no* really homogeneous business *heartland*; instead, businesses with different key success factors are allowed to remain within the portfolio
(8) A basic *lack of* willingness to be selective and *focus* investment, technology and management, for a sustained period, on growth in one product area
(9) *Lack of commitment to global expansion* in narrow product segments; too wide an initial product range, with most of its sales concentrated in too narrow a geographical theatre
(10) Uninspired and *incrementalist top management*, unable to lift everyone'e eyes to a radical expansion plan

(11) *Frequent changes* in top management and strategy

(12) *Myopia* or blindness in the face of new competitive threats

(13) A *defensive culture* that is neither open nor aggressive; focussed on a glorious past rather than a glorious future.

Given the failure rate, it is important to know whether this is the strategy for you.

Should you follow a Market Expansion Corporate Strategy?

(1) Does you firm have a powerful, ambitious, consistent and widely spread culture that emphasises internally-generated expansion?

(2) Is the firm good at internal co-operation and generally free of political game-playing and inter-divisional rivalry?

(3) Is top management genuinely charismatic and obsessed with market dominance?

(4) Are there important internal jumping-off points for organic growth, in terms of technology, customers, ways of doing business or value creation insights that can be used for expansion into businesses that are new, but quite adjacent to and similar to the firm's existing successful heartland businesses?

(5) Is the firm oriented towards, and good at, international expansion?

(6) Does the firm genuinely place a higher priority on long term market share growth than on short to medium term earnings growth?

(7) Is the head office both small and highly respected by the operating companies?

(8) Does the firm already know who its 2–3 main global competitors are, and how to beat them?

(9) Is there plenty of cash available, from internal operations, bankers and investors, to fund extremely aggressive expansion moves?

(10) Does the marketing director carry more weight in the boardroom than the finance director?

Scoring

Score ten points for each YES. Compare the total score to that for the other strategies (B, C, E, F) on pages 91, 99, 122 and 127.

Illustration 2.6 summarises the business conditions and skills within the firm that make the Market Expansion Corporate Strategy appropriate.

Illustration 2.6
When is Market Expansion Corporate Strategy appropriate?

Business Conditions	• Good business to be in • Global businesses with 2–3 main competitors • Plenty of cash for expansion
Skill Within Firm	• Powerful culture throughout firm stressing internally-led expansion • Little political game-playing • Top management obsessed with market leadership • Firm marketing-led, not finance-led • Long-termist managers and owners

7. COMPETENCE AND CULTURE BUILDING CORPORATE STRATEGY

Sometimes a corporation's greatness, or its mediocrity, lies not in what it does but in the way that it does it. In many multi-business firms, the business strategies being followed at the operating company level do not explain the consistent success, or consistent lack of success, experienced throughout the firm. The real force driving performance throughout the corporation's different businesses is the culture, the accumulated learning within parts of the firm (its 'competences' in English or 'competencies' in American), and the quality of its people and the strength of their motivation. Culture, competences and people lead to successful business unit strategy, not the other way round. Put another way, any two different real-life firms, given exactly the same strategy to execute, would have very different levels of success.

We can observe this easily enough from our own experience. Take a comparison between Marks & Spencer and British Home Stores. They are both UK mass market retailers, with similar premises, customers, technology and product lines. There are no compelling economic reasons why one should be more successful than the other. Yet over a generation or more, Marks & Spencer (M&S) has had much higher profitability, and has increased shareholder wealth to a much greater degree.

It is impossible to explain this except through the very strong and effective M&S culture, which stresses concern for both staff and customers, and where top management is highly visible, there are few layers of management, and there is very high identification of staff with the firm. Consequently, M&S tends to attract and keep the best people in the industry. M&S has outstanding skills in buying and merchandising, which result in market leadership in most product categories and low stock write-downs. M&S also has very close relationships with its suppliers, which enable it to buy cheaply and efficiently, while giving the supplier continuity and security in exchange for them accepting slightly lower than average margins. M&S also has low administration costs, as a result of few management layers and excellent communication between head office functions and the stores.

Once this culture is created, it confers an economic advantage that is difficult for competitors to break. Suppose that British Home Stores wanted to improve its buying and merchandising. It might decide the way to do this was to headhunt one of M&S's best buyers and one of its best merchandisers. But would they want to leave M&S? Even supposing they were enticed away, would they find it possible to operate in a different culture, without the natural supports and standards they were used to? If it were that easy, British Home Stores would have cracked the problem decades ago.

Similarly, one could compare Mars, the chocolate confectionery and pet food company, with all its competitors. The thing that sets Mars apart, and has led, for more than half a century, to superior growth and superior returns on assets, is its unique, winning, relentless culture. Mars attracts the brightest people in its industry, and forces them to work as a team, for the benefit of the company. It is not an experience that everyone likes, but those who stay are dedicated, enthusiastic and successful.

There is almost no difference in culture between the chocolate confectionery business and the pet food business of Mars, or between these operations in different countries. This is a remarkable achievement, given the marked differences in national business cultures. But Mars is a world, we might almost say a planet, entirely of its own.

A number of empirical studies have proved that companies with strong and constructive cultures, that stress teamwork and service to customers, and that create an unusual bond between employees and the firm, have been remarkably successful. Paradoxically, companies of this type actually compound shareholder wealth at a faster rate than those firms that stress profit making and shareholder wealth enhancement as their principal purpose.

For example, Robert Waterman, in his latest book (called *What America Does Right* in the US and *The Frontiers of Excellence* elsewhere) quotes two different studies demonstrating this paradox, that companies *not* focussing on shareholder wealth actually outperform on this very dimension. One recent study directed by James E Burke, the Business Roundtable, and the Ethics Resource Centre of Washington DC, found that companies taking unusual care to be socially responsible outperformed their peers in the Dow Jones Index, over a 30 year period, by 7.6 times! Similarly, work by Harvard professors Kotter and Heskett demonstrated that between 1977 and 1988 companies with a strong culture, that focussed as much or more on customers and employees as on shareholders, actually performed 12 times better on share price appreciation than a parallel sample of companies without this strong culture.

Some firms pay particular attention to building competences within key functional areas. We mentioned Marks & Spencer, which ensures that its buying and merchandising functions remain absolutely topnotch; in retailing, nothing is as important as buying and merchandising. A retailer with excellent skills in finance, information technology, store management, credit management and marketing, but mediocre buying and merchandising, would be less successful than one with excellent buying and merchandising and mediocre competence in all the other functions.

In other industries it is different. In fmcg (fast moving consumer goods), the key skills are brand building and marketing. The success of both IDV (part of Grand Metropolitan) and Guinness (in both the beer business, and especially in United Distillers) over the past decade has been due to exceptional competence in marketing and branding.

In pharmaceuticals, there are two alternative routes to success. One is to have drugs that are, in particular therapeutic areas, the best and the most cost effective. Clearly this is a matter of Research and Development competence, and this in turn is not a matter of luck: it is a function of corporate culture, the ability to attract the best scientists, and the links with outside universities. Some firms, like Astra of

Sweden, have demonstrated over decades an outstanding track record of R&D success, and those who have experienced the Astra culture at first-hand know that it is different – very Swedish, very long term, very persistent, very individualistic, very open to external collaboration, and extremely ethical. This culture would almost certainly be destroyed if Astra was to be taken over by an American firm.

The alternative route to success in pharmaceuticals has been scale and effectiveness in selling. A company that has locked up the US or Japanese markets, in terms of having the largest and best salesforce, can sell inferior products at higher prices, and can attract in-licensing deals from companies with excellent products but little or no sales presence (in the latter situation, the lion's share of the profits goes to the company with the salesforce, not the company with the best products). Recent changes in selling practices, where the wholesaler is acquiring more power, will change the pharmaceutical industry profoundly.

In other industries, the key to success has been quality and cost of manufacturing (e.g. automobiles), skill at exploration (e.g. oil and gas), competence in engineering applications and tailoring to customer requirements (e.g. process engineering), competence in recruitment and training (e.g. auditing and consulting), competence in site selection and judging the business cycle (e.g. property), resourcefulness in rolling out a standardised formula (e.g. middle market hotels, fast food restaurants), project management skills (e.g. turnkey contracting), or skill in trading assets (e.g. investment banking).

Whatever the key skill, it is clearly sensible for the firm to identify it and try to build the greatest competence in this skill alone in its industry. It may even make excellent sense to concentrate the majority of a firm's value added on one narrow part of the value chain, and outsource everything else. It is notable that the Japanese car industry outsources a much higher proportion of its value added, enabling it to concentrate on those functions (design and manufacturing) where it has the greatest comparative advantage.

Sometimes the definition of competence can be very specialised and recondite, or even unique to a particular company. Toyota invented Just-In-Time production, and is probably still the best at this technique of any manufacturer in any industry. Hitachi developed Management Improvement (MI), a proprietary and very effective method of value analysis, extending to all direct and indirect work. Hitachi's revenues are now well over $10bn and it has been one of Japan's most profitable firms.

For other firms, defining the competence narrowly may mean a focus on a particular type of technology. For instance, Sharp's strategy in calculators was to focus on liquid crystal technology, ignoring the rival LED technology. Sharp went further, and developed particular competence in making calculators as slim as possible. Sharp is now one of two clear world leaders in calculators, whereas for many years the industry resembled the Grand National in terms of the number of participants.

Technology-led strategies can very often lead firms into new markets and, provided the technology is good enough, and shared freely throughout a multi-business firm, this can be an excellent route to success. We mentioned earlier Honda's piston engine technology, that led from motorcycles to cars, lawnmowers and small generators, and NEC's semiconductor technology, that led to all manner of office automation and telecommunications products. We could equally cite Philips, Siemens, GE (US), and many much smaller firms, such as Oxford Instruments, whose skill in certain core technologies have been applied in a wide variety of high tech product applications.

And technology should not be defined too narrowly. Technology also includes ways of doing business that are effective and transferable. Coca-Cola corporation is the world's best marketer of a very narrow product line, but it is effective at this throughout the globe. Similarly, McDonalds' real competence lies in site selection, product sourcing, and standardisation of product quality, service and speed of delivery to the customer. These are universal skills, not confined to one product (McDonalds has now gone well beyond hamburgers to fish, salads and pizza) or one country.

Sometimes the real competence of a firm cannot be defined in product or functional terms, but exists in some other dimension. 3M's success, for example, comes from its skill in new product innovation and from its culture, that not only tolerates, but positively encourages, lateral thinking unrelated to employees' normal jobs. Arguably, McKinsey, the world's most successful management consultancy, derives most of its success from its installed base of ex-McKinsey consultants now running large companies throughout the world. McKinsey's key competence may be its skill in alumni relations.

Key competences may be dispersed throughout the multi-business firm, in each of the divisions and product areas; or these may be concentrated in certain central functions (at the Centre, or at a divisional head office); or there may be a combination, as when there is both central R&D, and product-based R&D, often with matrix reporting relationships. In some cases, such as Shell and RTZ, the key skills (especially in exploration and engineering) may reside at the Centre and represent a very large part of the firm's value added.

None of these dimensions of culture and competence can be reduced to business unit strategy. They are properly the subject of discussion at the level of the whole firm, and therefore legitimate territory for the Centre and for corporate strategy. But culture and competences are very slippery subjects, and we need to be very clear what we are talking about, and what are the different possible roles of the Centre. The odds of success are very different for different roles.

It is useful to distinguish between four different types of Competence and Culture Building Corporate Strategy:

(1) Maintenance, nurturing and fine-tuning of existing successful culture and competences

(2) Realising the potential of existing culture and competences, by focussing the firm's efforts on areas that best exploit these, and retrenching on areas that do not

(3) Maintenance and building of central functions where key competences reside, and effective dissemination of these competences to existing and new product businesses

(4) Radical change in culture and competences; a transformation strategy.

Let's deal with each of these in turn. As we go down the list, the risks become greater and the probability of the Centre adding rather than destroying value goes down.

Maintaining, nurturing and fine-tuning a successful culture or strong competences is clearly a suitable job for the Centre. In the happy situation – that of a minority of large European and American companies, perhaps as few as 10–20 per cent – where the culture is working throughout the firm, the Centre's most important job is to ensure that this continues to be the case for ever.

To do so requires (1) awareness of the key aspects of cultural success and of the exact nature of the key competences; (2) objective monitoring of these, so that there is early warning of any slippage; (3) awareness of any external events, such as a shift in the industry's key success factors, or changes in customers' purchase criteria, or the transformation of a competitor, that may render the culture and competences less unique and/or less valuable; and (4) a constant watch for the twin dangers of arrogance and complacency, that can often come with success. These themes are discussed in much more detail in *Wake Up and Shake Up Your Company*, by Koch and Andrew Campbell, and readers who wish to know exactly how to maintain a successful culture may want to consult the book, especially Chapter 10.

Maintaining a winning culture should require a very small, but very active Centre. In many ways the requirements for success are similar to those for the Olympian strategy (see pages 89–93 above), but the need to keep a constant watch on the culture distinguishes between the two approaches.

A second set of actions is necessary when the Centre recognises that the firm has winning competences and culture, but is not fully exploiting them throughout the corporation. The most common reason for this is that the firm is trying to do too much: it is in too many stages of the value added chain, and/or in too many product/market segments. The firm's strength in culture and competences may only be applicable in certain types of activity, but these may comprise less than the whole, and in some cases only a minority, of the firm's revenues and costs.

We have already alluded to some extreme examples. Firestone and Gestetner in 1980 were both good at sales and service; unfortunately, their main activity and value added at that date was in manufacturing, where they could not compete effectively.

More frequently, a multi-business firm comprises several divisions, perhaps as many as a dozen, which might have a poor fit with each other, and where perhaps only three divisions can use the firm's world class competence. In many cases, a firm may have two different types of activity, which superficially appear to be the same, because they are in the same broad industry, but which actually have very different requirements for success, and negative synergy between them. Examples include Zeneca and the old ICI, Courtaulds before the de-merger, Boots' retailing and drugs businesses, Cadbury's Food Division before the Premier Brands buy-out, and the British engineering firm TI, where Christopher Lewinton recognised in 1986–87 that the consumer engineering businesses were fundamentally alien to the skills TI possessed in industrial engineering products.

To deal with such misfits requires courage and radical surgery, commodities which appear to be in short supply. But it is far better to cut back a business to, say, 30 per cent of its turnover and 50 per cent of its profits, and then build up from there on the basis of distinctive and shared competences and cultures, than it is to continue to paper over the cracks and pretend that the businesses have more in common than they do.

I would even assert that if a company consists of businesses with more than one culture and key competence, businesses should be sold or de-merged until the original statement is no longer true. Managing different types of business and culture is a difficult and expensive process, where it is almost inevitable that the Centre will subtract more value than it adds.

Let us assume that you accept the message. How do you go about realising under-exploited advantages of competence and culture? The answer is quite simple: (1) Identify where the real advantages lie, ensuring that your answer on this derives from or is validated by a sample of key customers and other outsiders with a good feel for the business; (2) Identify and sell those business units that do not and cannot benefit from the culture and competences; (3) Identify the parts of the value added chain where the firm have competence superior to that of most competitors, and outsource all other activities; (4) Ensure that the cultural and competence advantages are strengthened, and made available throughout the new, simplified firm; and (5) Find and expand into new businesses where the culture and competences could significantly improve performance, organically at first, and by acquisition, if necessary, later.

The third type of Competence and Culture Building strategy is where the key competences of the firm belong largely or wholly to the Centre, as with RTZ and Shell, and with many Japanese companies discussed above that have central expertise in technology manufacturing and design. Here we are beginning to move onto ground that, at least for the West, is rather dangerous.

It is difficult to know, for example, whether Shell's centralisation of functional expertise really adds more value than it subtracts. To know for sure, you would have to split the company into two equivalent parts, and then maintain the current structure in one of the parts, while decentralising the other. No-one would undertake such a foolish experiment, but it is impossible to tell from comparative competitive performance whether Shell's organisation is sensible. Goold, Campbell and Alexander conclude that the functional centralisation adds more value than it subtracts; but I suspect that a majority of those who work in Shell, except at the very highest level, might have a different opinion.

What is clear, though, is how few examples Europe and America are able to provide where it can even be plausibly argued that large central resources are a net plus to the corporations concerned. Japanese examples are easier to find, and it seems probable that this is because of the skill of many large Japanese firms in creating consensus and managing the flow of information up and down large bureaucracies. Technology and other key competences really are shared across divisions in many Japanese companies, including most of those quoted above, (106) in a way that is rare in Western companies.

There are two possible but opposite reactions for Western firms. One would be to seek to emulate the successful Japanese firms, maintain or even create central pools of expertise, and ensure that they are well disseminated throughout the operating divisions. The alternative response is to give up, and avoid the central resources strategy altogether.

I would strongly urge anyone tempted towards the first reaction to reconsider. In this case, giving up is almost certain to be the more profitable reaction. Let's consider why.

We have seen earlier the weight of evidence against the ability of most Centres to add more value than they destroy. But there is an interesting sub-plot, specifically involving Japan versus the West. Japan's competitive advantage in the last 25 years has derived largely from having better product design and especially better factories, producing higher quality and lower cost goods. Now three developments are beginning to reverse Japan's advantage.

First, the West has finally tackled manufacturing seriously, emulating Japanese best practice in the same way that Japan had earlier copied and enhanced best Western practice from the 1950s and 1960s. The result is that many American and European firms are just as productive in their factories as the Japanese; for example, many observers claim that Ford is now more efficient in making cars than Honda.

The second change is that the very success in reducing manufacturing costs has made production a much less important component in total value added. The key battle is now being fought outside the factory, in all elements of overhead cost (research, marketing, selling, distribution, finance, and general management). And the pace in reducing such costs is clearly being made in the West, especially in the US, where the most ruthless forms of delayering, business process re-engineering, and downsizing are being deployed, leading to spectacular increases in productivity (and large increases in unemployment). Japanese firms in general are much less skilled at managing offices than factories, much less willing to pursue radical re-engineering solutions, and less willing to export the problem of unemployment to society at large.

The third development is that an increasing part of GNP is coming from service industries and 'soft' activities (e.g. from computer software rather than hardware), where productivity tends to be much higher in the West than in Japan.

Fourthly, there is an increasing tendency for the most valuable workers to want to work in autonomous work teams, and in smaller rather than larger units. This can be seen most clearly in the gravitation of top graduates (of both universities and business schools) into service industries and small firms rather than into large industrial concerns, but the forces of 'liberation management' and 'empowerment' are undermining traditional organisation structures, including those where the Centre is large and powerful. This trend is also one where the Japanese are behind, and, to the extent that one believes that the trend is driven by economics as well as ideology, at a disadvantage.

All of these developments directly or indirectly threaten the viability of traditional well-run bureaucracy, the middle-up-down organisation on which the industrial triumphs of the last century and a half have been built, and at which the Japanese so clearly excel. In this context, a decision to try to build or strengthen a Japanese-style central resource runs against the tide of history.

The contention here, which cannot be rigorously proved, is that skill in managing a large management network, and in particular one with large central resources, is of declining value. Given that it is a difficult thing to do in the West, why bother? The alternative approach, one that appears to be winning and where Western firms have a natural affinity, is to decentralise and build in expertise as close to the customer as much as possible.

In short, the risks of the third variant of this strategy, building up central expertise, will only rarely be proportionate to the benefit.

The fourth and final type of Competence and Culture Building strategy is even more risky than the third, but has such a high payoff in the event of success that it is sometimes worth the gamble. This is for the Centre, and in particular a new leader of a corporation, to attempt its transformation: to change the firm's culture and competences in a fundamental way, leading to markedly higher levels of financial and market performance.

Even a moment's thought should convince you that transforming a company is difficult. This is the flip side of the virtuous circle that Marks & Spencer finds itself in; the vicious circle facing someone trying to drag a firm up by its bootstraps. About 75 per cent of the transformation attempts of large American and British companies between 1970 and 1992 failed. Odds of three to one against are not appealing, particularly as failure to transform, though it may not worsen the firm's position, usually leads to ritual sacrifice of the failed leader.

There are, of course, many impressive examples of success. Guinness is now a totally different company from that confronting Ernest Saunders in 1980, and somewhat different from the company he left behind when higher authority beckoned. GE of the US is now getting to the stage where its transformation is sufficiently secure for it to survive the disappearance of Jack Welch. Christopher Lewinton is well on the way, after less than ten years, to transforming TI. Gestetner has changed out of all recognition since the days of family control. Other successful transformations include Nissan (under Kume, 1985–93), Borg Warner (under Bere, 1972–83), Ind Coope (under Cox, 1982–93), British Airways (under Marshall, 1983–93), Johnson & Johnson (under Burke, 1976–89), and Toshiba UK (1980–93).

What is interesting is that all examples of successful transformation that I have been able to trace have had six common characteristics (as well as a huge number of uncommon ones!):

(1) They all relied on the leadership of one person, who was always an unreasonably demanding character. This is a deeply unfashionable conclusion, but true. Can anyone name a corporate transformation that happened without one person being the initial driving force?

(2) Those who really ran the company – usually just 2–5 people, and always a much smaller group than the full board – shared an emotional commitment to the change, and to each other, to help make the change happen. Unity of purpose of this sort is very rare, and often only achieved by lowering the number of people who run the company.

(3) The change was helped along by a 'Cause', a short, pithy description, no more than five words, of the medium term change desired. The Cause must, directly or by contrast, describe something missing in the company today; it must be a standard for judging behaviour against; it

must be challenging; and it must be attainable within a 3–4 year horizon. Examples of good Causes include 'Putting people first', 'Simplify', 'Smash red tape', 'Outgrow Competitor X', 'One company', 'Close to the Customer', and 'Number One and Pulling Ahead'.

(4) The Centre had to have the power to see what was going on throughout the company, and to ensure that the culture change happened everywhere. Many attempts at transformation have collapsed, once it was clear that one division, one function (e.g. R&D) or one country (e.g. Germany) was going to resist the change and get away with it.

(5) The change process must be hard as well as soft, and in particular linked to new and more demanding, but simple, financial targets. For a company currently making 4 per cent return on sales, this might be 10 per cent return on sales, to be demanded from all business areas that wish to remain in the portfolio.

(6) The transformation must be supported by at least one world class competence, which must be identified and given full rein.

Other useful hints for leaders setting out on the transformation process include:

(1) Do not do it unless you can identify sufficient support within both top management and in the firm as a whole. If there is not a sufficient body of supporters that already exists, or can be created quickly, do not start out.

(2) Realise that transformation takes time: 10–12 years is typical; 3–5 years is the absolute minimum.

(3) Insist that hard results, in terms of financial returns and/or market share gains, come through in at least some areas within the first 18 months. Create early successes, even if this takes extraordinary effort. Once you have a few early successes, trumpet them throughout the firm.

(4) Do not make a big song and dance about the change process until you have early successes. Keep a low profile until then.

(5) Realise that you are setting out to convert people to a new way of doing things. Identify and nurture key supporters. Choose potential supporters not just on the basis of their enthusiasm for change, but on the basis of their power and personal competence. Spend time converting the latter. If you fail, ensure that they leave the firm.

(6) When you do publicise the change process, which should be after the early successes, and in general not less than 3 years after you start, ensure that people know what behaviour standards are now required. At this stage these new behaviour standards can and must be enforced. If you try to do this too soon, you will not have the power to enforce the standards, and they will become discredited because of lack of compliance.

(7) Do not talk to the investment community about the change process. Just leave them to observe the results.

(8) Realise that, as the leader, you will have to spend most of your time directly on the change process. Do not attempt to run a division or function yourself in the meantime. Do not attempt to do anything else that could become time-consuming. And, above all, do not make or attempt to make an acquisition during the first three years.

(9) Ensure that you have objective feedback on whether attitudes and behaviour are changing throughout the process. Top management frequently becomes lulled into a false sense of security, believing that things are changing, while at the grass roots life goes on as before, except for lip service to the changes.

(10) Finally, ensure that you are personally well prepared and supported for the demands of the change process. Delegate so that you always have plenty of time to deal with unexpected developments. Balance your home and work life so that you are always effective in the latter: do not work excessive hours or allow your family and personal life to atrophy. If your personal life is insecure or changing, do not start the transformation until you have a settled personal base from which to work. Remain fit throughout, taking exercise at least three times a week, and preferably every day. Do not book appointments before 10 o'clock on any day, so you always have time to think before events take control of you.

These hints are amplified in *Wake Up and Shake Up Your Company*, referred to earlier.

To sum up, building a firm's culture and competences is a legitimate and often much-needed form of corporate strategy. If the Centre does not do this, no-one else will. But that is far from saying that this is automatically, or even probably, the right strategy for the Centre to follow. The case against taking this route needs to be listed:

(1) The balance of risk and reward is often wrong. If culture and competences are already appropriate, the benefit from a focus on them may be slight. If culture and competences are not appropriate, or similar in different parts of the organisation, the task of changing them may be too difficult, or too risky.

(2) Any strategy built around a large phalanx of central corporate resource is likely to be flawed.

(3) Working on culture and competences requires an unusual leader: sensitive to these dimensions, both patient and demanding, and unusually skilled at leading change. These conditions will not normally be met. If not, little good will come, and valuable time and money may be wasted.

(4) Even with the right leader, and a strong need for change, success is not guaranteed or even probable. The top team must be united, supporters created, a Cause defined, simple financial targets propagated and attained, a world class competence identified and reinforced, early successes realised, new behaviour standards defined in due course, and a whole host of political pitfalls avoided. The time to start must be right, without economic time bombs that may blow the change process off-course, and no powerful enemies of change around.

(5) It is a long term strategy, requiring at least a decade of stable leadership.

(6) The leader and the supporters must be willing to take personal risks with their careers, in order to leave a legacy of change behind.

The list below will help you identify whether this form of corporate strategy is appropriate for your firm.

Should you follow a Competence and Culture Building Corporate Strategy?

(1) Is it clear that considerations of culture and competences are more important in explaining your firm's success or lack of success than any other factors?

(2) Is working on culture and competences the most obvious route to improving short and medium term financial performance?

(3) Do you have a small and well regarded Centre/Head Office?

(4) Do the chairman and chief executive share the same general views about the firm's culture and what aspects of it ought to change?

(5) Is this also true of everyone else who is very influential in running the company?

(6) Does the firm already have certain skills and competences that are world class but under-exploited?

(7) Are there opportunities to simplify the company and decrease the costs of complexity?

(8) If cultural change is necessary, is this the right time to start? Are there enough supporters of change, and are they powerful enough?

(9) Is the chief executive genuinely visionary, radical and charismatic?

(10) Will a programme to reinforce competences, re-focus the company. and/or change culture, be given time to work, given that several years are always necessary?

Scoring

Score ten points for each YES (up to a maximum of 100). Compare the total score to that for the other strategies (B, C, D, F) from pages 91, 99, 108 and 127.

Illustration 1.27 shows the appropriate conditions for Competence and Culture Building Corporate Strategy.

Illustration 2.7
When is Competence and Culture Building strategy appropriate?

Business Conditions	• Culture and competences more important than micro-strategy in explaining relative competitor performance... • ...and in improving firm's short to medium term financial performance
Skill Within Firm	• Truly united Board and Top management • Visionary CEO • Well regarded head office • Business interdependencies recognised and co-operative ethic in place • Change programme will be given many years to work

8. PERFORMANCE CONTROL CORPORATE STRATEGY

The final legitimate form of corporate strategy is where the Centre improves the financial performance of the operating companies through setting stretching financial targets in each year's budget, holding individual managers accountable for attaining budgets and motivating them to do so, and exercising tight budgetary control so that any incipient failure to meet budgets can be corrected. Performance Control companies also exercise authority over investment decisions, and, although nearly all Centres do this, the Performance Control companies do so in a particularly effective way, by looking carefully at short and medium term cash flows.

This form of central strategy may be unique, in that companies that follow it religiously appear, in aggregate, to have their Centres add more value than they subtract. Examples of successful practitioners (many of whom are also exponents of the Acquisition Driven Corporate Strategy, which fits well with Performance Control) include Associated British Foods, BBA Group, BTR, Hanson, Matsushita, Siebe, Tarmac, Tomkins, and Williams Holdings.

These and other companies following the Performance Control strategy all exhibit the following eight characteristics:

(1) They operate through close financial control, organised around budgets. The Centre has particular financial expertise and knows the financial idiosyncrasies of the operating companies intimately. The Centre is able to 'see through' to what is happening financially in the subsidiaries and cannot be deceived about the true financial position anywhere.

(2) They make one person, the chief executive of each operating company, responsible for attaining each budget. There is no ambiguity and no shared commitment.

(3) Budgets are prepared in a consistent and uniform way, according to rules laid down by the Centre.

(4) Budgets are set in such a way as to lead to continual improvement in financial results, often based around corporate earnings per share percentage improvement targets, as well as bottom-up projections of what is possible. There is relentless, persistent and pervasive pressure to squeeze out extra financial returns, against a cultural assumption that change and improvement must be the law of life for good managers.

(5) The Centre insists that budgets are serious commitments that must be met. Failure to meet budget results in dismissal or serious career set-back for the responsible manager.

(6) Close monitoring of monthly results occurs.

(7) Aside from financial control, the chief executives responsible for meeting budgets have very wide freedoms to run the businesses how they like. Financial control is centralised, but in all other respects there is a very high degree of de-centralisation. Those running the operating companies never have the frustration, or excuse, of central strategic or operating interference preventing them realising their results. In particular, these companies' Centres do not lay down market or competitive strategy.

(8) Despite point 7, the Centre may have some value creation insights, usually directly related to financial performance. Opportunities for margin enhancement or cost reduction are often highlighted, using financial comparisons and benchmarks, but usually supplemented by instinct or experience at the Centre related to the operating businesses.

BTR provides an excellent example of all these points. It is a diversified engineering-based British giant (with sales approaching £10 billion) that has demonstrated rapid and consistent growth in profits and earnings per share for over 20 years. Since 1983 it has made six large acquisitions and integrated them within the BTR profit planning process. Although it is successful at making acquisitions, BTR's success probably derives more from its financial controls than from skill at identifying and negotiating bid targets, and it is an excellent example of the eight attributes of Performance Control:

(1) BTR's management philosophy revolves around its 'profit planning' process, whose centre-piece is the annual budget.

(2) Each profit centre has a Managing Director who is on the line for achieving the results to which he or she has committed. There are 1,300 such people in BTR, each in charge of a profit centre.

(3) Each July, BTR's Centre issues guidelines to the profit centres, giving the overall performance improvement sought by the corporation in terms of specific financial ratios (such as return on sales, working capital to sales, value added per employee, etc.). Profit plans must then be prepared in accordance with 15 schedules and agreed by the relevant group chief executive (of which there are 25)

by September at two 'challenge meetings', during which the plans are rigorously tested to see if they are ambitious enough.

(4) The Centre's chief executives and financial people have vast experience of probing plans and monitoring their attainment. They can spot an undemanding plan miles away, and will land on it and its author from a great height. They are unlikely to accept any plan that does not conform to the corporate guidelines for overall improvement, and are adept at ferreting out business-specific profit improvement opportunities and getting commitment to them.

The profit planning process has many benefits. The common format facilitates communication between the operating companies and the Centre, and stimulates competition between the operating companies to produce the best results, as well as focussing the managers on profit improvement as their fundamental objective and raising their awareness of and proficiency in cash management. The Centre always gees up the operating companies, making them commit to more ambitious targets than would otherwise occur.

The focus on margin improvement is inescapable. And the corporate culture of continual improvement is highly motivating: pride is taken in it, there is no cynicism about the expertise of the Centre, and no doubt about what needs to be done to earn corporate advancement. Consequently, politics are minimised.

(5) Both individual profit centre managing directors, and the group chief executives in charge of a bundle profit centres, are vulnerable if planned results are not attained. The process is not totally Stalinist: explanations are listened to, especially if corrective action has already been taken, and temporary failure may be tolerated for a time. Still, consistent under-performers are ruthlessly weeded out.

(6) Each profit centre provides weekly reports on sales and order intake (the latter a key leading indicator that is watched closely), and a monthly account of orders, sales, operating profits, interest paid and number of employees, costs, balance sheet and all significant cash flow items. Each month the profit centre MD meets the relevant group chief executive to discuss the month's performance.

(7) Morale within BTR is very high, mainly from two causes: the independence that managers are given provided they meet results; and collective pride in BTR's track record of profit improvement.

(8) The group chief executives and the central financial team often provide indicative advice pinpointing specific profit improvement

opportunities within the businesses. Very often these relate to the possibility for price increases in industrial (as opposed to consumer) businesses, as well as how to achieve productivity improvements. The people from the Centre have a good understanding of and feel for how to run industrial businesses and are highly respected for their business judgment as well as their financial expertise. Nevertheless, it is crystal clear that the profit centre managing directors have the ultimate decision on how to achieve the profit plans.

It is important to note that BTR's system and expertise are models, and that few corporate Centres even begin to approach the quality of BTR's profit improvement process. Every multi-business corporation has a budgeting process, but only a small minority exhibit the eight attributes of Performance Control discussed above. If firms cannot meet these requirements (even though they may not be quite as adept at them as BTR), they would be better off following one of the other corporate strategies. Ultimately, the test of whether a company has a true Performance Control strategy is whether the profit centre managers respect and admire the Centre and its system, or whether they feel cynical and resentful about the Centre and the control process. If the latter, huge value will be subtracted by the Centre, because the profit centre managers will be motivated to deceive the Centre and play at politics, rather than strive to deliver the best possible results.

It is therefore easy for an outside interviewer to determine quite rapidly whether or not companies and their Centres that claim to add value via Performance Control really do so. In the majority of cases, the answer from the field is a resounding no, a lack of confidence in the process and the Centre. Thus, although true Performance Control is an excellent corporate strategy, it is also surprisingly rare, and most often not appropriate. Obtaining the necessary central skills, and producing the appropriate results-oriented corporate culture, where these do not already exist, is a very difficult and lengthy process. This is why firms like BTR have a sustainable competitive advantage that is quite unrelated to the specific micro-economics of business unit strategy.

Should you follow a Performance Control Corporate Strategy?

(1) Does the corporation have a long term record of above-average growth in earnings per share?

(2) Is there a culture throughout the firm of continual and ambitious profit improvement?

(3) Is the Centre highly respected by those running the operating companies?

(4) Does the firm have sophisticated financial controls that are uniformly applied throughout the firm?

(5) Are there clear and unambiguous profit centres, where it is crystal clear who is responsible for delivering financial results for each business?

(6) Is budget-setting and profit plan development a lengthy, detailed, challenging and carefully conducted process?

(7) Are monthly results closely scrutinised and discussed face to face by the Centre and the operating company managers together?

(8) Are profit centre managers praised and rewarded for meeting/exceeding their budgets, and punished if budgets are not met?

(9) Does the Centre contribute specific value creation insights, that help to pinpoint specific business opportunities to raise profits.

(10) Is there internal competition to produce the best results relative to budget, and great kudos from realising large profit improvements?

Scoring

Score ten points for each YES. Compare the total score to those for the other strategies (see pages 91, 99, 108 and 122 and fill in the scores on the summary sheet provided in Illustration 2.9).

Illustration 2.8 displays the business conditions and skills that make the Performance Control Corporate Strategy appropriate.

9. WHICH CORPORATE STRATEGY IS RIGHT FOR YOUR FIRM?

Now is the time to compare the scores for the fit with your firm of each of the five possible steady state (that is, non-emergency) corporate strategies. Simply transfer the relevant scores from pages 99, 108, 122 and 127 to Illustration 2.9.

Which Strategy is Right for You?

(1) If there is a tie for the highest score, you have to decide first of all whether the strategies are compatible and can be combined. In general, the Olympian strategy is incompatible with any other. The Acquisition Driven strategy fits very well with Performance Control to form a hybrid Acquisition and Performance Control strategy, but does not fit well with any other strategy. The Portfolio strategy can be combined with the Competence and Culture Building one, though you should be clear at any one time which is the more important role for the Centre. Neither of these two strategies fits well with any third strategy.

(2) If there is a tie between two incompatible strategies, choose the one with which top management is most comfortable.

(3) If no strategy scores 60 or more, you have a real problem. You will need to change the composition of top management and/or the firm's culture. Consider carefully which strategy can be followed (as judged by a future score of 80 or more) with the least risk and time.

(4) If the ranking of scores offends your intuition, go back to the questions and see why your intuitively favoured strategy scored poorly. I have to tell you that it is more likely that your intuition is wrong than that the scores are misleading. You are probably not paying enough attention to the sheer difficulty of changing your firm's culture and behaviour.

Illustration 2.8
When is Performance Control corporate strategy appropriate?

Business Conditions	● Market predictable ● Stable competitive environment
Skill Within Firm	● Above average EPS growth ● Culture of continous profit improvement ● Centre highly respected and adds insight ● Sophisticated financial controls throughout firm

Illustration 2.9
Fit with your firm of steady state Corporate Strategies

	Strategy	Checklist on page	Score
B	Olympian	91	
C	Acquisition Driven	99	
D	Portfolio	108	
E	Competence and Culture Building	122	
F	Performance Control	127	

(5) If you are personally strongly in favour or emotionally wedded to one approach, but the score shows that this strategy in inappropriate to your firm, consider moving to a firm that is following or able to follow your preferred strategy.

A Final Warning

Remember that corporate strategy resembles the Bermuda Triangle. Good intentions easily end in poor execution and de-motivation of those running the wealth-creating businesses. Relations between the latter and the Centre often degenerate into a downward spiral.

If you do not already have a clearly successful corporate strategy and matching style, be as modest in what you try to achieve as your ego will allow. Big egos sometimes create great value, but in the area of corporate strategy they far more often destroy it.

Part III

AN A–Z OF STRATEGIC THINKERS, TOOLS AND TECHNIQUES, AND CONCEPTS AND DEFINITIONS

A. STRATEGIC THINKERS

ANSOFF, H. IGOR (b. 1918)

Russian-American engineer, mathematician, military strategist and operations researcher who wrote the highly acclaimed *Corporate Strategy* in 1965. The book is quite readable and provides a model for deriving a corporate strategy. The model assumes that the purpose of a firm is to maximise long term profitability (return on investment) and then gives a host of checklists and charts for deriving objectives, assessing SYNERGY between different parts of the firm (functions and businesses), appraising the firm's COMPETENCE profile and deciding how to expand (how to diversify, how to assess whether entry to an industry is likely to give the desired ROI, whether to acquire or go for organic growth, and how to weight alternatives taking into account a large number of highlighted factors. He stresses the need for a 'common thread' for all a company's businesses if it is to add value to them.

Re-reading *Corporate Strategy* today is disappointing. The book has not aged well, the methodology overwhelms the substance, and it is difficult to gain much insight from the mechanistic procedures suggested. The concept of competitive advantage is only introduced systematically on page 161 (out of a total of 191 pages in my edition) and is then only given four and half pages. On the other hand the books' checklists are useful for analysts who want to know whether they have looked at everything they should, for example in conducting an industry analysis. The ANSOFF MATRIX is definitely a useful framework for considering expansion into new areas.

Since 1965 Ansoff has written at least 5 full-length books on strategic management. The later Ansoff is much more contingent in his prescriptions.

BOWER, MARVIN

The real founder of McKinsey, who gave it its backbone and values in the 1940s and has kept watch over the Firm's soul ever since. Bower was a lawyer by background and his great innovation was to think that management consulting – up to then a rather fly-by-night and *ad hoc* activity – could become a profession comparable to the law. Professionalism was partly a matter of high intelligence and codification of all useful knowledge relating to management science, but it was far more than that: it was anchored in the quality and integrity of the client-professional relationship. Bower insisted that McKinsey should put the client's interests first, rather than those of McKinsey or of the individual consultant. Client service, client confidentiality, client responsiveness and integrity in telling the client the truth, as perceived by the professional, were all drummed into the Firm by Bower. He made McKinsey the most prestigious and envied firm in management consulting throughout the world, based on his ethic of professionalism. Bower, who is now over 90, still has a desk at McKinsey, and is deeply revered. Since his retirement a generation ago, he has still been influential, stopping in its tracks all discussion of 'selling out' by taking the Firm public or selling to another firm. He regards his heritage as largely intact, though insiders say that he worries about the materialism and concern for high earnings of the top professionals today.

CAMPBELL, ANDREW (b. 1950)

Scottish management guru, ex-McKinsey consultant and founder of the Ashridge Strategic Management Centre, who is the world's leading authority on issues related to MISSION and has (with Michael GOOLD) been a pioneer in the area of parenting and management styles. In 1990 his book *A Sense of Mission* stressed that mission statements could be unnecessary or even counter-productive: what mattered was whether a company had a driving sense of purpose, a consistent set of values, a commercial strategy that was also aligned with the purpose and values, and a set of behaviour standards that underpinned the value system. See MISSION, VISION and PARENTING ADVANTAGE and GOOLD.

CHANDLER, ALFRED (b. 1918)

Influential American economic historian whose book *Strategy and Structure* (1962) was based on studying major US corporations between 1850 and 1920. He is important for having made three points clearly:

(1) He highlighted the close relationship between strategy and structure, and said that firms should first determine their strategy, then their structure. This was more unusual for the emphasis on strategy than the sequencing, because very few writers had paid attention to strategy: it is almost completely lacking in the earlier theorists like Taylor and Weber.

(2) He believed that the role of the salaried manager and technician was vital, and talked about the 'visible hand' of management co-ordinating the flow of product to customers more efficiently than Adam Smith's 'invisible hand' of the market. This is an early recognition that corporations, in their internal dealings, favour a planned economy.

(3) He was an advocate of decentralisation in large corporations, contributing to the divisionalisation and decentralisation trend of the 1960s and 1970s. He praised Alfred SLOAN's decentralisation of General Motors in the 1920s before Sloan published his book (in 1963), and was influential in the transformation of AT&T in the 1980s from a production-based bureaucracy to a marketing organisation.

Chandler provided much of the vocabulary for the subsequent management debate: it is still very much a live issue whether strategy should follow structure. Tom PETERS holds that Chandler 'got it exactly wrong': that structure inevitably determines strategy, and that the socialist principle of management must be broken down and subjected to market pressures. The truth is probably that Chandler was more right than wrong when he wrote, and that Peters is now. See PETERS.

DEMING, W. EDWARDS (b. 1900)

American originator of the quality revolution: consulted to many major Japanese firms in the late 1940s and 1950s and was the single greatest external influence on Japanese industry. Until Deming, Japanese goods were inferior. Became known in America only in the 1980s, when he helped to stem the tide of superior Japanese imports into the West that he had earlier contributed towards. He was a statistician who emphasised the importance of the consumer ('the consumer is the most important part of the production line') and that reducing variation was the key to superior profitability. See also Joseph Duran, a contemporary and compatriot who also influenced Japan.

GOOLD, MICHAEL (b.1945)

British management writer and founding director of the Ashridge Strategic Management Centre after a career with BCG. Made his name with the excellent book, *Strategies and Styles* (1987) which looked at the way in which the Centre of large, diversified firms managed their businesses. More recently he has developed a framework for corporate level strategy built round the concept of parenting advantage described in another landmark book, *Corporate-Level Strategy: Creating Value in the Multibusiness Company* (1994). It looks at the justification for multibusiness companies and concludes that sound corporate strategies are based on the advantage created by the parent organisation. Goold's work is always original, measured, incisive and important.

HAMPDEN-TURNER, CHARLES

British academic and consultant, one of the leading international experience authorities on CULTURE, both at the corporate and at the national level. He has a holistic understanding of management processes and combines a refreshing, high-level view of the world with nitty-gritty examples of how to make the most out of each firm's unique culture.

He has written several highly acclaimed books, but in my opinion the two best are *Corporate Culture* (1990) and *The Seven Cultures of Capitalism* (1993, written with Fons TROMPENAARS). The first of these starts with some insights about corporate culture: cultures provide firm members with continuity and identity ('without a shared culture Volvo would not be recognisably Volvo'); cultures are patterns, where behaviour at one level (bosses to subordinates) are repeated, for good or ill, in relation to customers; cultures facilitate the sharing of experience and information; cultures are the mechanism through which organisations can learn (there is no other way); and changing culture is increasingly the only way that a leader can achieve anything; culture is a stronger and cheaper way to motivate than money; cultures are deeply rooted, but can be changed by intervention by managers and consultants, provided this is skilful and does not attack the culture head-on.

Hampden-Turner believes that the key issues facing companies are *dilemmas*: safety and productivity, the need to cut staff and demonstrate a new caring view of employees; the need to exercise personal initiative and the need to maintain group solidarity; the need to raise profits and also spend money to improve infrastructure; and so on. The culture of a firm will respond to a new leader if he or she can find constructive ways of resolving these dilemmas, in a way that satisfies both its horns. Culture can be negative or positive, and the change process is seen as subtly turning what is negative (and a strong cultural belief or trait of the organisation) into something that is positive (and equally strong, using the same cultural substrate). At times Hampden-Turner comes close to making 'culture' almost the 'General Will' of an organisation, which must warm to a new task or way of doing things for it to be effective. He presents organisational dynamics as a series of either vicious circles or VIRTUOUS CIRCLES, and shows how new initiatives can use the same cultural attributes to turn a downward spiral into an upward one.

Seven detailed examples are given. One of the greatest challenges quoted was the attempt of a new Swedish manager in 1982–86 to turn Volvo's unsuccessful and loss-making business in France into a success. The French team and Volvo dealers in the country had convinced themselves that failure was inevitable: the French people would never warm to Swedish cars, which, like the Swedes, were seen as melancholic, cold and dull. The French subsidiary talked down to the dealers, attempting to motivate them by threatening to replace them if they failed to sell more. The dealers passed this indifference on the customers, and having a pessimistic view of their task failed to invest in their showrooms, resulting in a depressing sales picture which in turn reinforced the view that the 'hot' French would never buy 'cold' Volvos. Instead of hitting the dealers over the head, the new manager held a series of meetings with them, listening, breaking down the hierarchy, inviting the entire French dealer network to visit Sweden, giving them pride in the company and their role, encouraging them to invest in their showrooms and treat customers differently ... and doubling sales within two years.

The case examples all stress the importance of positive 'rituals', corporate events that build on the existing culture but help to stress the desired values.

See also: CULTURE, FLAT ORGANISATION, and TROMPENAARS.

HANDY, CHARLES (b. 1932)

Leading management thinker, and fun to read, because both style and content are original, provocative and engaging. British, but the son of an Irish vicar, and only just being properly appreciated in America.

As an introduction to Handy, read both *The Age of Unreason* (1989), and *The Empty Raincoat* (1994), and then if you are interested (as you should be) in CULTURE, read *Gods of Management* (1978). Handy believes that the nature of work and the type of organisation needed today is changing profoundly: that the number of core workers in firms will continue to fall sharply and that the future firm will be a SHAM-ROCK comprising core workers, a network of qualified contractors, and the hired help. Many talented people will increasingly not think in terms of a career, but a succession of roles and after a time a portfolio of part-time activities: soon, he says, there won't be any promotions after 30. Handy is a radical humanist who believes that both govern-ment and business organisations in the West need to transform the way they think and act: he both prefers the Eastern model of company-as-community to the Western model of company-as-property, and thinks it is more effective. Ultimately the market will clear: those who have knowledge will insist on being treated as partners, and the role and rights of shareholders will be reduced.

The Empty Raincoat develops the themes contained in *The Age of Unreason*, but puts a much more pessimistic gloss on them. The famous Handy formula of $\frac{1}{2} \times 2 \times 3$ – firms employing half as many people, paying them twice as much, and getting three times the output – is still here, but rather than emphasising the increase in incomes and produc-tivity implied, Handy dwells more on the adverse personal and social implications. Longer hours and a flawed lifestyle for the core workers, the difficulty for young people to find their first conventional job, and the ever increasing problem of unemployment ('governments seem sur-prised when each recovery soaks up fewer unemployed ... organisations belatedly have realised that it is possible to grow without growing the labour force') are put into stark relief. The liberated ex-core workers with their portfolio of part-time activities beloved of the earlier book turn into 'reluctant independents. They may be the way of the future but few wanted to be the pathfinders'. *The Empty Raincoat*'s final words are characteristic of a much less gung-ho Handy: 'It is up to us to light our own small fires in the darkness.'

I much preferred the upbeat message of *The Age of Unreason*, and I believe its tone will seem more appropriate to those looking back from the twenty-first century. But whether you are an optimist or a pessimist, read at least one of Handy's books. A boiled-down version of his views is no substitute for the instructive pleasure of reading them first-hand.

HENDERSON, BRUCE (1915–92)

Founder of the Boston Consulting Group (BCG) and one of the most original and far sighted American business thinkers of all time. He and a handful of colleagues invented the GROWTH/SHARE MATRIX (BCG MATRIX), as well as developing the best view of BUSINESS SEGMENTATION that yet exists. Bruce weaved it all together in a coherent philosophy of business that highlighted more clearly than ever before the compelling importance of market leadership, a low cost position, selectivity in business, and looking at cash flows. He was ahead of his time in seeing the threat to American business posed both by Japan and by America's (and Britain's) obsession with return on investment, which he roundly condemned. Although a capitalist, red in tooth and claw, he understood the importance of corporate CULTURE long before it became fashionable: he was a weird but ultimately consistent mix of right wing economist and revolutionary critic of standard American corporate practice. His love of paradox, and unique style, which alternates short and shocking sentences with Gibbonesque long ones, are all of a piece with his revolutionary mind.

Bruce changed the way we think about strategy and through BCG has had a major impact on many Western companies. Yet perhaps he achieved much less than a man of his energy and vision should have. He was always a loner, and did not stamp his personality on BCG in the same way that Marvin BOWER had on McKinsey. Consultants in BCG were always apprehensive about encounters with Bruce, which were always challenging and often disturbing. BCG has continued his heritage of providing new ideas for management, but no-one after Bruce has had his single-minded crusading drive, and after being a tremendous hothouse of ideas in the late 1960s and early 1970s, BCG soon became (even when Bruce was still active in it) an only slightly unconventional commercial consultancy, which would often undertake work where it had little chance, and often no desire, to change the client's thinking and behaviour fundamentally. In short, BCG became domesticated, more concerned to do good professional work and to make money for its vice presidents than to change the world. Bruce realised that this was happening, but lacked the practical management skills or close colleagues to stop it.

Even in terms of ideas, Bruce and BCG never fully exploited the force of the original insights, which even today are not evangelised to the extent that they should be. America continued to lose global market share for the same reasons Bruce had pinpointed so well. One is tempted to conclude that, if BCG had had an organising genius interested in implementation but deeply committed to Bruce's vision, history could have been different. Bruce never developed around him a school of thought that took root in academia either: he could have done with his own Michael PORTER to develop and codify the ideas and help market them to business schools.

Bruce Henderson was a genius. That his achievements fell well short of his insights is much to be regretted.

JURAN, JOSEPH M. (b. 1904)

Romanian-born American electrical engineer and quality guru, who was jointly responsible (with W. Edwards DEMING) for the quality revolution in Japan after 1950. He published his *Quality Control Handbook* in 1951 and began work in Tokyo in 1953. He developed Company-Wide Quality Management (CWQM), a systematic methodology for spreading the gospel of quality throughout a firm. He insisted that quality could not be delegated and was an early exponent of what has come to be known as EMPOWERMENT: for him quality had to be the goal of each employee, individually and in teams, through self-supervision. He was less mechanistic than DEMING and placed greater stress on human relations. In 1988 he published *Juran on Planning for Quality* which included his quality trilogy of quality planning, quality management and quality improvement. A firm and all its people must commit to and be obsessive about quality: it must become a way of life built into the firm's CULTURE. Well worth reading, though not the lightest of reads.

KANTER, ROSABETH MOSS (b. 1943)

US sociologist, Harvard Business School professor and editor of the Harvard Business Review and the driving force behind empowerment as a change management crusade. Three of her books are important.

Men and Women of the Corporation (1977) criticised the way that human talent was cramped within bureaucratic structures, hurting both the corporation and the individuals. She proposed career development mechanisms to move more women (and some other 'powerless' groups) into more senior jobs, and also urged empowering strategies leading to flatter structures and autonomous work groups.

The Change Masters (1983) profiled companies that were good at innovation and identified their underlying characteristics. The most significant finding was that such firms have an 'integrative' view of the world and were iconoclastic; firms poor at innovation were analytical, compartmentalised, 'segmentalist' and conservative. The book developed the theme that individuals should be made more powerful, but within a framework of common corporate purpose.

When Giants Learn to Dance (1989) stresses the need for even giant corporations to become 'post-entrepreneurial': demonstrating all the attributes of an entrepreneur such as flexibility, responsiveness and personal initiative, but combining this with the discipline of a large firm and the realisation of SYNERGY between different parts of the firm by having a vision of the firm overall and where it can go. In a striking metaphor, she talks about the dancing elephant: 'the power of an elephant with the agility of a dancer'. Another useful phrase is 'the corporation as a switchboard, where a small centre helps to direct other parts of the organisation to realise synergies'. She also invents PAL, not a type of dog food but rather '*pool* resources with others, *ally* to exploit an opportunity, or *link* systems in a partnership'. The wise corporation becomes PALs with customers, suppliers, joint venture partners and outside contractors. The company of the future will be lean but not mean, able to do more with less (fewer layers), but operating within a framework of shared values.

Kanter is right about all of this, though to me she misses (or chooses not to stress) the key role that an individual leader has in transforming a corporation. See also STRATEGIC ALLIANCES, SYNERGY, and KEIRETSU.

LEAVITT, HAROLD J.

American management psychologist who is one of the most stimulating and original thinkers in the field. His 1978 book, *Managerial Psychology*, is one of the best texts on the subject, and in particular on the interactions and communication patterns of groups, and the distortions that arise from links in a chain. But his most interesting, landmark, work is his recent *Corporate Pathfinders*, which examines the characteristic personalities of leaders. In particular, he has a very useful typology into TYPE 1, TYPE 2 and TYPE 3 EXECUTIVES.

LEVITT, THEODORE (b. 1925)

German-born American marketing guru, professor at Harvard Business School. Wrote the legendary *Harvard Business Review* article on 'Marketing Myopia' in 1960: it has since sold half a million reprints. The article said that firms and industries should be 'customer-satisfying' rather than 'goods-producing' in their orientation: marketing-led not production-led. He said that it was not good enough to meet customer demand with a new product, and then believe that the key to continued success was low cost production. He criticised 'Fordism' for giving the customer what was thought to be good for him, rather than continually being alert to what the customer wanted. Hence Ford's decline in the face of General Motors' policy of offering cars in any colour and later in the face of the compact car from Japan and Europe. He also castigated the myopia of the US railroad industry in thinking that they were in the railroad business (a production-led view) rather than consumer transport: if they had had the latter view they would have diversified into airlines and not seen their business wither.

Levitt was wholly right and partly wrong. He was well ahead of his time in telling firms to be customer-obsessed. But his railroads example and the other he gave (such as buggywhips) were simplistic and possibly wrong. What possible expertise or cost sharing did the railroads have for entering the airline business? Perhaps they should have been experts at marketing transport to passengers, expertise that would have been transferable. But they weren't, and if Penn Central had bought an airline it would have gone bust much quicker than it did. The criticism was right, the remedy wrong.

More recently, Levitt has become a prophet of global brands. Levitt is fun to read, stimulating and bursting with ideas. We should not complain if some of them are flawed.

MAGAZINER, IRA C.

Important American writer and consultant who has written on industrial policy in Japan, Sweden and Ireland and whose 1982 book, *Minding America's Business* (co-authored with Robert B. Reich) is still the best account of how and why the US has lost market share to Japan. It stresses the need for the US Government and industrialists to focus on competitive productivity and to develop industrial policy for specific industries in a discrete and precise way. In 1989 he wrote *The Silent War* (with Mark Patinkin), providing new examples of how American firms had lost out to Europe (Airbus Industrie), Korea (Samsung, now the world's largest maker of microwave ovens), and Japan (many examples), but also how Corning Glass beat the Japanese in fibre optics. The book advocated an American fight back and outlined measures for both companies and corporations to follow in dealing with foreign competition.

Magaziner is iconoclastic, populist and an adviser to President Clinton (in healthcare). He clearly has a future in Democratic party politics, despite swimming firmly against the prevailing tide of economic liberalism. Meanwhile, America's relative industrial decline is being reversed, although in the main not by the means Magaziner advocates. Yet his work is always fresh, stimulating and worth a quick read.

OHMAE, KENICHI (b. 1943)

Brilliant, un-Japanese, Japanese, whose book *The Mind of the Strategist* (published in Japan in 1975, but not in the US until 1982) remains one of the best on strategy, and who contributed towards the development of Toyota's JUST-IN-TIME system. An analyst who gives a higher place to intuition and insight, Ohmae was amongst the first to drive everything from the customer, and place the customer at the heart of the firm's value system: 'customer-based strategies are the basis of all strategy'. *The Mind of the Strategist* is an eloquent plea for creative, customer-based strategies, while giving a large number of hints and prompts in the form of analytical diagnoses and examples of unconventional strategies successfully pursued by Japanese companies. See also KEY FACTORS FOR SUCCESS (KFS) and STRATEGIC DEGREES OF FREEDOM (SDF).

In recent years, notably in his landmark 1990 book, *The Borderless World*, Ohmae has turned his attention to the way that the world's largest companies are creating what he calls the ILE (Inter-Linked Economy) of the US, Europe and Japan/Asia, based largely on the need to meet the requirements of demanding consumers in all important economies. He argues persuasively the case for inevitable and beneficient GLOBALISATION, albeit based on LOCAL GLOBALISATION rather than UNIVERSAL PRODUCTS, a process being slowed down but not stopped by the rearguard actions of protectionists, bureaucrats and governments around the world. The companies forcing the change are becoming multilocals rather than multinationals. According to Ohmae, 'nothing is "overseas" any longer'; the word is banned from Honda's vocabulary, for example, 'because [Honda] sees itself as equidistant from all customers'. Multilocals must become 'insiders' to each important market (a process he describes usefully as INSIDERISATION) and be driven by a determination to serve customers better wherever they are: 'Global players must have the engine and knowledge to propel themselves. They must be directly familiar with the key markets. That knowledge is the secret of success in the borderless world.' See GLOBILI-SATION (definition 2), GLOBAL LOCALISATION and ILE.

PETERS, TOM (b. 1942)

Probably the world's foremost management guru and the one who has made most money out of the profession. His achievements are real: a McKinsey consultant until after he and Bob WATERMAN wrote *In Search of Excellence* (1982), which now has sales approaching six million (absolutely unprecedented for a business book), Peters shortly after left McKinsey to publish, lecture and evangelise for passionate management. He has built up a massive and highly profitable business in merchandising himself and his artefacts: books, videos, cassettes, TV series, consultancy, and personal appearances. He is the Billy Graham of management, though in his cases the profits go back to The Tom Peters Group.

The Excellence project had prosaic origins in a McKinsey business development exercise that started in 1977. The simple and relatively uninspired idea was to isolate the best performing US companies over the previous 20 years, looking at the top decile of the Fortune 500. In the end, Peters and Waterman chose 43 companies and tried to describe what common characteristics had led to their success.

The methodology was sensible, if rather loose; the conclusions questionable; and the glorification of some of the companies naive, the product of hindsight and corporate propaganda as much as a real understanding of what had gone on Within five years after publication, two thirds of the 'excellent' companies celebrated had hit trouble, and one, People Express, went bust. Yet the success of the book was well deserved. It was an inspiring read, quite unlike any previous book on management: it made readers want to go out there and do great deeds, like those celebrated in the book. It put passion, leadership, VALUES, and the customer at the centre of excellence, and in these respects was 100 per cent correct, even if the particulars it used to celebrate excellence were often flawed. The Gospels and other great religious writings do not depend for their meaning on literal truth. Simply because people can respond to them, and achieve subsequent miracles, is testimony enough. So it was, and is, with Excellence.

Peters wrote a sequel (with Nancy Austin), *A Passion for Excellence* (1985), then changed tack significantly by writing *Thriving on Chaos* (1987), demonstrating enormous chutzpa by starting with the sentence, '*There are no excellent companies*'. Clearly true, but not many opinion formers would have demonstrated such bravado, and fewer still would have emerged with their reputations enhanced rather than tarnished by such a U-turn two years after another book celebrating more excellent companies. *Thriving on Chaos* is about change and whether it is possible to manage it, and if so, how. In the book Peters took a relatively optimistic view about change management, broadly advocating a move from hierarchical bureaucracies to customer-centred adhocracies. In classic Anglo-Saxon style he provided a checklist of 45 precepts for managers, of which the most important are:

- *Specialise/create niches/differentiate.*
- *Provide top quality.*
- *Become a service addict.*
- *Make manufacturing the prime marketing tool.*
- *Over-invest in people, front line sales, service, distribution (make these the company heroes.*
- *Become customer-obsessed.*
- *Support failures by publicly rewarding well thought-out mistakes.*
- *Make innovation a way of life for everyone.*
- *Guarantee continuous employment for the core workforce.*
- *Radically reduce layers of management.*
- *Become a compulsive listener.*
- *Demand total integrity in all dealings, both inside and outside the firm.*

Not many of these are original, but the synthesis is good and the way in which they are urged is, well, excellent.

Since then Peters has moved on, and become much more 'pessimistic about *planned* change'. It is true that 75 per cent of such efforts at TRANS-FORMATION fail, but should he not say that the cup is a quarter full rather than three quarters empty. Concentrating on the 25 per cent and trying to move that to, say, 50 per cent, might be a better use of Peters' talents than defeatism. His latest book *Liberation Management* (1992) is important but difficult to handle: long, rambling, poorly organised, easy to put down and full of American jargon. It reads more like *Bonfire of the Vanities* than *In Search of Excellence*, though without the plot of either. There are five main points being made in *Liberation Management*:

(1) All business is becoming FASHION.
(2) Create mini-SBUs everywhere.
(3) Organise everything and everyone around projects.
(4) Destroy functional departments.
(5) Use partners outside the formal organisation.

The book is very concerned with structure, because Peters believes that without changing the structure of organisations very little can be achieved. He is probably right, but the message in *Liberation Management* is not put across as eloquently as in his previous books. See CHANGE MANAGEMENT, WATERMAN, passion and leadership.

PORTER, MICHAEL (b. 1947)

The second highest paid management lecturer after Tom Peters: Harvard Business School professor, consultant, and the star of corporate strategy worldwide. Porter even talks about the 'Porter brand'. In two books, *Competitive Strategy: Techniques for Analysing Industries and Competitors* (1980) and *Competitive Advantage* (1985), Porter summarises and builds on the main concepts of corporate strategy. A brilliant synthesizer, formulator and packager. Porter defines two kinds of competitive advantage: low cost, or differentiation. He places a firm in the context of its industry (see PORTER'S FIVE COMPETITIVE FORCES) and identifies the firm's own value chain (all the ways it adds value from start to finish by activity) systematically. Since the mid 1980s he has looked at global competition and the comparative advantage of nations, building on work done earlier by Ira Magaziner. He stresses the need for clusters of mutually supporting industries (see also KEIRETSU) and comes as close as a mainstream American could to recommending industrial policy: *The Competitive Advantage of Nations* (1990) should be compulsory reading for all politicians. Like Peters, Porter has come up with some useful and insightful strategic prescriptions, including:

- *Sell to the most demanding buyers, as they will set standards for your people.*
- *Seek buyers with the most difficult needs, so they become your R&D lab.*
- *Establish norms exceeding the world's toughest regulations.*
- *Source from the world's best suppliers: scour the world for them.*
- *Treat employees as permanent partners.*
- *Use outstanding competitors as motivators.*

Precisely.

Porter's competitive analysis, Michael PORTER's *Competitive Strategy* (1980) codified how to gain competitive advantage. His analysis suggests four diagnostic components of looking at any specific competitor: (1) Future goals: what are they trying to achieve, including their ambitions in terms of market leadership and technology; (2) Assumptions: how does the competitor perceive himself, and what assumptions does he make about the industry and his competition? (3) Current Strategy; and (4) Opportunities: what do they think they have? Armed with this framework, one can then construct scenarios about competitors' possible reactions to any action by one's firm.

SCHEIN, EDGAR H.

Ed Schein is a distinguished and commercially astute American social psychologist based at MIT. He is 'well networked', having worked with and been influenced by Doug McGregor, as well as having close links with Warren Bennis, Chris Argyris and Charles HANDY, whom he taught. Schein was one of the first to focus on process consulting, the title of his 1969 book, which involves looking at how a firm operates and its CULTURE and helping it be more effective, rather than supplying expert content-oriented consulting. Schein has been influential for the past 20 years, and has added three concepts to management language: beside process consulting, there are also the Psychological Contract and the Career Anchor.

The 'psychological contract' is the bargain struck between employees and the firm, covering not only the normal economic contractual terms but what is expected more broadly, both by the firm and the employee, of each other. Unless the terms of the psychological contract are understood (at least intuitively) by each side, the basis for a long term relationship does not exist, and there may be unexpected friction in the short term. The psychological contract relates to trust and expected patterns of behaviour.

The 'career anchor' is the self-image of an individual in an organisation that holds him or her in place. Early on in a career the individual may develop (or fail to develop) a sense of worth, satisfaction and confidence in his or her role in the organisation. Without the anchor, the individual may strive for a new role inside or outside the organisation.

Schein was an early writer on corporate culture, which he defines as 'what [an organisation] has learned as a total social unit over the course of its history'. He stressed the importance of VALUES, modes of behaviour, and artefacts (the external manifestations of a firm's culture, like Mars' white coats and clocking-in, IBM's white shirts, open-plan or compartmentalised offices, the way that people in the firm talk to each other, and so on). Schein emphasises also the role of leadership in change management. See MISSION.

SCHONBERGER, RICHARD J. (b. 1937)

Interesting and creative American industrial engineer and the author of the two best selling books on manufacturing: *Japanese Manufacturing Techniques* (1982) and *World Class Manufacturing* (1986). Introduced JUST-IN-TIME and other techniques used in Japan to the US market in the early 1980s. But his most interesting book is *Building a Chain of Customers* (1990), which argues boldly that world class business can only be built if each function in a business is viewed as the customer of the preceding stage, all the way to the final customer. Each part of the corporation must satisfy its (internal or external) customer's four needs: 'ever-better quality, ever-lower costs, ever-increasing flexibility, and ever-quicker response'. Schonberger packaged the idea of cellular manufacturing as the way to meet these needs: clusters of employees and the operations are deployed according to the work flow rather than on artificial functional or departmental lines. Schonberger thus laid the foundations for BUSINESS PROCESS RE-ENGINEERING and for the recent theories of Tom PETERS and other prophets of customer obsession.

SLOAN, ALFRED P. (1875–1966)

One of the very few industrialists to be referred to as an authority on management; head of General Motors from 1923 to 1955; author of *My Years with General Motors* (1963) and notable for three reasons. First, he virtually invented the decentralised, divisionalised firm, establishing what he called federal decentralisation, when he transformed General Motors in the early 1920s from a mass of untidy and overlapping entities, with sporadic but ineffective central control, into eight separate divisions (five car divisions and three component divisions) which were treated as though they were separate businesses, but which were subject to professional controls on finance and policy from the Centre.

Second, Sloan changed the structure of the car industry and its SEGMENTATION, and provided a model for how other firms could do the same. When he took over, there were just two car segments in the US: the mass market, dominated by the black Ford Model T, which had 60 per cent of the total car market volume; and the very low-volume, high-class market. Sloan aimed to plug the gap between these two markets by creating five price and performance segments and aiming that the five markets so created should be dominated by one of the new five GM car ranges: the Chevrolet, Oldsmobile, Pontiac, Buick and Cadillac (this represented a range rationalisation for GM from eight competing models). He turned Ford's no-choice policy on its head by introducing a range of colours and features so that cars could be 'customised' at relatively little extra cost, as well as introducing new models each year to encourage trading up.

The segmentation fitted neatly with the divisionalisation: each of the five car segments and models had its own division, thus inventing the idea of the SBU (Strategic Business Unit) about fifty years before GE actually articulated it.

Sloan's third innovation was to establish the three component divisions as separate profit centres that supplied not only the five car divisions but also outside customers. Again, this concept has had to wait 50–70 years before its virtues became fully appreciated.

Sloan is fascinating because he had a foot in the old management camp of scientific management, drawing on many of the nineteenth century ideas of Henri Fayol, as well as anticipating some of the tenets of very contemporary theory, including decentralisation, segmentation as a basis for organisation, and the value of creative dissent. The latter side can, however, be exaggerated. Sloan was at heart a mechanistic autocrat who was also a marketing genius, and to expect him to be a liberation manager into the bargain is to expect too much. MIT named its business school after him, a fitting tribute for both.

TROMPENAARS, FONS

Dutch expert on international cultural differences between managers. Co-authors with Charles HAMPDEN-TURNER of the excellent *Seven Cultures of Capitalism*, and author of *Riding the Waves of Culture* (1993) that covers some of the same ground but focusses particularly on how the transnational corporation should maximise effective co-opera-tion between operations in different countries and between these and the centre. Trompenaars insists that cultural diversity must be recog-nised and that the transnational corporation is 'polycentric' rather than a hub and spoke from the Centre. The transnational corporation must synthesise the advantages of all the national cultures and facilitate com-munication, but leave local operations free to reward their people in the way most effective for their culture. An important message from an increasingly prominent guru.

See GLOBAL LOCALISATION, CULTURE, FLAT ORGANISATION, HAMPDEN-TURNER and COMPETITIVE ADVANTAGE.

WATERMAN, ROBERT H. JR (b. 1936)

Forever linked with Tom PETERS as joint author of *In Search of Excellence* (1982), Waterman is the older, more reflective and, many would say, more original of the two writers. A laid-back Californian, he has written two outstanding books since: *The Renewal Factor* and *Adhocracy: the Power to Change*. Both are concerned with how organi-sations learn, manage change and chaos, use taskforces and develop their distinctive roles in life. Waterman has pointed out that most managers still live in the shadow of TAYLOR, and practise the opposite of what they preach. Waterman's latest (1994) book, called *What America Does Right* in the US edition, and *The Frontiers of Excellence* in the UK, looks at ten US organisations that 'put people first', including Federal Express, Levi Strauss, Motorola, Procter & Gamble and Rubbermaid. It is a useful and enjoyable read that asserts that the most successful companies do not put shareholders first, paying primary attention to customers and employees. A side-effect is excellent stock market performance. The case examples are fresh, but a little rose-tinted; the general argument is not original, but well argued, inspirational and broadly correct. See PETERS.

B. STRATEGIC TOOLS AND TECHNIQUES

ANSOFF MATRIX

As shown in Illustration 3.1, this gives 4 options for increasing sales.

Box 1, selling more of existing products in existing markets, is a low risk, market share gain strategy. To be useful, this must specify how this objective is to be attained, for example by enlarging the salesforce, increasing advertising or cutting price.

Box 2 implies product development to sell new (or modified) products to existing customers: fine as long as the firm has a good track record of new product development and provided the new products share enough costs and skills with the existing products, and do not face a very strong incumbent competitor (see also ADJACENT SEGMENT).

Illustration 3.1
The Ansoff Matrix for business development

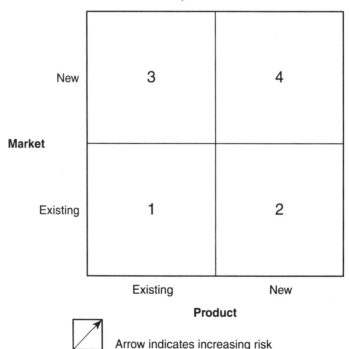

Box 3 takes existing products and sells them to new markets or customers. This is clearly sensible if the new markets can be cultivated at relatively little extra cost, but can be risky if a new market requires investment in fixed cost (for example, a new salesforce), if the customers have different requirements, or if there are entrenched competitors.

Box 4 – new products to new markets – is the highest risk strategy: the segments being entered are not adjacent to the existing business and it is almost like starting a new business from scratch. The presumption is that Box 4 strategies are inherently unsound and should only be taken either in desperation or because there is a compelling short term opportunity not being exploited by others.

BCG MATRIX

The popular name for the GROWTH/SHARE MATRIX, an abused but powerful tool encapsulating the most important insights into business of the past 50 years. See GROWTH/SHARE MATRIX.

BPR (BUSINESS PROCESS RE-ENGINEERING)

A new way of rethinking what a company does and re-designing its processes from first principles in order to produce dramatic improvements in cost, quality, speed and service. BPR is the hottest management concept of the 1990s so far. Its advocates claim that Re-engineering (which they spell, incorrectly, without a hyphen) will be for the 1990s what Strategy was for the 1970s and Quality for the 1980s. This is certainly true as far as consulting revenues are concerned. But BPR is not just a management fad and deserves to be taken seriously. Many leading US companies (such as Eastman Kodak, Ford and Texas Instruments) have used BPR to change their way of doing business, leading to cost reductions in excess of 25 per cent, and in some specific areas of up to 90 per cent.

BPR claims to reinvent the way that companies do business, from first principles, by throwing out the view that firms should be organised into functions and departments to perform tasks, and paying attention instead to processes. A process here is a set of activities that in total produce a result of value to a customer, for example, developing a new product. Who is in charge of this? In the non-BPR-ed company the answer is 'no-one', despite the involvement of a large number of traditional functions such as R&D, marketing.

The essence of BPR is reversing the task specialisation built into most management thinking since Adam Smith's 1776 pin factory, and focussing instead on completing a total process with value to customers in one fell swoop. A good example is IBM Credit, which used to take 7 days to process applications for credit for people wishing to buy computers. Before BPR, there were five separate specialist stages through which an application progressed: logging the credit request; credit checking; modifying the standard loan covenant; pricing the loan; and compiling a quote letter. Experiments then proved that the actual work involved only took ninety minutes; the real delay was caused by having different departments that did the work in stages and had to pass it on to each other. The solution hit upon was to replace the specialists with generalists called deal structurers who handled all the steps in the process. The average turnaround time was reduced from seven days to four hours, and productivity was increased 100 times.

'Doing' BPR means taking a clean sheet of paper and asking fundamental questions like: Why do we do this at all? How does it help to meet customer needs? Could we eliminate the task or process if we changed something else? How can we get away from specialisation, so that several jobs are combined into one?

'BPR-ed' companies have thrown away their 'assembly lines', particularly in respect of clerical and overhead functions. One person, such as a 'customer service representative', may for example act as the single point of contact for a customer, taking care of selling, order taking, finding the equipment to be purchased, and delivering it personally. Performance improvement comes from eliminating the expense and misunderstandings implicit in 'handoffs' from one part of the organisation to another, as well as eliminating internal overheads necessary to manage the complexity brought on by task specialisation.

The process claims several benefits:

(1) Customers can deal with a single point of contact (the 'case manager').

(2) Several jobs can be combined into one, where the primary need to satisfy the customer is not lost in organisational complexity.

(3) Workers make decisions, compressing work horizontally (that is, doing without supervisors and other overhead functions that are necessary as a result of specialisation), resulting in fewer delays, lower overhead costs, better customer response, and greater motivation of staff through empowerment.

(4) The steps in the process are performed in a sensible order, and removing specialisation enables many more jobs to be done in parallel, as well as lowering the need for rework.

(5) Processes can be easily adapted to cope with work of greater or lesser complexity, instead of forcing everything to go through the same lengthy work steps.
(6) Work can be performed where it makes most sense, which is often not by specialists.
(7) Checks and controls and reconciliations can be reduced without loss of quality.

Like all forms of radical change, BPR often fails: objective estimates are that this is so in almost 75 per cent of cases. The most frequent causes of failure are lack of top management commitment, an insufficiently broad canvass on which to operate (as when parts of the organisation refuse to take the effort seriously), and lack of readiness to adapt corporate CULTURE. Nevertheless, BPR has achieved such stunning results in many documented cases that it cannot be ignored. In the most successful cases it is clear that BPR as a technique was the catalyst for more far reaching changes in culture and standards.

Two points about BPR are not sufficiently well made by its protagonists, for obvious reasons. One is that certain types of company and business are more likely to benefit from BPR than others. The most susceptible companies are those where manufacturing is a relatively small part of the cost structure, where overheads are a large part, where customer needs have been neglected, and where the potential benefits of information technology (IT) have not yet been exploited.

The other point is that BPR is not a Do It Yourself technique: serious attempts at BPR nearly always involve help from consultants. As BPR has boomed, so too has the supply of consultant help, but often at the expense of quality. Many consultants reduce BPR to cost reduction techniques or re-badge their existing methodologies under the BPR banner, without having the imagination and creativity required for effective BPR. The likely result is that as most companies come to undertake some form of BPR, most will become disillusioned, and the technique itself may fall into disrepute. See also Part I, pages 69–71.

BUSINESS ATTRACTIVENESS

An assessment of how attractive a business or market is, based on a number of criteria. Often a distinction is made between the attractiveness of the market, on the one hand, based on desiderata like market growth, average industry profitability, BARRIERS TO ENTRY (which should be high), BARRIERS TO EXIT (preferably low), the bargaining power of customers and suppliers (ideally low), the predictability of technological change, the protection against substitutes, and on the other hand, the strength of the individual company's business within the market, based on relative market share, brand strength, cost position, technological expertise and other such assessments. One can then produce a matrix such as that shown in Ilustration 3.2 and plot all a firm's businesses on the matrix to see where scarce corporate resources such as cash and good management should be allocated.

Illustration 3.2
Business attractiveness matrix

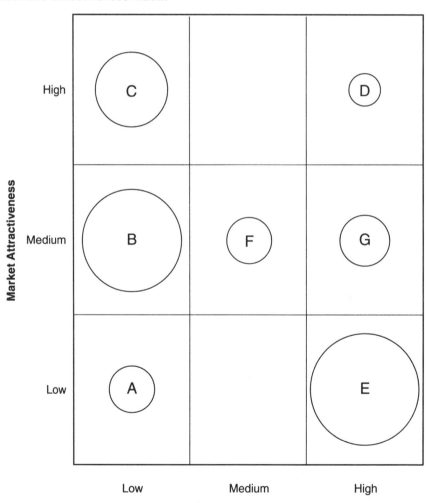

In the example above, the most obviously attractive businesses for investment would be D, followed by G, and then probably C or F. Business C could be a very good investment target, but only if the investment could drive it to a very strong position within the market (i.e. move it from the top left to the top right). If this is reckoned unlikely, it may be best to sell C for a high price. Businesses B and A are also disposal candidates if a reasonable price could be obtained.

The matrix is an alternative to the BCG MATRIX and has the advantage that it can take into account several factors in evaluating the attractiveness of both business and market. On the other hand the lack of quantification of the axes can be a subjective trap, with management unwilling to admit that businesses are not attractive. For any overall corporate plan it is useful to position all businesses on both matrices, and see whether the prescriptions are at all different. If they are, you should carefully examine the assumptions leading to the difference.

COMB ANALYSIS

A very useful and simple technique for comparing customers' purchase criteria with their rating of suppliers. Let us assume that you are a textile manufacturer producing women's clothes and selling them to retailers who are fashion specialists. You want to find out what the most important reasons are for them to choose supply from one manufacturer rather than another. You also want to find out what the retailers think about you and your competitors on each of these purchase criteria.

You should then engage independent researchers to interview the retailers and ask them two questions. First, the researchers should ask the retailers to score on a 1–5 scale the importance of various purchase criteria. Let us assume that the average results are as shown in Illustration 3.3.

Illustration 3.3
Example of comb analysis

Criterion	Importance Score
Fashion appeal of garments	4.9
Strength of brand name	4.6
Service & speed of delivery	4.5
Willingness to deliver small orders	3.5
Price from manufacturer to them	3.0
Durability of garments	2.3

These results can now be displayed on the first part of the 'comb' chart (Illustration 3.4).

Illustration 3.4
Comb chart: retailers' purchase criteria

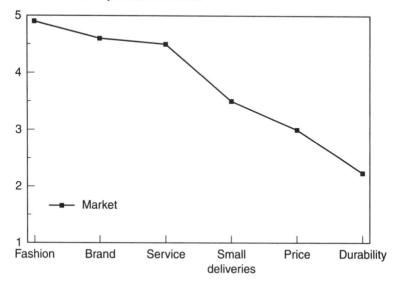

The second question the researchers ask is how each of the competing suppliers rates on each of these criteria, again on a 1–5 scale. Let us start by overlaying on the previous results (the retailers' purchase criteria) their rating of the company sponsoring the research, which we will call Gertrude Textiles (Illustration 3.5).

These results should be of great interest to Gertrude Textiles. Except on one criterion, Gertrude manages to score above the importance of the criterion to the retailer. Unfortunately, the one criterion on which Gertrude scores below market expectations is the most important one: the fashion appeal of its clothes. To increase market share, the one thing that Gertrude Textiles must focus on is improving its garments' fashion appeal. Of interest too is that on the last three criteria – willingness to deliver small quantities, price, and the durability of its clothes – Gertrude scores *above* what the market requires. No doubt this is costing Gertrude a lot of money. This comb profile suggests that Gertrude could afford to not be so accommodating on small deliveries, could raise prices, and could stop building in long life to its clothes. The money saved should be invested in doing whatever is necessary to improve perceptions of its fashion appeal: perhaps by hiring away the top designer team from a rival.

Illustration 3.5
Comb chart: retailers' purchase criteria and their rating of Gertrude Textiles on these criteria

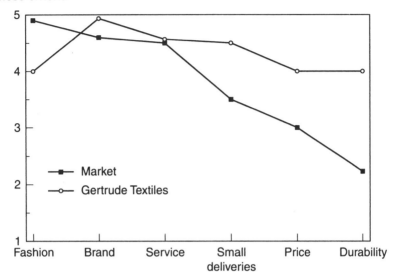

This is where the rating of competitors adds to the picture. We can now overlay on the previous picture the ratings given by retailers to two of Gertrude's rivals: Fast Fashions and Sandy's Styles (Illustration 3.6).

Illustration 3.6
Comb chart: rating of three competitors against market criteria

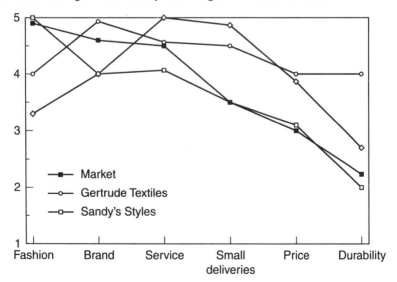

From this we can make three important observations:

(1) The only competitor that meets the market's very high fashion requirements is Sandy's Styles. This is the team for Gertrude Textiles to poach or beat.

(2) Gertrude has the best brand name, according to the retailers, and can meet all the other purchase criteria apart from fashion. If this criterion can be met, Gertrude will be in a very strong position to increase market share.

(3) Only Gertrude is significantly over-performing on the price requirements of retailers. This helps to confirm that some price increases to retailers may be possible for Gertrude, particularly if the fashion element improves.

DECISION TREE

A flow chart that sets out possible future events and highlights the effects of decisions or chance occurrences in a sequential order. Can be very useful in estimating the probability that any event may happen, or simply in pinpointing the critical decisions that have to be made. For some peculiar reason decision trees are nearly always drawn from left to right, although I much prefer to draw them from top to bottom. Two examples are given in Illustration 3.7 and Illustration 3.8. In Illustration 3.7 a manufacturer is trying to decide whether to open a new factory, in the face of uncertainty about whether his main rival will decide to do the same thing and whether the economy will move into recession or boom. The decision tree helps him to lay out the possibilities and calculate the returns under all eight possible outcomes (Illustration 3.7).

So far the decision tree has helped by laying out the possibilities, although it does not yet tell Superior Sproggetts Limited (SSL) what to do. For this we need to overlay on the decision tree the *probabilities* of each of the four possible outcomes arising from (a) an investment by SSL and (b) a decision by SSL not to invest. Illustration 3.8 overlays these probabilities and therefore allows a calculation of the EXPECTED VALUE (the weighted average value) in terms of ROCE (Return on Capital Employed) under both (a) and (b).

From this it can be seen that investment has a much higher expected return on capital, at 22 per cent, than the decision not to invest, which has an expected value of 8 per cent. One important reason for this is that the competitor is much less likely to invest if SSL does so first. Adding the probabilities helps to highlight the importance of this judgment.

Decision trees can be used for a wide variety of purposes and are a great help in clarifying what should be done when events are uncertain and outcomes depend to some degree on earlier uncertain events.

Illustration 3.7
Decision tree for Superior Sproggetts Limited

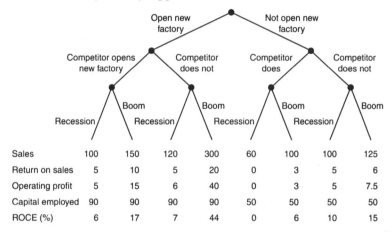

Sales	100	150	120	300	60	100	100	125
Return on sales	5	10	5	20	0	3	5	6
Operating profit	5	15	6	40	0	3	5	7.5
Capital employed	90	90	90	90	50	50	50	50
ROCE (%)	6	17	7	44	0	6	10	15

Illustration 3.8
Decision tree with probabilities and expected values

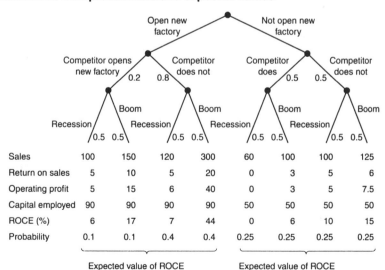

Sales	100	150	120	300	60	100	100	125
Return on sales	5	10	5	20	0	3	5	6
Operating profit	5	15	6	40	0	3	5	7.5
Capital employed	90	90	90	90	50	50	50	50
ROCE (%)	6	17	7	44	0	6	10	15
Probability	0.1	0.1	0.4	0.4	0.25	0.25	0.25	0.25

Expected value of ROCE
=0.1(6) + 0.1(17) + 0.4(7) + 0.4(44)
= 22.2%

Expected value of ROCE
= 0.25(0) + 0.25(6) + 0.25(10) + 0.25(15)
= 7.8%

DELPHI TECHNIQUE

Forecasting technique using a number of experts (or managers) who each make estimates in round one, then receive everyone else's estimates and re-estimate in round two, and so on until consensus is reached.

EXPERIENCE CURVE

Along with the BCG MATRIX, the greatest discovery of Bruce HENDERSON, although it started life in 1926 as the 'learning curve'. Briefly it states that when the accumulated production of any good or service doubles, unit costs in real terms (i.e adjusted for inflation) have the potential to fall by 20 per cent. Accumulated production is not a concept much used, nor is it usually very easy to calculate: it is the total number of units of a product that have ever been made by a firm, or the total number of units of a product ever made by all participants in the market. It is not related to time, because accumulated production can double within one year for a new or very fast growth product, or take centuries for a very old or slow growth one.

BCG found and documented many exciting instances in the late 1960s and 1970s where accumulated production had increased rapidly and deflated (inflation adjusted) costs had fallen to 70–80 per cent of their previous level each time this happened. One of the most important examples is the decline in the cost of integrated circuits (ICs), which explains why the cost of calculators was able to plummet so dramatically. A typical example of a cost experience curve is shown in Illustration 3.9.

BCG used the experience tool both to identify cost reduction opportunities and as a dynamic tool for describing and influencing the battle between competitors in a particular product. If a particular firm was found *not* to have cut costs in line with the experience curve, this was held to be a cost reduction opportunity. The beauty of the method was that it described precisely the point that costs should have reached (although not how to get there), and therefore set a firm and seemingly objective target for management to meet. A great deal of cost reduction was actually achieved this way.

In terms of competitive strategy, BCG invented a second type of experience curve: related not to costs but to prices. For any market as a whole, but particularly for an individual firm, BCG would chart how

Illustration 3.9
Cost experience curve
Source: **Automobile Manufacturer's Association, BCG Analysis**

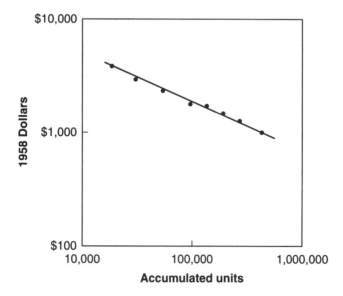

real prices (after adjusting for inflation) had behaved in relation to accumulated production of the product. The price experience curve might or might not follow the shape of the cost experience curve. In Illustration 3.10 we show a cost experience curve of 80 per cent (that is, costs behaved as they should, reducing by 20 per cent each time accumulated production doubled), but different cost behaviour in three phases. In the first phase, prices did not come down at all: in other words, the deflated price experience curve was 100 per cent (or in other words, prices were increased in line with inflation). In the second phase, prices come down very sharply, to compensate for the earlier failure to match cost reductions. In the third phase, prices fall in parallel with costs, that is, the price experience curve is also 80 per cent.

BCG explained the first phase as one of complacency and excess profits, where consumers are willing to continue paying a high price and where competitors all enjoy higher margins by not passing cost savings on to customers. Eventually, however, these high profits encourage new players into the marketplace, and at least one of these new players cuts costs to try to gain market share. The other players have to respond, and prices are therefore reduced until 'normal' margins obtain again.

Illustration 3.10
Price experience curve in three phases compared to cost experience curve

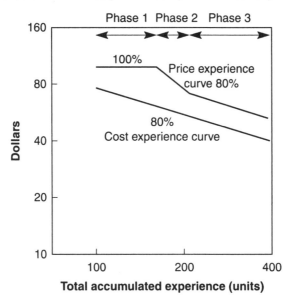

BCG preached that it was doubly foolish to have a flatter price experience curve than cost experience curve (i.e. to widen margins in the first phase): firstly, because it would lead to loss of market share initially, and secondly because the player with the greater market share himself would have lower costs, so that a market leader who held market share (by having competitive prices, so that his price might be below new entrants' cost) would continually compound his competitive advantage of low cost and make it impossible for new players to enter unless they were willing to lose money initially. Prices should therefore be reduced by the market leader at least as fast as costs, in order to keep competitors out or unprofitable, and thus consolidate market leadership and compound the low cost position.

BCG was able to explain the success of Japanese companies such as Honda in motorcycles by reference to 'experience curve cost reduction' and 'experience curve pricing'. Ultimately the experience curve effect was used to explain the incidence of short-termism in Western industry and the consequent loss of global market share.

The concepts behind the experience curve are wholly correct. It must be admitted that calculating accumulated volume was often a black art, and that BCG sometimes exaggerated the scientific and empirical nature of the experience curve. Since the late 1970s the experience curve as a practical management tool has fallen into disuse, though lone adherents still persist (and use it effectively). Experience curve thinking, even if no experience curves are drawn (and one suspects that very few Japanese executives ever drew such curves), should be an integral part of good management. The mysterious disappearance of the experience curve from Western boardrooms is much to be deplored, even though experience curve thinking is in part imbedded in the Quality Revolution of the 1980s and the BPR Revolution of the 1990s.

GROWTH/GROWTH MATRIX

Useful two-by-two chart (invented by BCG) which compares the growth of a firm's business in one product or BUSINESS SEGMENT to the growth of the market as a whole, thus enabling one to see whether market share was being won or lost and by whom (Illustration 3.11).

Illustration 3.11 shows an example, using imaginary data, of three competitors in a particular market at a particular time (three, five or ten years are generally used). According to the (made up) data, the largest competitor is McKinsey, which is growing slower than the market as a whole (and therefore losing share); the next largest in BCG, which is growing at the same rate as the market); and the smallest but fastest growing competitor is Bain & Company. Note that companies on a growth/growth chart are always at the same vertical height, since this represents the overall market growth and must by definition be common for all.

Growth/growth charts are not much used nowadays but are very useful, especially if used in conjunction with the main BCG MATRIX (the GROWTH/SHARE MATRIX).

GROWTH/SHARE MATRIX

The Boston Consulting Group has invented several matrices, having consultants trained to think in terms of two-by-two displays, but this is the most famous and useful one (it is also sometimes called the BCG MATRIX). Invented in the late 1960s and still of great importance today, it measures market growth and relative market share for all the business a particular firm has. An example is shown in Illustration 3.12.

It is important to define the axes properly. The horizontal axis is of fundamental importance and measures the market share that a firm has

Illustration 3.11
Examples of Growth/Growth Matrix with competitors arrayed

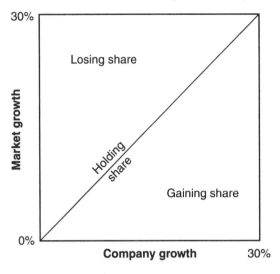

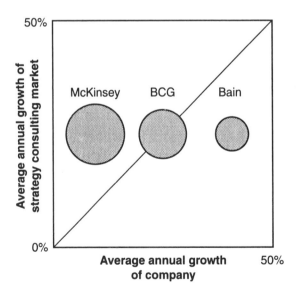

in a particular business *relative to the share enjoyed in that business by its largest competitor*. Thus if Engulf & Devour Plc has a 40 per cent market share in Business A and its nearest competitor has a 10 per cent market share, its relative market share ('RMS') is 400 per cent or 4 times (written as 4.0×). In Business B, Engulf & Devour may have a

Illustration 3.12
Engulf & Devour Plc, Growth/Share Matrix

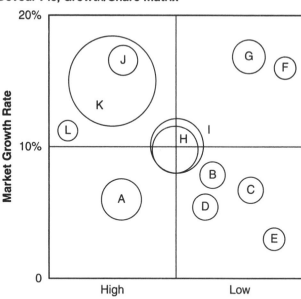

5 per cent share and the leading competitor 10 per cent, in which case Engulf & Devour's relative market share is 50 per cent or 0.5×. Note that absolute market share (for example, 20 per cent of a market) means little, because it would mean a relative market share of 0.33 per cent (if the dominant competitor has 60 per cent market share), or of 10.0× (if the rest of the market is very fragmented and the next largest player only has 2 per cent).

The vertical axis is the growth rate of the market in which the business competes. Much confusion surrounds the precise definition of this market growth rate. The correct definition is the *expected future annual growth rate* (over the next five years) *in volume* (units of production) *of the market as a whole*, not of the particular Engulf & Devour business.

Before going on, it is important to understand the reasons why BCG and I think that the axes are significant. The relative market share is key because a business that is larger than its competitors (has a high relative market share, over 1.0×) *ought to have lower costs, or higher prices, or both, and therefore higher profitability* than a competitor in that business with a lower share. This is generally, although not always, true, as confirmed by databases such as the PIMS studies.

It is also logical: a business with higher volume ought to be able to spread its fixed costs over more units, and therefore have lower fixed and overhead costs, as well as make better use of any expensive machinery or people that are the best for that particular business. The higher share business may also be able to charge a higher price, either because it has the best brand or because it has the best distribution or simply because it is the preferred choice of most people. Since price minus cost equals profit, the higher share competitor should have the highest margins, or be ploughing back his advantage in the form of extra customer benefits that will reinforce his market share advantage.

Note that we say that the higher share competitor *ought* to have lower costs or higher prices. It does not necessarily follow, since he may squander his potential advantage by inefficiency, sharing costs with unprofitable products, or by having poorer customer service than a rival. Where the higher share player does not have profits higher than competitors there is usually an unstable competitive relationship which can create both opportunity and vulnerability in that market (see the OPPORTUNITY/VULNERABILITY INDEX).

In some cases having a higher share of a business does not confer any benefit or potential benefit, for example where a one-man plumbing business faces a ten-man plumbing business, and the costs of labour are the same for everyone. Many people have claimed that the importance of market share, and the value of the Growth/Share Matrix, have been greatly overstated, and produce examples of cases where larger businesses are *less* profitable than smaller businesses, or where there is no systematic difference in profitability according to scale. On detailed examination, however, there are few individual business segments where it is not or cannot be a real advantage to be larger, all other things being equal. The qualification in the last phrase is absolutely crucial: relative market share is not the only influence on profitability, and it may be overwhelmed by different competitors' operating skills or strategies or random influences on profitability.

One of the major causes of confusion is that businesses are often not defined properly, in a sufficiently disaggregated way, before measuring market share. The niche player who focusses on a limited product range or customer base is playing in just one segment from the broad line supplier, who may be playing in several segments and may actually not be very large in any one segment despite appearing to have a high overall market share. For example, a national supermarket chain may be bigger than competitors who have regional chains, but the relevant basis of competition may be local scale and customer awareness. See BUSINESS SEGMENT and SEGMENTATION for the importance of correct business definition and some hints on how to do it.

If businesses are defined properly, the higher share competitor should have an advantage at least nine times out of ten. It therefore follows that the further to the left a business is on the BCG MATRIX, the stronger it should be.

What about the vertical axis: the growth rate of the market? BCG claimed that there was a real difference between high growth businesses (where demand is growing at 10 per cent or more) and lower growth ones, because of greater fluidity in the former: that is, if the market is growing fast, there is more opportunity to gain market share. This is logical, both because more new business is up for grabs, and because competitors will react much more vigorously to defend their absolute share (to avoid a loss of turnover) than to defend loss of relative share, which they do not even notice in a fast changing market.

Having understood these points, we can go on to characterise the four quadrants of the BCG MATRIX (see Illustration 3.13).

The bottom left hand box contains the CASH COWS (also called gold mines in some early versions of the matrix: in many ways a better name). These businesses have high relative market share (they are by definition market leaders) and therefore ought to be profitable. They are very valuable and should be protected at all costs. They throw off a lot of cash, which can be reinvested in the business, used elsewhere in the business portfolio, used to buy other businesses, or paid out to shareholders.

The top left box comprises STARS: high relative market share businesses in high growth markets. These are very profitable but may need a

Illustration 3.13
The Growth/Share Matrix four quadrants

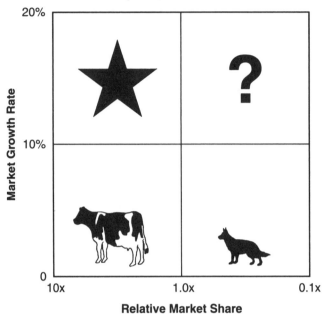

lot of cash to maintain their position. This cash should be made available. Whatever it takes to hold or gain share in star businesses should be undertake If they hold RMS, star businesses will become cash cows when the market growth slows down, and therefore hugely valuable over a long time. But if star businesses lose relative market share, as they are often allowed to do, they will end up as DOGS and be of limited value.

The top right box holds QUESTION-MARKS (sometimes called wild-cats): low RMS positions but in high growth markets. In this case 'question-mark' is a very good description of the business, since it has an uncertain future, and the decision on whether to invest in the business is both important and difficult. If a question-mark does not improve its relative market share – that is, if it remains a follower – it will end life as a DOG. On the other hand, if the volatility that market growth bestows is used and investment made in a question-mark to drive it into a leadership position, the business will migrate to being a star (profitable) and ends its days as a cash cow (very profitable and very cash positive). The problem is that question-mark businesses very often turn into CASH TRAPS, as money can be invested without any guarantee (and in some cases much chance) of attaining a leadership position. A business that is invested in heavily without ever attaining market leadership (like much of the British computer industry) will simply be an investment in failure and a gross waste of money.

The bottom right box is the DOG kennel. Dogs are low relative market share positions in low growth businesses. The theory therefore says that they should not be very profitable and should not be able to gain share to migrate into cash cows. Given that the majority of most firm's businesses may be in this box, this is not a very cheerful notion.

In fact, the greatest weakness in the BCG theory relates to dogs, largely because of this fatalism. The entry later on DOGS puts the case for their defence and stresses the ways in which dogs can often be made valuable parts of a firm's business portfolio. Briefly, dogs *can* migrate into cash cows, by re-segmenting the business or simply by having greater customer responsiveness than the market leader. Even if leadership is not possible, it is usually worth while to improve market share position within the dog category. A business with a relative market share of 0.7 × (70 per cent of the leader) may be quite profitable, highly cash positive, and quite different from a business with an RMS of only 0.3× (30 per cent of the leader).

Nevertheless, it may be true that there is limited room for manoeuvre with dog businesses, and they will generally be less attractive than stars or cash cows.

BCG super-imposed on the Growth/Share Matrix a theory of cash management (sometimes confusingly called PORTFOLIO MANAGEMENT) which is intriguing and makes some useful points, although it is also somewhat flawed. The theory looks at the cash characteristics of each of the quadrants (Illustration 3.14).

BCG's theory then came up with a hierarchy of uses of cash, numbered from 1 to 4 in their order of priority (Illustration 3.15).

(1) The best use of cash, we can agree, is to defend cash cows. They should not need to use cash very often, but if investment in a new factory or technology is required, it should be made unstintingly.

(2) We can also agree that the next call on cash should normally be in stars. These will need a great deal of investment to hold (or gain) relative market share.

Illustration 3.14
The Growth/Share Matrix cash characteristics

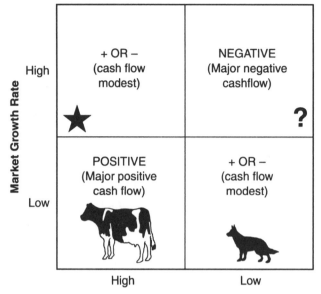

Relative Market Share

Illustration 3.15
How to use the cash

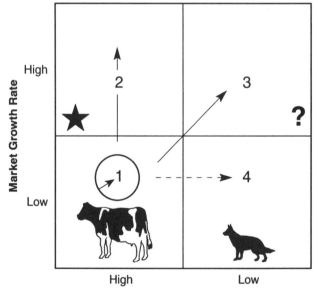

Relative Market Share

(3) The trouble begins here, with BCG's third priority, to take money from cash cows and invest in question-marks. The bastardised version of the theory stressed this cash flow in particular. BCG countered by stressing that investment in question-marks should be selective, confined to those cases where there was a real chance of attaining market leadership. With this qualification, BCG's point is sensible.

(4) The lowest priority was investment in dogs, which BCG said should be minimal or even negative, if they were run for cash. This may be a sensible prescription, but the problem is that the dog kennel may contain a large range of breeds with different qualities, and a differentiated cash strategy is generally required within the dog kennel.

One real weakness of the BCG cash management theory, however, as BCG came to realise, was the assumption that the portfolio had to be in balance in respect of cash on an annual or three year basis. In fact, the cash invested in the overall business portfolio does *not* have to equal the cash generated. Surplus cash can be invested outside of the existing portfolio, either by acquiring new businesses, by entering them from scratch, or by reducing debt or giving cash back to the shareholders. Conversely, if a business needs to invest more cash (for example, in an important and cash-guzzling star) than the business portfolio is generating, it should go out and raise the cash from bankers and/or shareholders to fund the cash gap. The business portfolio should not be thought of as a closed system.

The second major weakness of BCG views on cash, and one not fully realised until much later, was the implicit assumption that *all* businesses should be managed from the centre in a cashbox-plus-strategic-control way. See management styles for a refutation of this view. BCG's theory was immensely attractive to chairmen and chief executives seeking a sensible role for the Centre, and probably did a great deal more good than harm, but it is only a small minority of businesses that are actually run in this way. Indeed, the recent work by GOOLD and CAMPBELL largely divides businesses into those that are run by financial control and those that follow strategic control or strategic planning. These are two very different approaches, the former decentralised, the latter more centralised, and it is difficult to combine the two styles, as BCG's approach assumed. Perhaps, in the future, someone will devise a method of control which does incorporate the strong points of both styles, but it will take much more than a two-by-two matrix to realise this vision.

The BCG MATRIX marked a major contribution to management thinking. From the mid to late 1970s BCG tended to retreat too much under the weight of critical comment, and the matrix is not much used today. It is well overdue for a revival. Anyone who tries to apply it thoughtfully to his or her business will learn a lot during the process.

JUST-IN-TIME (JIT)

Valuable system developed first in Japan for production management aimed at minimising stock by having materials and work-in-progress delivered to the right place at the right time. As well as lowering costs, JIT can have other major benefits: the systematic identification of operational problems and their resolution by technology-based tools; higher levels of customer service and speeding up the time to market; higher quality standards by being 'RIGHT FIRST TIME'; and higher standards of COMPETENCE in the production function generally. To be most effective, JIT should be introduced as part of TQM (Total Quality Management), and it should be recognised at the outset that JIT is not just a technique, but a way of changing behaviour. A full JIT programme such as introduced by Toyota or Matsushita may take years to complete. But companies without JIT who compete against those with JIT will have a major handicap.

Properly conceived, JIT should be seen as a synchronising way of life: jobs must be completed quickly, but even more important is that they be completed just in time to fit in with the next step in the dance. This is a radically different concept from traditional assembly line thinking, which is sequential rather than synchronising. Charles HAMPDEN-TURNER and Fons TROMPENAARS point out that culturally, the US, UK, Sweden and Holland are disposed towards trying to speed things up sequentially, whereas Japan, Germany and France are more geared towards synchronisation. This means that when installing JIT and other synchronising techniques in 'Anglo-Saxon' and similar countries, it should be realised that JIT can go against the cultural grain: people need to be re-trained to think and act in a synchronised way.

OPPORTUNITY/VULNERABILITY INDEX

An interesting outgrowth from the BCG MATRIX, although not developed until the late 1970s/early 1980s (mainly by Bain & Company) and refined later that decade by The LEK Partnership, another strategy boutique. BCG had posited that high relative market share businesses (leaders) should be highly profitable, and the logic of the experience curve certainly suggested that the higher the market share, the higher the profitability (unless the firm was not using its potential advantages, or pricing to penetrate the market still further). It followed that it should be possible to construct a 'normative curve' to describe the profitability of the average BUSINESS SEGMENT in a particular industry, or, with a wider band, all industries, according to a normal expectation given the segment's relative market share. This normative band is shown on the matrix in Illustration 3.16.

The parallel area between the two curved lines represents the normative curve: depending on the exact data used, perhaps 80 per cent of observations would fall between these broad limits, and it would be unusual (only 20 per cent of business segment positions) for businesses to fall outside the bands. (The normative band can be constructed based on actual data of business segment positions and profitability, but only correct segmentation: in practice such data can only be obtained with any degree of confidence after working within a client organisation, and building up an anonymous database of the relationships.) In fact empirical data did enable the normative band to be built

Illustration 3.16
Opportunity Vulnerability Matrix

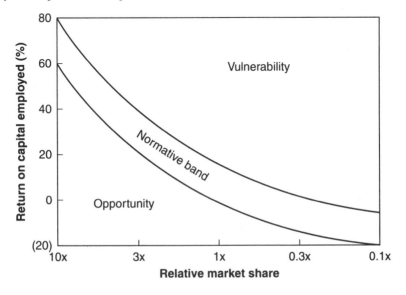

up in this way. The band used to be shown coloured in yellow, hence the chart became known in some circles as a bananagram.

So what? Well, one implication is that high relative market share positions, correctly segmented, are as valuable as BCG said, whatever reservations one has about the experience curve. Managers should therefore strive to be in such businesses and cannot expect to have profitability above the required rate of return of investors unless a majority of their sales are in leaders or strong followers (at least .7× Relative Market Share, that is, at least 70 per cent as the leader in the segment). Another implication, not really made clearly by BCG, and in some ways obscured by the doctrine of the BCG matrix about DOGS, was that it was useful to improve relative market share in a business segment *whatever the starting position*: useful to take a .3× RMS business and move it to a .6× RMS position, to take a .5× position and take it to 1.0×, to take a 2× position and move it to 4×, and so on. The chart enables one to calculate roughly what equilibrium profitability can be expected from any particular position, so that it is possible to state roughly the benefit of moving any particular segment position in this way and compare it to the expected short term cost of doing so (by extra marketing or service, product development or lower prices). In this way it can be seen (a) whether it is worth trying to raise RMS, and (b) which segments give the biggest bang for the buck.

But the most valuable use of the matrix lies not in the 80 per cent of positions that fall within the banana (normative curve), but rather in the 20 per cent that fall outside. Two examples of possible such positions are given in Illustration 3.17.

Business A is earning (say) 20 per cent Return On Capital Employed, a good return, but is in a weak Relative Market Share position (say .3×, or only 30 per cent the size of the segment leader). The theory and empirical data from the matrix suggest that the combination of these two positions is at best anomalous, and probably unsustainable. Business A is therefore in the 'VULNERABILITY' part of the matrix. The expectation must be that in the medium term, either the business must improve its Relative Market Share position to sustain its profitability (the dotted arrow moving left), or that it will decline in profitability (to about break even). Why should this happen? Well, the banana indicates that the market leader in this business may well be earning 40 per cent or even more ROCE in the segment (the beauty of the method is that this

Illustration 3.17
Opportunity Vulnerability Matrix Illustrative positions of business outside the Banana

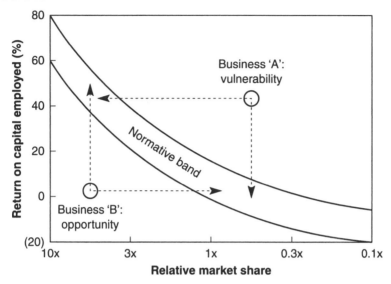

can be investigated empirically). What may be happening is that the leader is holding a price umbrella over the market: that is, is pricing unsustainably high, so that even the competitors with weak market share are protected from normal competitive rainfall. What happens if the market leader suddenly cuts prices by 20 per cent? He will still earn a good return, but the weaker competitors will not. (The leader may not cut prices, but instead provide extra product benefits or service or other features, but the effect would still be a margin cut). It is as well to know that business A is vulnerable. If relative market share cannot be improved, it is sensible to sell it before the profitability degrades.

Now let's look at Business B. This is a business in a strong relative market share position: the leader in its segment, four times larger than its nearest rival. It is earning 8 per cent ROCE. This is a wonderful business to find. The theory and practical data suggest that such a business should be making 40 per cent ROCE, not 8 per cent. Nine times out of ten when such businesses are found, it is possible to make them *very* much more profitable, usually by radical cost reduction (often involving BPR), but sometimes through radical improvement of the service and product offering to the customer at low extra cost to the supplier, but enabling a large price hike to be made. Managements of particular businesses very often become complacent with historical returns and think it is impossible to raise profits in a step function to three, four or five times their current level. The bananagram challenges that thinking for leadership segment positions, and usually the bananagram is proved right. After all, high relative market share implies huge potential advantages: but these must be earned and exploited, as they do not automatically disgorge huge profits.

PORTER'S FIVE COMPETITIVE FORCES

Porter was an innovator in structural analysis of markets, which previously, even with BCG, tended to focus largely on direct competition in the industry, without looking systematically at the context in other stages of the industry VALUE CHAIN. Porter's five forces to analyse are:

(1) Threat of potential new entrants
(2) Threat from substitutes using different technology
(3) Bargaining power of customers
(4) Bargaining power of suppliers
(5) Competition amongst existing suppliers.

The interactions amongst the five forces are shown in Illustration 3.18.

From this Porter builds a useful model of industry attractiveness and how this might change over time, both because of objective economic changes and also because of the ambitions of the players themselves.

PRODUCT LINE PROFITABILITY

Much neglected, highly useful analysis of how much money a firm makes (fully costed) on each of its products or services. Usually throws up results that surprise managers, often showing that a majority of products lose money on a fully costed basis, and 100 per cent or more than 100 per cent of the profits are made by a small proportion of exceptional money spinners. No-one has yet standardised a universally applicable way of conducting this analysis. Traditional accounting systems make it very difficult, and accurate product line profitability is nearly always supplied by outside consultants.

Illustration 3.18
Michael Porter's Five Competitive Forces

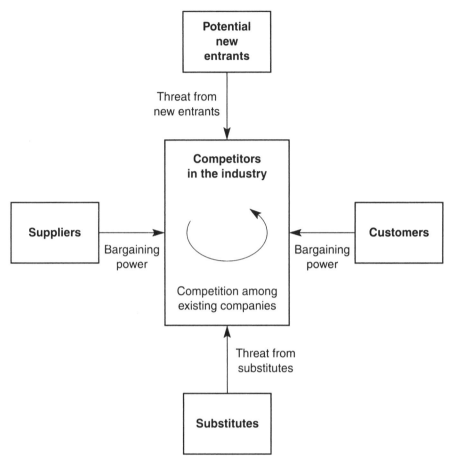

RCP (RELATIVE COST POSITION)

The cost position of a firm in a product relative to that of a competitor. For example, if it costs Heinz 10p to manufacture a can of beans, and it costs Crosse & Blackwell 11p for the same can, Heinz has an RCP advantage of about 10 per cent, or an RCP of 91 (C&B = 100). Classical economics assumes that firms in an industry will come to have the same cost position, but in the real world this is almost never true. RCP can be quite difficult to establish (usually requiring the use of specialist consultants) but it is often not what managers imagined, and the differences between competitors usually emerge as much greater than previously thought. It is useful (and necessary anyway, to arrive at the total answer) to look at RCP at each stage of the VALUE CHAIN: for example, X may have a 30 per cent cost advantage in production but have an inefficient salesforce, and be at a 10 per cent cost disadvantage in selling. Relative cost advantage is often, but by no means always, related to scale or experience advantages (expressed in RMS: Relative Market Share).

RCP analysis is not invalidated by differences in quality, or the fact that one supplier may have a better brand. The cost position can be looked at with the price realisation of each supplier indexed at 100, so that if Heinz receives 12p for its can of beans and C&B only 10p, Heinz's total and sub-divided costs can be looked at relative to the 12p, and C&B's relative to the 10p that they receive. On this basis, Heinz would have a total cost of 83 (10/12) and C&B a total cost of 110 (11/10): Heinz would be making a profit margin of 17 per cent but C&B would be losing 10 per cent. The real cost difference between the two firms (adjusted for price realisation) would be 27 per cent (110 minus 83). Heinz might be spending more on marketing, to help capture the extra price realisation, but the analysis would show this as well.

RCP analysis is expensive and only worth doing when there is a lot of turnover in the products being compared and there is a good chance that it will reveal things that can be acted upon, or help to set a competitive strategy in a battle worth winning. RCP analysis can lead to cost savings through imitation: for example, a competitor may miss out a process step altogether that the firm can also eliminate; or lead to a dramatic re-design of production to take out perhaps 30 per cent of cost.

RCP is little practised but where it has been used it has generally been extremely insightful and effective, saving tens of millions of pounds and giving a return of about 20–50 times the amount paid for the analysis (which will be several hundred thousand pounds). RCP cannot be conducted vis-à-vis most Japanese competitors, because it is impossible to discover their real costs, partly because of deliberate obfuscation, and partly because of the KEIRETSU system. See also RPP (Relative Price Position), and RMS.

RMS (RELATIVE MARKET SHARE)

The share of a firm in a BUSINESS SEGMENT divided by the share of the largest competitor that the firm has. Much more important than market share as an absolute number. For example, if Sony's nearest competitor in making Walkman-type products is one tenth the size, Sony will have an RMS of 10 times (written as 10×, or 10.0×, or sometimes simply 10). The competitor, on the other hand, will have an RMS that is the reciprocal of this: it will have an RMS of 0.1×. One more example will suffice: if Coca-Cola in one national market has a market share of 60 per cent, and Pepsi-Cola, 30 per cent, then Coke has an RMS of 2×, and Pepsi 0.5×.

Relative market share should correlate with profitability. If it does not, one (or more) of five things is happening: either (1) the business segment has been defined incorrectly; or (2) the smaller competitor is much cleverer than the bigger: the leader is not using his potential advantage properly, and/or the follower has found a nifty way to lower costs or higher prices that has overcome the advantages of scale and experience; or (3) the leader is deliberately forfeiting profit now by expense reinvestment that will compound his advantage in the future, and lead to much higher profits then; or (4) there is over-capacity in the industry, so that the key concern is capacity utilisation, and the bigger competitors may simply have too much of the excess; or (5) it is a business not susceptible to normal scale, status and experience effects.

Let us take each of these in turn. (1) Incorrect business definition: more often than not, this is the reason. In most cases, the segment will not have been defined in a sufficiently disaggregated way. See Business Definition. (2) A clever follower. This does happen, and is usually manifest in a refusal to play by the usual rules of the game. See: MAVERICK and DELIVERY SYSTEM. (3) Long term compounding strategy by the leader. May be true if it is Japanese or Korean, almost certainly not otherwise. (4) Excess capacity: yes, sometimes. (5) Industry and business not susceptible to scale, experience or status: very rare. Even service businesses generally are skewed in favour of the bigger players, who have greater advantages in terms of branding, reputation, lower marketing and selling costs, and greater expertise and ability to attract the best recruits.

One of the most useful charts to draw for any business, if the data can be collected, is shown in Illustration 3.19, which looks at the profitability (in terms of ROS or ROCE) of different competitors in a business segment.

Illustration 3.19
Typical pattern of profitability by RMS

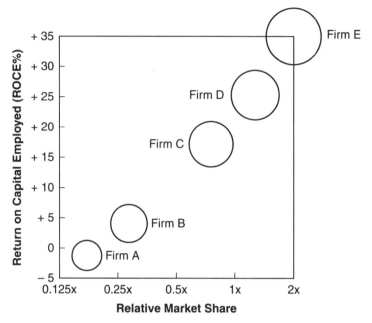

The chart shows a typical pattern, but the beauty of the method is that empirical data can be displayed to see whether and how far the expected pattern applies. If there is deviance from the normal pattern, the reasons given in (1) to (5) above can be systematically investigated.

The chart stops at 2× (two times) RMS only because in this case the leader was here. In other examples the relationship has been observed to continue working over whatever range of RMS applies: businesses with a 10× RMS really do make very high ROCE: normally in the 60–90 per cent range.

Observation of this relationship led to the development of a very useful tool – the OPPORTUNITY/VULNERABILITY MATRIX. See this entry for the action implications of RMS and profit relationships. See also RCP.

RPP (RELATIVE PRICE POSITION)

A complement to RCP (Relative Cost Position). RPP looks at the price realisation for two or more competitors in the same product or service. If two identical packets of crisps are sold in the same outlet, one under the KP brand, and one a retailer's private label, and the former is 20p and the latter 18p, then the KP RPP is 20/18 = 111 and the RPP of the retailer's brand is 18/20 = 90. RPP shows how far there is a brand, quality or distribution advantage. See also RCP.

S-CURVE

The growth pattern resembling an S: slow to pick up, followed by a period of maximum growth, then a point of inflection leading to gradually slower growth. Study of the 1665 Plague in England led to the conclusion that the spread of disease followed a mathematically predictable path, and the same methodology has been used with some success to predict the rate at which a new product will penetrate into any given population, given the early experience. If, for example, you knew that the penetration of dishwashers into Korea was 1 per cent in the first year, 2 per cent in the second year and 4.5 per cent in the third year, you could calculate a prediction for future years.

The formula to be used to calculate each year's observation is f/1–f, where:

f $\quad$ = $\quad$ the penetration (expressed as a fraction: e.g. 1 per cent = 0.01), and

1–f $\quad$ = $\quad$ one minus the penetration fraction (e.g. 1 – 0.01 = 0.99)

f/1–f = $\quad$ 0.0101 in this case, or for the 2 per cent observation
$\qquad$ = $\quad$ 0.02/0.98
$\qquad$ = $\quad$ 0.0204

If the observations are plotted on semi-log paper and a straight line is drawn through the observations, predictions for future years emerge in the form of the 'answer' above (e.g. 0.0204), which can then be converted by algebra into the percentage prediction. A simple computer program will perform the calculations without the need to resort to plotting on semi-log paper.

The same procedure can be used in modified form where you know that there will be a saturation level at a given point. In dishwashers in Korea, for example, you may know from similar cases that no-one below a certain income level will ever own a dishwasher. Let us assume that this cuts out 40 per cent of the population: the saturation level is therefore 60 per cent. Instead of using 1.0 as the maximum point, therefore, we would use 0.6, the saturation point(s). The calculation would then be f/s–f, and the first observation (at 1 per cent) would become:

$$0.01/.6–0.01 = 0.1695.$$

Many people are sceptical of the power of this methodology until they actually use it. It is not, of course, a magic predictor, but it does enable you to calculate what the answer would be if the current momentum persists. It will work out when the growth will slow because there is a diminishing pool of people to be 'converted' to the new product.

SEGMENTATION

Most usefully, the process of analysing customers, costs and competitors in order to decide where and how to wage the competitive battle; or a description of the competitive map according to the contours of the business segments. Sadly, segmentation is often used to describe a more limited (and often misleading) exercise in dividing up customer groups. See BUSINESS SEGMENT. Proper segmentation only takes place at the level of identifying the BUSINESS SEGMENTS: this is at the root of any firm's business strategy. Segmentation in this most useful sense is what is discussed below.

It is crucial for any firm to know which segments it is operating in, to know its relative market share in those segments, and to focus on those segments where it has or can build a leadership position. A segment is a competitive system, or arena, where it is possible to build barriers against other firms, by having lower costs or customer-satisfying differentiation (which will be expressed in higher prices, and/or in higher customer volume which itself will lead to lower costs). A segment can be a particular product, or a particular customer group being sold a standard product, or a particular customer group being sold a special product or provided with a special service, or a particular distribution channel or region, or any combination of the above. What matters is that the following conditions for a genuine segment are *all* satisfied:

(1) The segment must be capable of clear distinction, so that there is no doubt what customers and products fall inside and outside the segment.
(2) The segment must have a clear and limited set of competitors that serve it.

(3) It must be possible to organise supply of a product or service to the segment in a way that represents some specialisation, and is differentiated from supply to another or other segments.

(4) The segment must have purchase criteria that are different in important ways from other segments.

(5) The segment must be one where competitors specialise, and where there is a characteristic market share ranking that can be described.

(6) The segment must be capable of giving at least one competitor a profitability advantage, either by having lower costs, or higher prices, than other competitors, or both.

(7) It must be possible to build barriers around the segment to deter new entrants.

Segmentation may change over time. To take the example of the motor car, Henry Ford created his own segment around the black model-T Ford: the mass produced, standard automobile. Initially, he had 100 per cent of this segment, and it satisfied all of the rules above. Then it became possible to provide other colours at relatively low cost, and General Motors changed the mass automobile market to include any colour, standard car: the 'black car' segment ceased to exist and became part of a wider competitive arena. Subsequently new segments emerged, based on sports/high performance criteria, and later on 'compact' low fuel consumption cars.

Geography is a fascinating and changing dimension of segmentation. Most products and services start out by having a very limited geographical reach: one region or one country. The UK crisp (what Americans call potato chips) market is an interesting example. At one time the market was dominated by Smiths, then by Golden Wonder (who innovated with a range of flavours), both national competitors. But slowly but surely a new regional competitor, Walkers, emerged, based on superior quality. Initially the segment boundaries of Walkers were very restricted, based around the Midlands where the company was based. Within these regions the national segmentation did not rule: Walkers was the number one supplier by a long way, although nationally very small. Gradually, with greater production and improved distribution, Walkers became a national competitor, and for a time market leader, again causing the segmentation to revert to a national level.

An increasing number of markets are global: the battle between Pepsi and Coke is fought out beyond the boundaries of individual countries.

Nevertheless, segment RELATIVE MARKET SHARE positions often vary significantly in different countries: if Pepsi outsells Coke in one national market, against the global trend, that national market is today a separate segment. If, on the other hand, relative market shares around the world converge, the whole world can become one segment for cola drinks. Economics comes into this as well. To take one far-fetched example, assume that Coke came to have a two to one advantage over Pepsi everywhere in the world except New Zealand, where Pepsi was by far the leader, it would be correct to speak of New Zealand as a separate segment, but the rest of the world would be one segment and the marketing scale advantage enjoyed by Coke everywhere else would make New Zealand a barely tenable separate segment for Pepsi: at some point, the most interesting segmentation would have become global, even if national segment enclaves temporarily continued to exist.

Similarly, segments can be carved out or relinquished within a product range. At one time, British motorcycles were the market leaders throughout the world whatever type or power of bike was being considered: motorcycles were one global segment. Then the Japanese began to develop bikes, based around the low-powered bikes for which there was greatest domestic demand. What happened first was that this low c.c. market became a separate segment in Japan, because the market leaders (Honda and Yamaha) were different from the leaders in the rest of the world market (and in Japan in mid and high performance bikes). Then the Japanese companies, by trial and error, managed to develop a market for these low c.c. bikes in America, and later throughout the world, so that low c.c. bikes became a separate global segment. Later, using modular designs and high cost sharing, the Japanese suppliers entered mid size bikes, became market leaders in these, thus changing the segmentation around the world by annexing the mid market, so that there were two global segments: the low-to-mid segment (dominated by the Japanese), and the high performance segment, still dominated by Norton and BSA. Then, in the early 1970s, the Japanese began to edge their way into the high performance segment, and BMW created a separate high-comfort, high-safety segment, so that the world motorcycle market had two major segments: the 'BMW' segment, and the rest (the majority) of the market, served largely by Japanese competitors.

In diagnosing what segments you are in today – whether the market is one big segment or several small ones – the best way is to set up hypotheses that X market is a separate segment from Y market, and then test according to the following rules. The short set of rules, that will give you the correct answer 95 per cent of the time, is to ask just two questions:

(1) Are there separate competitors, with significant market share, in segment X that do not participate in segment Y? If so, it is a separate segment.

(2) Are the relative market share positions in market X different from those in market Y, even if the same competitors compete? If so, it is a separate segment. For example, Heinz and HP compete in both the red sauce (ketchup) and thick brown sauce markets in the UK, but in the first Heinz is miles ahead of HP, and in the latter HP is way ahead: so they are separate segments.

To be absolutely sure, apply the following additional rules:

(3) Is your firm's profitability different in market X from market Y? If so, even if it is the same product being supplied to different customers, it may be a separate segment.

(4) Are the COST STRUCTURES different in the two markets?

(5) Are there technological barriers between the two markets that only some competitors can surmount?

(6) Are prices different (for the same product or service) in the different markets?

(7) Is it possible to gain an economic advantage by specialising in one of the markets, by gaining lower costs or higher prices in that market.

Because segmentation changes over time, it is interesting to look both at the empirical segmentation today, which is defined particularly by the first two questions above, and also at potential segmentation based on the economics of the business: what is called economic segmentation. Economic segmentation applies questions (3) to (7) above to ask, not just whether the segmentation is distinct today, but whether it could be distinct. Economic segmentation can be used as a technique to re-segment a market, either by creating a new, smaller segment out of an existing segment (as with the initial Japanese move to create a below-250 c.c. motorcycle segment), or to merge two segments together (as with the later annexation of first the mid and then the high performance motorcycle segments) in order to realise ECONOMIES OF SCALE. Economic segmentation asks: could we obtain lower costs or higher prices or both by redefining the segment and changing the rules of the game?

SEVEN Ss, 7S FRAMEWORK

A framework for thinking about a firm's personality; a diagnostic tool for describing any company, developed by Peters & Waterman and their then colleagues in McKinsey around 1980. Seven elements of an organisation, all beginning with S – strategy, structure, systems, style, skills, staff and shared values – can be used as a checklist. Do the Ss fit well together, or are they inconsistent or unclear? When the Ss fit well together and reinforce each other, the organisation is likely to be moving forward purposefully; where the Ss are in conflict, it is likely to lack unity and momentum. The Seven Ss are shown in Illustration 3.20.

Note, however, that an organisation with seven consistent Ss will be much harder to change than one where the Ss are visibly in disarray.

Illustration 3.20
The Seven Ss

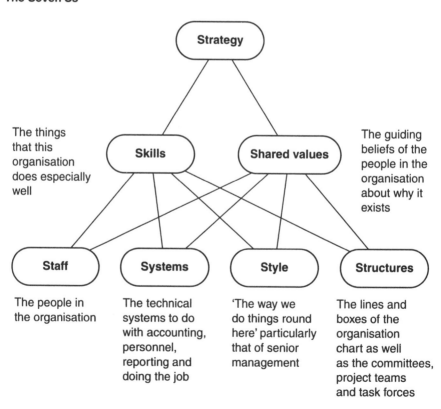

SUSTAINABLE GROWTH RATE (SGR)

Concept invented by BCG in the early 1970s to measure and demonstrate the effects of leverage and the proportion of earnings retained on the rate at which a company could grow. The point was that a firm could be constrained from growing (in the absence of new equity) if it had too little debt or retained too low a proportion of its earnings (that is, if dividends were too high a proportion of earnings). Since BCG believed (correctly) that the successful firm should aim to grow market share in its major markets, it tended to use the SGR to urge firms to become high debt, low dividend corporations, channelling as much money as possible back into investment. For the algebraicly inclined, the SGR formula is:

$$SGR = D/E\,(R - i)p + Rp$$

where:

D/E	=	Debt/Equity
R	=	return on assets, after tax
i	=	interest rate, after tax
p	=	percentage of earnings retained.

The SGR is more an interesting curiosity than a useful management tool, except where firms are competing pretty much head to head in a single segment business. The flaw in the thinking is that very few firms are that: there are usually a very large number of businesses and funds for one can come from one or more other businesses, or from the sale of one or more businesses. It is rarely the case that financial policy constrains growth.

TIME-BASED COMPETITION

Concept invented by BCG which holds that the time it takes a firm to get a product from conception to the customer, or to complete its tasks and provide goods or services to market can be the key to COMPETITIVE ADVANTAGE. Time is a crucial factor in the internal and external chain of customers-and-suppliers. At each internal or external customer/supplier interface there is not just a risk, but a near-certainty, that time will be wasted. And time really is money, as well as being service to boot. The total time taken through the chain – throughput time – determines not only the firm's costs, but is also a litmus test of the firm's responsiveness to customers. Concentration of time to market therefore kills two birds with one concept: service and cost. If quality is free, reducing the time to market has negative costs as well as customer benefits. Notwithstanding its importance, time-based competition is basically a package of earlier discoveries, and it in turn has been repackaged as just a part of BPR (BUSINESS PROCESS RE-ENGINEERING).

It has been long realised that most of the time taken to make a product or provide a service is generally not 'productive' time but the gaps between different stages of the process. An example is given in the entry on BPR of IBM Credit, which at one time took 7 days to process a credit application for a would-be computer buyer: but the actual work involved took only 90 minutes. By cutting out the gaps and giving responsibility to one person, costs can be cut, customer satisfaction and retention increased, and profits dramatically increased. Another example, this time quoted in the 'bible' of time-based competition (*Competing Against Time: How Time-Based Competition is Reshaping Global Markets*, by George Stalk, Jr., and Thomas M. Hout), is the 'H-Y War' in the early 1980s between Honda and Yamaha. This revolved around the speed with which new motorcycles could be produced. Honda won the war by producing first 60 new motorcycle models in a year, and then another 113 new models in 18 months, speed that Yamaha could not match.

Most organisations, even well run ones like Yamaha, soak up time like a sponge. Stalk and Hout invented the '0.05 to 5 rule', which says that most products are receiving value for between one-half of one per cent and five per cent of the time that they are in the value delivery system of the firm. In other words, over 95 per cent of the time products spend in their companies is wasted; eliminate the wasted time, and time to market can be increased between 20 and 200 times!

The time to market a product can be calculated and compared to that of several competitors; the idea behind time-based competition is to become the shortest time-to-market competitor. It is worth stopping to think through the implications for your own business.

TIME ELASTICITY OF PROFITABILITY

BCG's term for the relationship between a supplier's profit and the speed with which the product is supplied (the elapsed time between the customer's decision to buy and his receipt of the product or service). Short elapsed time equals high profit; long elapsed time equals low profit. This is because the customer will pay top whack if he can obtain the product at once, but if he has to wait he will shop around and may lower the price he will pay. Customers made to wait may also cancel their orders.

The firm's value-delivery system therefore needs to be changed to speed up time to market. Any extra costs will be more than compensated for by higher prices and greater market share.

C. STRATEGIC CONCEPTS AND DEFINITIONS

ADHOCRACY

Invented by Warren Bennis in 1968 and popularised by Alvin Toffler. Crudely the opposite of bureaucracy: an adhocracy is an organisation that disregards the classical principles of management where everyone has a defined and permanent role. Adhocracies are usually fun to work in, chaotic, task and project team based, disrespectful of authority if not accompanied by expertise, and fast changing. Adhocracy suits cultures and individuals used to thinking for themselves and willing to tolerate ambiguity. Adhocracy is most suited to workforces that are highly educated and motivated and where the work requires creativity and responsiveness to unpredictable and volatile customer needs. Most car plants are not adhocracies, most advertising agencies are.

Mintzberg supplies a more formal definition: 'Highly organic structure, with little formalisation of behaviour, high horizontal job specialisation, based on formal training; a tendency to group the specialists in functional units for housekeeping purposes, but to deploy them in small market-based teams to do their work' (*Structure in Firms*).

ADJACENT SEGMENT

A product or product-customer combination that is 'close' or similar to another one and that could be served by a company with relatively little extra effort. Marketing executives often list their adjacent segments as a prelude to deciding which new customers to target or new business areas to enter. For example, a local newspaper serving one area may decide to enter another area (the adjacent segment) either by extending the coverage of its existing paper or by bringing out an additional edition. Entering an adjacent segment is normally a more sensible step than going after a more distant segment (in this case, a distant newspaper area).

The skill in describing and evaluating adjacent segments lies in thinking about dimensions of the adjacency that may not be obvious. It is easy to think of a geographically adjacent market, but the newspaper may also be adjacent to other segments if it can use its skills, cost base or market franchise to enter that market. In this case, local radio, local magazines, or even the promotion of concerts may be adjacent segments for the newspaper.

In choosing adjacent segments it is important to avoid potential new segments that are already dominated by existing competitors, or that are themselves adjacent to other segments controlled by powerful players. For instance, a pet-accessory maker may think that pet food is an adjacent segment, but if it is already dominated by a large and well run pet food manufacturer he should steer clear. A better bet may be to enter an adjacent segment unrelated to pets, for example the manufacture of leather belts (if these have high cost sharing with making cat and dog collars) or other accessories that have high cost sharing with existing operations. See also ANSOFF MATRIX.

APOLLO

One of Charles HANDY's four GODS OF MANAGEMENT. In 1978 Handy made a breakthrough in thinking about organisational styles by gracing four typical ways of running companies with the names of Greek gods. Apollo represents 'role culture', being the god of order and rules. This CULTURE assumes that reason should prevail and that tasks can be parcelled out logically. An organisation chart that has a series of boxes describing jobs and that is a classic pyramid represents 'Apollonian' thinking. Everyone knows their role and works on their delegated activities according to their job description.

Apollo represents bureaucracy in the pure sense invented by Max Weber rather than the modern pejorative sense. The Apollo style can be the most efficient way of running firms operating in a stable and predictable environment. Everyone can be given their individual accountabilities and a system like management by objectives can ensure that individuals are treated fairly according to their performance rather than the personal opinion or liking of their bosses. Because responsibilities are clear and fixed, many people find the Apollo style easy to deal with, secure and stress-free.

Life insurance companies, monopolies, state industries, the civil service and local government are good examples of Apollo cultures.

Private companies operating in slow-changing industries with protected market positions may also exemplify Apollo. This style is unlikely to be effective, however, where there is rapid technological or market change or where teamwork is vital. Nor does it suit creative, restless or questioning individuals, or those who like the firm to be highly personal.

ATHENA

One of Charles HANDY's four GODS OF MANAGEMENT, representing a task-oriented way of running companies. Athena was a young warrior goddess, the patron saint of craftsmen and explorers. Athena firms have a problem-solving CULTURE, are not hierarchical, respect professional expertise and encourage teamwork, creativity and energy. They tend to work in project teams which may be dismantled once a problem is solved and be re-assembled, perhaps with different membership, to attack a new challenge. The teams are like guerilla commando units rather than massed armies.

Athena firms are most appropriate to 'knowledge industries' and professional firms, to times of expansion, and to people who think for themselves and can tolerate ambiguity and rapid change. The Athena culture may fit badly and be vulnerable if a firm hits a crisis, stops growing or if the work becomes more routine.

AVERAGE COSTING

A term coined by the Boston Consulting Group to indicate inadequately accurate costing systems that average costs across products or services taking in reality quite different amounts of cost, especially indirect and overhead costs. For example, a special or one-off product for a particular customer may cause unusual levels of cost in terms of specification, selling, quality control and so forth yet when the costing is done be charged no more for these elements of cost than standard products. It is almost always true that traditional cost-centre based methods of costing understate the cost of top-of-the-line and special products and services and overstate the cost of high volume standard products. This can be very damaging if (as usual) it leads to AVERAGE PRICING. The way in which average costing and pricing works is illustrated in Illustration 3.21.

Illustration 3.21
Average costing and pricing

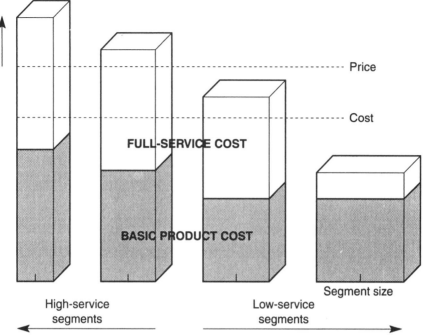

AVERAGE PRICING

Traditional costing systems understate the cost of producing special or one-off products. This AVERAGE COSTING leads to average pricing, which as the name suggests means failing to charge enough of a price premium for top-of-the-line or special products, and conversely charging too much for standard products (because the prices of the two types of product are averaged rather than sharply differentiated).

Average pricing is still rife, to a much greater extent than most managers realise. They may charge more for higher specification products, but rarely enough to reflect the real (but hidden) extra cost. For example, a firm making coin mechanisms for vending machines made a special one for the London tube (metro/subway) system. In tendering for the business the firm put in what they considered a very high price, so that the managers believed the work to be highly profitable. After the contract had been completed, a consulting study using ABC analysis (activity-based costing) showed that it had been highly unprofitable, because of the extra time of engineers and service people needed. 'If we had understood then about average costing and average pricing,' the managers concluded, 'we would have charged 30 per cent more for the work.'

Average pricing is dangerous, not just because of losses on special products, but because it can also lead to loss of market share through over-pricing on the high volume, standard products. A producer who just concentrates on the latter, 'commodity' business may be able to have a much lower overhead structure, lower prices, and higher profits. Over time, the specialist may gain market share of this profitable business and leave the high-overhead broad-line producer with a higher share of the unprofitable business. If costs are not correctly allocated and prices set accordingly the commercial consequences can be dire.

BARRIERS TO ENTRY

Obstacles making it difficult or impossible for competitors to enter a particular business segment. Barriers sometimes exist naturally but astute managers will try to raise these barriers and introduce new ones in order to restrict competition amongst their customers. It is worth while reflecting from time to time on what can be done to raise barriers, by examining a checklist of potential barriers (Illustration 3.22).

BARRIERS TO EXIT

Exit barriers are undesirable forces that keep too many competitors in a market, and lead to over-capacity and low profitability, because it is thought too expensive for a firm to leave the business. Barriers to exit may be real or imagined, economic or illusory, as Illustration 3.23 illustrates.

In general, barriers to exit are given too much thought and barriers to entry too little.

BRAND

A visual design and/or name that is given to a product or service by an organisation in order to differentiate it from competing products and which assures consumers that the product will be of high and consistent quality. Examples include manufacturers' brand such as Coca-Cola and Ford, retailers' brands such as St Michael or Sainsbury's, and even a

Illustration 3.22
Barriers to entry

Barrier to Entry	Comment
1. Investment scale	**Building a bigger or better plant, service network or retail outlet** can discourage competitors from trying to compete with you, especially if your installed customer base means it would take longer for them to get the scale of business to cover the cost of the initial investment, or if your investment gives you a lower cost base than existing competitors
2. Branding	**Making your product or service synonymous with superior and consistent quality,** whether or not a 'brand' in the conventional sense is used
3. Service	**Providing such a high level of service** that customers will be naturally loyal and not want to switch to competitors
4. Building in 'Cost to Switch'	**Locking customers in**, for example by promotional schemes such as 'Air Miles' where customers are saving up for incentives and will not want to switch to another supplier, or by giving OVER-RIDING DISCOUNTS once a level of sales has been triggered, or even by supplying equipment (such as freezer cabinets for newsagents selling ice cream) which can be withdrawn if a competitor's product is bought, or in professional services by knowing so much about a client's business that it would take another supplier too long to 'come up to speed'
5. Locking up distribution channels	**Buying or having a special relationship with distributors** that makes it difficult or impossible for a new supplier to get his product to the ultimate consumer: a policy followed for many years with great success, for example, in petrol retailing, where the superior siting of major oil companies' service stations helped them sell their oil
6. Locking up sources of raw material supply	**Obtaining the best (or all) the product from its source** either by owning the raw material (as with many large dairy companies) or by having a special relationship with suppliers, or by paying them more
7. Property/ Location	**Obtaining the best sites** can be crucial in businesses as diverse as oil production and retailing. It is worth asking from time to time whether the desired location might change in the future and then moving to lock up suitable new sites, as for example in edge of town/out of town superstores

Barrier to Entry	Comment
8. Expertise/ hiring the best people	**Knowing how best to do something that is important to customers** is an under-rated barrier. The key thing is to locate the functional expertise that is most important and then make sure that your firm is better than any other at this. For example, in mass market retailing the buying and merchandising function is crucial, and Marks & Spencer has a huge advantage because it has the best buyers and best relationships with suppliers. Hiring in the best people available to an industry can be a winning tactic, although only if the people can fit into the culture or the culture can be adapted to make best use of the newcomers
9. Proprietary expertise/ patents	**The logical extension to 8 above** in many businesses is a patent and in some businesses such as pharmaceuticals patents are hugely important in leading to much higher margins than would otherwise apply. Intellectual property can apply to a surprising range of businesses and it is worth checking whether anything your firm possesses can be patented
10. Lowest cost producer	**One of the very best barriers is to be able to produce a particular product or service for a particular market at a lower cost than competitors,** usually by having larger scale in that SEGMENT than competitors and defending that relative advantage ferociously. To be most effective the cost advantage should be passed through in the form of lower prices, although spending more than competitors can match in terms of advertising, sales force or research can also be effective ways of using a cost (and margin) advantage to build barriers
11. Competitive response	**Making it clear to competitors that you will defend 'your patch',** if necessary by 'crazy' actions, is a very effective barrier to entry. If a competitor ignores the warnings and enters, the response must be immediate and crushing, for example by dropping prices to their potential customers
12. Secrecy	**Sometimes a profitable market is relatively small** and its existence or profitability may not be known by competitors. **Keeping these segments well hidden from competitors** can be very important, if necessary by obscuring or playing down their importance to your firm. Conversely, someone seeking to enter a new market should invest properly in information about all potential customers.

Illustration 3.23
Barriers to exit

Barrier to Exit	Comment
1. Redundancy costs	**The cost of paying off employees** may be very heavy and much larger than the annual loss in a business. If a company is strapped for cash, it may find it easier to carry on in the short-term and hope that others in the business will remove capacity first, thus postponing and perhaps removing the need to spend cash laying off the workforce. More of a problem in the US than most developing countries, more in the UK than the US, and more in most Continental countries than the UK, because of higher statutory redundancy provisions
2. Investment write-offs	**Exiting from a business may cause a write-off of expensive plant and machinery that can only be used in that business.** This leads to a feeling that the investment is being wasted and to a large one-time loss going through the PROFIT AND LOSS STATEMENT and a reduction of net assets in the BALANCE SHEET. This reason is, however, usually a very bad one for not exiting from a loss-making business, since it refers to paper entries and not to industrial reality. A business which ought to have a write-off but does not is no more valuable, and probably less valuable, than a business that bites the bullet. The stock market understands this, and often large losses and write-offs from exiting a business lead to an increase in share price, as investors are relieved by management's realism and look forward to the elimination of losses in the business
3. Real disengagement costs	Leaving a business may sometimes lead to real, one-off costs other than labour ones; for example, a quarry may have to pay to restore the countryside to its previous glory, or a shop may have to carry out improvements before leaving. Recently one of the most serious disengagement costs has been long leases on property which cannot be re-let at rates as high as the business is paying, and which would still need to be paid once the business has closed
4. Shared costs	Often leaving one loss-making business is difficult because it would leave another profit-making business with higher costs, where these are shared between the two. For example, a factory may make two products and have shared overhead (and sometimes labour) costs,

Barrier to Exit	Comment
	or a sales force may sell two products to the same customers. Very often, however, shared costs are an excuse for inaction. The proper answer, wherever possible (and however painful) is to slim down the overheads for the profitable business to what is necessary for that business after exiting the unprofitable one
5. Customers require a 'package'	**Customers sometimes value the provision of multiple products by the same supplier** and would be reluctant or unwilling to buy from one that just supplies the profitable products. For instance, a supermarket that refused to sell loss leaders such as baked beans or milk might find itself short of customers. Very often, however, this claim is a spurious excuse, and customers would continue to buy a narrower product range provided this has a real advantage to them
6. Non-economic reasons	Barriers to exit are very often openly non-economic, as when a government or trade union requires the business to be kept open and has the power to enforce this. More covert non-economic reasons include management ego or emotional attachment to a business, fear (normally unfounded or exaggerated) that it will affect a business's image and relationships in the trade, or simply opting for the line of least resistance. Non-economic reasons are increasingly becoming discredited, although they can work to your advantage when you are less sentimental than your competitors or when they face less economically numerate governments

brand which is synonymous with a whole company like British Airways or Air Canada. Firms often create 'sub-brands' or new brands within a particular category, such as Diet Coke or Club Europe.

Branding goes back to the time when medieval guilds required tradesmen to put trademarks on their products to protect themselves and buyers against inferior imitations. Nowadays virtually everything has been branded. Consumers prefer brands because they dislike uncertainty and need quick reference points. A brand is particularly powerful if it can gain a slot in the brain and be identified either with whole product categories ('hoovers' for vacuum cleaners or 'filofax' for personal organiser) or with particular attributes (a Rolls Royce will always be high quality, a Mars bar will supply energy, Avis will always try harder). Many brands have helped companies remain market leaders in particular products throughout the last sixty years, including Bird's in custard, Heinz in soup and tomato ketchup, Kellogg's in cornflakes, McVitie's in digestive biscuits, Schweppes in mixers, Colgate in toothpaste, Kodak in film, Gillette in razors, and Johnson's in floor polish.

Despite the longevity of brands, it is always possible to develop new, powerful brands, although this requires a real new product advantage and usually very heavy investment in advertising and other marketing (there are exceptions to the latter requirement, such as Filofax, Laura Ashley and Walkers Crisps, where a cult develops almost spontaneously, but they are few and far between). Examples of strong new brands include Flora, Ariel, Canon, Sony, Heineken, Diamond White cider, Mr Kipling and (regrettably) The Sun.

Brands have seven major advantages for suppliers:

(1) They can help to build *consumer loyalty* and thus give a higher and more enduring market share

(2) Most brands involve a *price premium* which can be very substantial and which greatly exceeds the extra cost in terms of superior ingredients and marketing. The most profitable food companies in the UK in terms of return on sales are Kellogg's and Walkers Crisps, whose sales are exclusively branded. Cider is another recent UK industry where clever branding and product innovation turned a low-price industry into one with high prices. Market research has often asked consumers what they would pay for a particular new product, both unnamed, and with a trusted brand name, and it is not unusual for the latter to attract a 30 per cent price premium in the research.

(3) By virtue of their premium price (which widens margins for wholesalers and retailers as well as the manufacturer) and consumer pull, brands can make it easier for manufacturers to gain *vital distribution*. This is particularly crucial for new products and for smaller suppliers.

(4) Brands can sometimes *change the balance of power* between different parts of an industry. The development of manufacturers' grocery brands between 1918 and 1960 helped to put manufacturers in the driving seat and give them higher margins than retailers. In the past 25 years consolidation in food retailing and the development of

retailers' (own label) brands has handed higher margins to retailers and enabled them to introduce new products from smaller suppliers, including some high margin innovations such as chilled ready meals.

(5) Brands can make it easier to *introduce new products* and get consumers to try them, so that often a new product will use some of the brand equity in an existing brand by using it while adding a differentiating sub-brand, such as Miller Lite or Guinness Draft Bitter.

(6) Closely associated with point 5, branding facilitates the *creation of new market segments* within an established product category: for instance, low-calory or low-fat versions of almost any food or drink product, the creation of at least three classes of airline travel, or longer-lasting products such as Duracell.

(7) Finally, the combination of trust and razzmatazz that brands carry can enable whole industries to defy the market maturity stage of the alleged product life cycle, taking a fusty and declining market and injecting *new growth into an industry*. Besides the cider and stout examples, successful branding has helped to revive markets as diverse as shampoo, hand razors, bicycles and newspapers, all of which once seemed stuck in steady decline.

BRAND STRETCHING

The process whereby an existing well-known brand name is used on new products that compete in a different market from the brand's existing core product(s). A great deal of brand stretching is currently being undertake. Some examples from the UK are given in Illustration 3.24.

The basic reason for brand stretching is the increased probability of success using an established brand. Of new product launches examined by OC&C Strategy Consultants from 1984 to 1993, only 30 per cent of new brands survived at least 4 years, but brand extensions had over double the survival rate, at 65 per cent. It is easier to get brand stretches into the trade and consumers are more likely to experiment with, and repeat purchase, the brand extensions. Moreover, the cost of launching new products is much lower using existing brands.

We appear to be moving into a new era, where brands are positioned as having emotional and life-style benefits that are transferable across several products, rather than being narrowly identified with a particular product.

Illustration 3.24
Recent examples of brand stretching in the UK

Brand	Core Market Category	New Market Category
Bisto	Gravy	Casserole sauces
Bowyers	Meat products	Chilled salads
Flora	Margarine/spreads	Salad dressings
KP	Crisps and peanuts	Peanut butter spread
Mars	Confectionary	Ice cream & Milk drinks
Mr Kipling	Cakes	Frozen puddings
Quaker	Cereals	Bread
Ryvita	Crispbread	Cereals

Source: OC&C Strategy Consultants

The benefits of brand stretching are clear, but there are also risks, principally the danger of diluting the core brand image. These risks can, however, be contained to acceptable limits by (1) providing an excellent new product, at least comparable in quality to the current brand leader, and (2) by *not* putting a lot of advertising support behind the stretched product, so that if consumers give it the thumbs down it can be allowed to die a decent death without contaminating the core branded product.

Brand stretching is here to stay and is an accelerating trend. It increases both the rewards and the risks for established brands, in whatever market. See NPD.

BUSINESS SEGMENT

A defensible competitive arena within which market leadership is valuable. Contrast market segment, which is usually defined by market researchers' pre-ordained categorisations of the population into social class or psychologically defined groups, and much less useful. A business segment is an area within which a firm can specialise and gain COMPETITIVE ADVANTAGE. An example of a business segment would be high performance sports cars, which is a defensible market against mass market cars (at least for the time being). Thus Ferrari does not have to worry about its share of the overall car market, if it can be the leader in its own segment. On the other hand, companies cannot define the market in a way that gives them market leadership and *ipso facto* call that a business segment. For example, red cars are not a separate segment from black cars, because specialising in red cars would not result in either extra consumer appeal or lower cost for producing red cars, and would therefore not be a defensible segmentation. See also SEGMENTATION for a much fuller discussion.

CANNIBALISATION

When a new product or service is introduced in the knowledge that it will eat into the market for an existing product or service already being provided by the supplier. Diet Coke, for example, cannibalised the existing market for Coke, or Turkey flavoured Whiskas cannibalised the demand for existing Whiskas variants. Suppliers know that these goods will to some extent reduce existing product demand, but expect this to be more than compensated for by the extra demand created by the new product introduction (and in some cases higher prices too, as when Whiskas was originally introduced and cannibalised Kit-e-Kat). Moreover, if one supplier does not introduce a new product to cater for a potential new product category, the competitor might: causing loss of market share, which is always a greater evil than cannibalisation.

CASH COW

A business that is highly cash positive as a result of being a market leader in a low growth market. Such a business typically requires only moderate investment in physical assets or working capital, so that high profits result in high cash flow.

Cash cows are one of the four positions on the BCG MATRIX. In the BCG theory cash from cash cows can be used to support other businesses that are leaders or potential leaders in high growth markets and that need cash to improve or maintain their market share positions.

The BCG theory has often been misinterpreted, partly as a result of the tag 'cash cow'. Cows need to be milked, so the natural (but incorrect) inference is that the main role of cash cows is to give cash to the rest of the portfolio. Yet the original BCG theory stressed the key point that cash cows should have the first call on their own cash: whatever investment was necessary to support and reinforce the cash cows' position should come first. This common-sense prescription is often overlooked. Cash cows are not glamorous, and generally require only moderate amounts of grass, but they should still be allowed to graze on the most verdant pastures. It would have saved us all a great deal of trouble if BCG had stuck to the alternative name for cash cows, namely gold mines. Nobody would dream of denying a gold mine its required share of the maintenance budget.

CASH TRAP

Useful jargon invented by the Boston Consulting Group to describe businesses that absorb cash but will never repay it fully or at all. BCG even went so far as to say in 1972 that 'the majority of the products in most companies are cash traps. They will absorb more money forever than they will generate. This is true even though they may show a profit in the books.' Typically question-mark businesses (poor market share positions in high growth businesses) are the worst cash traps, although some DOGS may also be. BCG crusaded against cash traps, urging managers to cut their losses in these businesses and focus cash on businesses that were or could become market leaders. The crusade has had real impact in the past two decades or so, partly through the action of managers but even more through hostile acquisitions that have led to UNBUNDLING, which is often little more than the sale or closure of cash traps. Are you sure you know what your cash traps are?

CATEGORY KILLER

Retailer that specialises in a particular type of product, like toys, baby products or furniture, and offers both the widest range and the greatest value, usually by means of very large and 'fun' out-of-town stores. See destination retailing.

CAUSE

Recent pioneering work on change management has stressed the need for all companies to have an overall medium term objective that can unite everyone's efforts and focus on what the company as a whole is trying to achieve. Causes should be snappy phrases that encapsulate the company's forward momentum and help to guide individual behaviour. Examples of good Causes include 'Putting People First' (British Airways), 'Encircle Caterpillar' (Komatsu), 'Number One and Pulling Ahead' (Coca-Cola Schweppes Beverages) and 'Become larger than BCG' (Bain & Company).

CHERRY-PICKING

Specialising in parts of a product range that are most profitable and/or easiest to access rather than providing a full line of product. Large, full-line suppliers are often vulnerable to smaller cherry-pickers, especially if the larger player has made the mistake of AVERAGE COSTING and AVERAGE PRICING.

COMMODITY

Undifferentiated product, where suppliers are doomed to compete on price, branding has no value, and the low-cost competitor will be able to earn higher returns and/or gain market share at the expense of his weaker (higher cost) brethren. Actually, commodity markets are often the result of a lack of imagination and marketing flair on the part of the participants. Almost anything can be successfully branded, and a price premium extracted. Take baked beans as an example: easy to produce and you might think a classic commodity market. Yet brilliant advertising based on brand identity – 'Beans Means Heinz' – has made it possible for Heinz to be market leader and extract a high price premium too. Or take a more recent example where a commodity market has been transformed into a branded market: flour. This is a large market where the competing products are almost indistinguishable in functional performance. Competition used, accordingly, to be based on fierce price discounting. Until, that is, RHM turned the market upside down with its branded marketing campaign for Homepride based on the bowler-hatted flour-grader and the slogan: 'Graded Grains make Finer Flour'. RHM gained both market share and a price premium. Many industrial companies have discovered also that markets previously thought to be 'commodity' bear gardens can be turned into higher margin ones where one competitor gains an advantage based on service, technical excellence, industrial branding, or some other attribute of value to buyers.

COMPETENCES, COMPETENCIES

Skills that an organisation has: what it is good at. Much recent thinking has stressed that an organisation's operating skills relative to competition are at least as important to its success as the strategy it has. To be successful an organisation must be at least as good as its competition in certain core competences. For example, in retailing one of the most important skills is Buying and Merchandising, that is, procuring goods that consumers will want to buy and displaying them attractively. This very obvious statement explains in large part why some retailers, like The Gap or Marks & Spencer, are consistently more successful than their market rivals. Assessing and improving competences (relative to competition) has rightly become the top priority for many managements.

COMPETITIVE ADVANTAGE

One of the most enduring and valuable catchwords of strategy. Competitive advantage obtains when one player has identified a market or market niche where it is possible to have a price advantage, or a cost advantage, or both, over competitors.

Price advantage means that the product or service is thought sufficiently superior by its buyers to make a price premium (for equivalent quality and cost to produce) possible. Brand leaders usually command a price premium over secondary brands or own label products, sometimes as much as 20–40 per cent, which far exceeds the additional cost of advertising and superior product formulation.

Cost advantage can come from superior scale (and therefore greater spreading of fixed costs), from having lower factor costs (for example, by using cheap labour), from superior technology, or simply having workers who perform their tasks more intelligently or quickly.

Competitive advantage is usually, although not invariably, related to superior market share in a defined segment. Even if not caused by competitive advantage, market leadership should be the result of competitive advantage: otherwise it is being under-exploited.

CONCENTRATION

The extent to which few suppliers cover the market. The UK grocery retailing market is highly concentrated, with 75 per cent of it being provided by five supermarket chains; the American grocery retailing market is much less concentrated. Concentration is often measured by the market share controlled by the largest four or five suppliers, known respectively as the C4 ratio and the C5 ratio. Another measure is the Herfindahl Index.

Most markets have the potential to be concentrated and a fragmented market should be a challenge for suppliers to undertake the process of concentration. In the absence of misguided anti-trust constraints, it is economically logical to have up to 80 per cent of a market controlled by three competitors, with perhaps 40 per cent, 25 per cent and 15 per cent of the market for the number one, two and three respectively.

CONTINUOUS IMPROVEMENT

A Japanese concept holding that COMPETITIVE ADVANTAGE of a company accrues from the persistent search for improvement and a series of tiny steps made continuously, rather than from great leaps forward. The latter are more consistent with Anglo-Saxon cultures, which helps to explain the popularity of BPR (BUSINESS PROCESS RE-ENGINEERING). The evidence is that the Japanese approach works very effectively for Asian cultures, while more revolutionary techniques are both more necessary and more acceptable for Anglo-Saxons.

CONTRACTING-OUT

Process of using outside suppliers of services to a corporation or public authority rather than using an internal department. There is a strong and increasing trend towards contracting-out in both business and government, largely to cut cost, but partly also motivated by the belief that organisations should concentrate on their core competences and leave other specialists to fulfil other roles. Some astute observers, such as Charles HANDY, believe that contracting-out will eventually transform our economic landscape, leading most organisations to employ far fewer people, the CORE WORKERS, while using armies of contractors from several smaller, specialist firms. One result will be that many people will leave larger organisations half-way through their working lives to found or join contracting organisations. See also SHAMROCK ORGANISATION.

CORE WORKERS

Those people who are central to an organisation's success and who need to be nurtured and rewarded accordingly. This professional core, increasingly made up of qualified professionals, technicians and managers, comprise the knowledge and skills that explain an organisation's success (or lack thereof). Core workers are precious, hard to replace, expensive and increasingly footloose. Because they are expensive, organisations are tending to be more discriminating in defining what functions and which people should be regarded as core workers, resulting both in downsizing, and also in contracting-out functions that used to be performed by core workers. Core workers are coming to be a privileged but hard-working élite, who in return for high pay, rewarding work and a CAUSE they can believe in, are willing to dedicate themselves to the success of their firms. See also Contractors and SHAMROCK ORGANISATION.

COSTS OF COMPLEXITY

Very important idea that the more complex a business, the higher the costs, for any given level of scale. Complexity can mitigate the advantages of additional scale or even overturn them altogether. Complexity arises when a firm extends its product line, customers, areas of expertise and/or use of different technologies in order to expand. The wise firm seeks extra scale without extra complexity, or reduces complexity without sacrificing scale.

Complexity cannot be totally avoided, and is often market-driven. What separates the operationally skilful firm from others is very often its ability to manage customer-demanded complexity simply: providing CUSTOMISED or preferably CUSTOMERISED products with little added internal complexity.

But very often complexity is self-inflicted rather than market-driven. Customers may say they want a special product or service, but be unwilling to pay for the real extra cost: they do not want it badly enough. And in many cases complexity is nothing at all to do with the customer, but just reflects bad management, and is often against the interests of both the firm and the customer. Production systems that resemble spaghetti, poor factory lay-outs, unnecessary stages in the production process, quality control departments (instead of building quality in on the line), excess staff numbers and too many functional boundaries, insistence on doing everything within the firm rather than outsourcing wherever possible, interfering head office functions: all of these are complexity own-goals.

Waging war on complexity can lead simultaneously to stunning cost reductions and improvements in customer value. About half of all the value-added costs in the average firm are complexity-related, and half of these provide opportunities for radical cost reduction. Some clues to reducing the costs of complexity are: reducing the number of current suppliers and entering more collaborative relationships with them; buying in components and services rather than 'making' them oneself wherever possible; avoiding products or customers where added complexity is not fully compensated; eliminating complexity from product design and making product families modular; reducing the number of process steps; improving factory lay-out; creating small business units within the firm that take charge of a whole product/process from design to customer delivery; decimating head office; abolishing management hierarchy; reducing the information collected and disseminated; and generally not doing anything that is not essential to making customers happy. See BPR, AVERAGE COSTING and VALUE CHAIN.

COST STRUCTURE

The total cost elements of a company broken down into key elements and often shown in the form of a bar, which can then be compared to the cost structure of a competitor making the same product, or to the cost structure of other products in the same firm, as in Illustration 3.25.

Cost structures have changed over time: as the 'typical' cost structures in Illustration 3.26 show.

The major change has been the decrease in direct labour, due to greater automation, and the increases in indirect labour and other overhead. This makes the allocation of fixed costs to products much more important than previously. In fact, 'fixed' cost very often

Illustration 3.25
Competitive cost structures

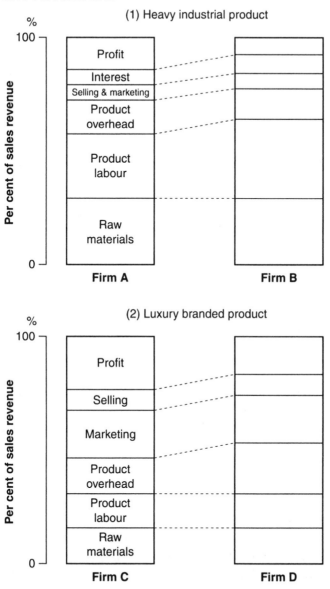

(1) Heavy industrial product

Firm A / Firm B

Per cent of sales revenue

Profit
Interest
Selling & marketing
Product overhead
Product labour
Raw materials

(2) Luxury branded product

Firm C / Firm D

Per cent of sales revenue

Profit
Selling
Marketing
Product overhead
Product labour
Raw materials

increases as turnover goes up, particularly if the firm is adding additional product lines or product variants, or additional customer service and after-sales support in an effort to appeal to a new customer group or just to gain more market share. Product proliferation and more

Illustration 3.26
Typical cost structures in 1950 and 1990

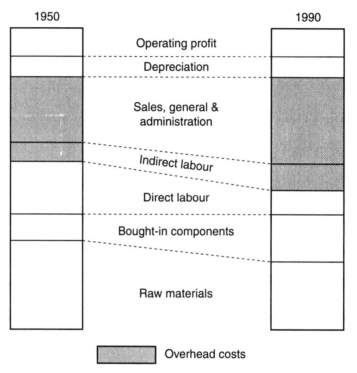

demanding customers have increased the proportion of overhead costs, and the latter, if not carefully controlled, can negate or overturn the advantage of increased turnover. See AVERAGE COSTING, AVERAGE PRICING, and COSTS OF COMPLEXITY.

COST TO SWITCH, COSTS TO SWITCH

The psychological and/or financial cost to move from one supplier to another. Classical micro-economic theory held that buyers would switch from one supplier to another if there was even a very slight difference in price, provided product quality was equivalent. In practice, there are very often high costs to switch suppliers, even if they are of equal quality. A supplier may know a customer's business well and educating a new supplier may take time and effort. This is an often hidden BARRIER TO ENTRY that can make market shares 'sticky' and make it difficult to gain share. Consultants who know a company well can often rely on the cost to switch to keep out competitors.

CULTURE

The personality and character of a company, derived from generations of people and experience and leading people inside a firm to behave in certain characteristic ways without thinking about it. Different firms in the same country and industry may have radically different cultures, and the difference may be far more important in determining relative success than any other factor, including differences in strategy, which may themselves be partly explained by the culture. Increasing but still insufficient attention is being paid to creating and sustaining winning cultures within firms. It is impossible to succeed in a corporate TRANS-FORMATION without such radical culture change, though this takes many years and single-minded determination by the leader of a firm. See also Charles HANDY's useful description of four GODS OF MAN-AGEMENT – APOLLO, ATHENA, DIONYSUS and ZEUS, which describe four broad cultural groups. Other useful dimensions of culture are:

- *by class/background of senior staff*
- *open and collaborative versus 'dinosaur' and backbiting culture*
- *traditional/clubby versus professional*
- *forgiving/low standards versus relentless/high standards*
- *marketing and customer-led versus production/internal orientation*
- *personal versus bureaucratic*
- *intellectual versus street-smart*
- *'learning' versus know-it-all*
- *'believed in' by staff versus 'not believed in'.*

Such categorisations can be thought-provoking but cannot fully capture the richness of each company's unique culture. Nothing is more important for management than understanding culture and how to change it. See *Wake Up and Shake Up Your Company* by Richard Koch and Andrew Campbell and *The Seven Cultures of Capitalism* by Charles HAMPDEN-TURNER and Fons TROMPENAARS.

CUSTOMER RETENTION

The extent to which customers repeat-purchase. Customers defect at average rates of 10–30 per cent, and far more in some businesses like car dealing. Losing customers is expensive, because the marketing costs to win them over in the first place are so high. Differential customer retention can often explain a significant part of profit differences between firms. Increasing attention is being given to monitoring and increasing customer retention, since it has been discovered that a 5 per cent shift in customer retention can result in 25–100 per cent profit swings. Customer retention arises from customer loyalty, which arises when superior value has been delivered. Loyalty in turn leads to higher market share of the chosen customer base, which is often the most value-conscious and least price-conscious part of the market, and therefore the most desirable. High share of value-conscious customers leads to lower costs, both directly through added volume, and indirectly through referrals and word-of-mouth appreciation, which lowers marketing and selling costs. The effect can carry through to employees, who are proud to be offering such good value to customers, and who in turn reinforce the value proposition by particularly good service. With turnover going up and costs going down, profits increase, which in turn allows further investment in product quality and service and in hiring and retaining the best employees: these effects further reinforce the competitive advantage of customer value and loyalty. This VIRTUOUS CIRCLE can carry on *ad infinitum*, until competitors with inferior value and loyalty go out of business, or are contained to unprofitable commodity segments.

The most besotted adherents of customer retention claim that relative customer retention (RCR) explains differential competitor profitability much better than RELATIVE MARKET SHARE (RMS), RELATIVE COST POSITION (RCP) or any other variable. Whether this is true or not, providing customers with the best product and service is clearly one of the best ways to engender loyalty, customer retention and high relative market share, and it therefore makes sense to monitor both absolute and relative customer retention. It is clearly also true that the way to deliver SHAREHOLDER VALUE in the long term is to provide the best value to customers in the short, medium and long terms, so that the debates about whether to put customers or shareholders 'first' is largely sterile. A good starting point for creating trust between the firm and its customers, employees and shareholders alike is to provide the best possible customer value and obtain the highest relative retention rates.

CUSTOMERISED, CUSTOMERISING

Allowing customers to adapt products themselves: in Tom PETERS' words 'produced by, directed by and starring our customers'. The customer, not the firm, is the initiator. Why does Peters have a penchant for coining useful but ugly words?

DECLINING INDUSTRY

One where demand is falling and expected to continue to do so. Two comments can be made about declining industries. One is that there is no inevitability about secular decline in many cases. An industry may continue declining solely because of lack of investment and imagination. Railroads in the US is an example, where poor service, lack of investment and industry fatalism wrecked the industry, and more recent initiatives reversed the decline. Similarly, newspapers declined in most countries as TV gained ground, but the growth of segmented titles and freesheets have turned declining into growing markets. Cider in the UK is another example, as is 'real ale'. An example from Japan is the way that Yamaha has revived the piano industry by creating a PC-based retrofit and a new digital electronic piano, turning a market declining at 10 per cent annually into an explosive growth market.

The second comment is that even if a market continues to decline, the last one or two players in the market can end up with a very profitable, extremely cash positive business. Often there is a greater payoff to gaining market share in declining than in growing markets, particularly if a position of dominance can be attained. Decline is often a mirage or an opportunity.

DELAYERING

Removing whole layers of management, resulting in a more FLAT STRUCTURE, lower costs, less bureaucracy, and greater accountability of executives. Very often, a high proportion (often in the range of 30–50 per cent, sometimes even 90 per cent) of overhead and head office staff can be removed by delayering. A typical example is removing two whole tiers of management from a firm that starts with five. This is not just cost reduction in response to crisis or recession, but a secular trend.

DELIVERY SYSTEM

The activities a firm performs in delivering a product and/or service to the customer. The concept of the delivery system far transcends physical distribution and can be used to think about new ways of delivering value to the customer. A good example is IKEA, the Swedish furniture and home furnishing company that has grabbed global leadership in an industry previously characterised by local suppliers. IKEA did this by developing a totally new delivery system by rethinking the structure, processes and skills across the entire supply chain from timber to customer. IKEA offers customers a new division of labour: in return for high design and low prices the customer takes on key tasks previously performed by manufacturers or retailers, such as assembly of products and delivery to the home. Every aspect of the IKEA business system facilitates customers taking on this new role, from the time that customers at the front door are given catalogues, tape measures, pens and paper, to the time that they leave with a loaned roof rack.

DE-MERGER

Split of one company into two (or very rarely, more than two) new companies. Most common where a company already has two divisions engaged in different businesses. Generally involves shareholders in the original company being given shares in both the new companies, with the new shares being quoted separately. An alternative is where a company de-merges one division by selling it and pays out a one-time dividend to shareholders.

De-mergers are increasingly common but not common enough. Where two businesses have different CULTURES and little SYNERGY they should be separated, both to allow management in each business to focus and have full control, and to enable investors to have a 'purer play'.

DESTINATION, DESTINATION RETAILING

The practice of running large, out-of-town or edge-of-town superstores that are themselves a 'destination' rather than just part of the high street or a shopping mall. The retailer therefore needs to offer a sense of excitement, fun and facilities for the whole family in order to attract people to the destination. IKEA, the Swedish furniture retailer, is a classic example (see DELIVERY SYSTEM); so too is Toys R Us. Increasingly, retailing is polarising between the high street, which is still economic for frequent and generally low ticket items, and destination retailers out of town, for infrequent and high ticket items. Destination retailing is increasing its share of total retailing in the UK and many other countries, particularly when associated with CATEGORY KILLERS, that is, specialists in a particular product range like toys, baby products, CDs or furniture.

DIONYSUS

In Charles HANDY's GODS OF MANAGEMENT, Dionysus is the god of existential culture, and Dionysians are the most individualistic and anarchic of those found in organisations. The Dionysian culture is found in universities, research institutions, some professions, and some 'way out' professional service firms, especially small ones, as well as in many self-employed businesses, the arts, and crafts. Dionysians often comprise outposts within large firms, notably in R&D or any other rarefied, highly qualified technical post. Dionysians are difficult to manage and often impossible to motivate: they are self-motivated, inner-directed, self-contained, and concerned about the quality of their work, not what anyone else thinks about it or them. It is difficult to make Dionysians behave as team players, unless they have strong personal bonds with the rest of the team. They are most effective in very small firms or as one-person units.

DIVERSIFICATION

1. Being in or moving towards being a group of companies engaged in several different products and markets. Diversification is usually driven by the wish (or financial ability) to expand beyond the apparent limits of existing markets, and/or by the wish to reduce business risk by developing new 'legs'.

Many forests have been destroyed by writers praising and damning diversification. The balance of recent opinion has been against diversification (as in 'stick to the knitting'), although this has not stopped conglomerates (diversified companies) gaining a larger and larger share of corporate activity throughout the world, and especially in Britain.

The main justifications behind diversification are:

(1) financial. The BCG MATRIX developed a theory in the late 1960s/early 1970s that central management of successful firms can

and should shovel cash around the corporation in order to move it away from businesses that would always consume cash and into those few businesses that have the potential for market leadership and thus for long term cash generation. This was a rather selective theory of diversification, but Bruce HENDERSON became an apostle of conglomerates, convinced that the strategically directed conglomerate could continually compound its cash generation capability and expand the scope of its operations. Modern financial theorists counter that shareholders, not managers, should diversify their holdings and that it is better for shareholders to be offered a selection of 'pure plays' of non-diversified companies.

(2) management skills. Several diversified companies such as Hanson and BTR are highly skilled at identifying under-performing companies and at changing management structures and behaviour in order to improve performance. Diversification of this type involves buying, fixing, and at the right time selling, such companies.

(3) core skills or COMPETENCES. A company's expertise may not really reside in knowing a particular market, but in certain skills that are applicable across several markets. This is well illustrated in Illustration 3.27, a list of examples of successful diversification compiled by Charles Coates.

Companies must not fool themselves about whether they have competences that are applicable in new areas. But a moment's thought is usually all that is necessary to dismiss many instances of clear wishful thinking. The most notorious instances of unsuccessful diversification could not have been justified by the principle of core skills. Had this principle been the touchstone, Cummins, the world leader in diesel engines, would not have gone into ski resort development; Letraset, the world specialist in dry transfers, would not have bought stamp dealer Stanley Gibbons; General Mills would not have ventured from its core area of food manufacturing into toys; Cola-Cola would not have gone into the film industry by buying Columbia Pictures; and Lex Service, the car dealer and importer, would not have gone into the specialist world of electronic distribution.

All good diversification builds on competitive advantage in core businesses and reinforces rather than detracts from that by strengthening still further the competences that drive success in the existing businesses. This is true even though the product areas may seem only tangentially related,

Illustration 3.27
Diversification using core competences

Company	Country of origin	Original Core Business	Key Skills	Growth Path
Honda	Japan	Motorcycles	Piston engine design and development	Cars, lawnmowers, small generators
Gillette	USA	Shaving products	Advertising effectiveness	Other toiletries, e.g. deodorants
Hanson	UK		Financial control; acquisition evaluation	Post-acquisition cash maximisation in low technology businesses
McDonalds	USA	Hamburger restaurants	Site selection; quality standardisation	Extension of opening hours to include breakfast; products innovation (fish, pizza, salads)
Marks & Spencer	UK	Clothes retailing	Supplier management; value-for-money branding	Diversification into food, furniture, flowers
Sony	Japan	Transistor radios	Production innovation; evaluation of future customer desires	Broad consumer electronics; TV cameras; computer components
NEC	Japan	PABX; Semiconductors	Semiconductor technology	Telecommunications products (mobile phones, faxes, etc). Lap-top computers; office automation
Toyota	Japan	Cars	Flexible manufacturing; quality control	Geographical expansion

Source: Coates, Charles (1994) *The Total Manager*

as in Marks & Spencers' inspired move from clothes retailing to selling a narrow line of up-market foods. The core competences of buying and merchandising, branding, stock management and customer care were reinforced by the diversification, even though at the time it seemed to many observers an odd move. See also ANSOFF MATRIX.

DIVERSIFICATION

2. Investment diversification is the process of spreading risk by buying a number of different assets. Analysis of share diversification suggests

that this sort of risk reduction can be achieved by buying as few as 15 shares (provided they have a reasonably low beta coefficient).

DOG

1. Bad business, candidate for disposal. 2. Term invented by BCG to describe a company's low relative market share businesses (i.e. those that are not market leaders) in low-growth markets (those growing at less than 10 per cent per annum). BCG originally said that dogs (which it called 'pets' in the early days) were unlikely to be very cash positive or to be capable of being driven to market leadership; dogs should therefore be sold or closed. Since a majority of nearly all firms' businesses are dogs, this advice is draconian indeed, and was later soft-pedalled by BCG. Dogs are in fact often quite cash positive, especially if they are STRONG FOLLOWERS (i.e. not very much smaller than the market leader). It is also untrue that dogs cannot be driven to market leadership (i.e. become CASH COWS). though this is less usual than for followers in high growth markets (QUESTION-MARKS). See GROWTH/SHARE MATRIX and MARKET CHALLENGER.

DOMINANT FIRM

One that has a RELATIVE MARKET SHARE well above that of competitors in a particular market. There is no accepted definition of how much larger a firm should be to be considered dominant, but it should be at least double the size of the next largest competitor (i.e., have a relative market share of at least 2), and probably be at least four times as large. A dominant firm should be highly profitable.

DOOM LOOP

Consultantese for vicious circle. A doom loop is a self-reinforcing downward spiral that follows from inadequate response to competitor initiatives. Illustration 3.28 shows a typical doom loop. Doom loops are easier to describe than to correct, so the first priority must be to avoid getting in one in the first place, which requires continual effort to upgrade the customer product proposition and service and to improve the efficiency of the DELIVERY SYSTEM. Once in a doom loop, the only

Illustration 3.28
Example of Doom Loop for firm XYZ

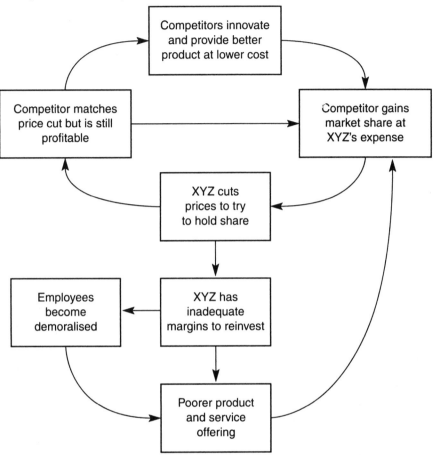

way out is to do something quite radical, usually involving a major re-focus of the firm on a smaller number of businesses and a fundamental change in the firm's CULTURE and way of conducting itself. Existing top management can almost never escape from a doom loop if it affects the firm's most important business.

ECONOMIES OF SCALE

Reduction in unit costs through having greater scale. One of the main reasons why the high market share competitor has lower costs than the smaller player. Economies of scale can cease to operate (or more precisely, are thought incorrectly to exist) when additional revenue is not exactly of the same type, that is, requires additional cost. See COSTS OF COMPLEXITY.

ECONOMIES OF SCOPE

Economies that come from having a broad product line that can utilise the same skills or cost infrastructure. Relies upon cost sharing between two different lines of business. Even if such sharing is not perfect, that is, only part of the costs can be shared, the importance of economies of scope may outweigh economies of scale. For example, the supplier of product A may have 100 units and an average cost of $10, and a smaller supplier of product A may have only 50 units and an average cost of $12. This means that the larger supplier has economies of scale, the smaller supplier suffers diseconomies of scale. But assume that the smaller supplier now enters two other markets, producing 100 units of product B and 100 units of product C. Assume also that products B and C each manage to share half of their costs with product A. The smaller supplier of product A now has economies of scope, and his unit costs for producing A will effectively be based on 150 units equivalent of A (the 50 actual units of A, and half of the 200 units of B and C, giving a total scale for cost sharing purposes equivalent to 150 units of A). The economies of scope mean that the smaller player in the A market can have lower costs even in that market: in the example above, the economies of scope may reduce the unit cost from $12 to $9.

Economies of scope only exist if there is genuine cost sharing and if there are no additional, hidden costs (such as additional supervision or overhead) required by having a broader product line. See COSTS OF COMPLEXITY.

EIGHTY/TWENTY RULE, 80/20 RULE

The Pareto rule, that 80 per cent of sales or profits or any other variable may come from 20 per cent of the products. Can clearly be looked at empirically in any case, and usually one of the most valuable simple steps to understanding any business. Invented by Alfredo Pareto, the nineteenth century economist. Looked at in retrospect, many of the major insights of business in the last half century are derived from the Pareto principle, including BCG's focus on those few high relative market share businesses that generate most of the cash for a company, the insight that COSTS OF COMPLEXITY derive from too extensive a product range, and that therefore maximum use should be made of out-sourcing, as well as the movement to rationalise stock-holding, restrict the numbers of SKUs (Stock Holding Units), and conduct ABC analy-sis of true profitability. The 80/20 rule applies to individuals as well: 80 per cent of the value you provide in your job may come from 20 per cent of your time, so if you delegated the activities that take the remain-ing 80 per cent of your time to a lower cost or less experienced person (or stopped doing them altogether), you could multiply your impact up to five times. For both firms and individuals, some of the low-value 80 per cent may actually have negative value. Perhaps firms should legis-late that all of their people spend at least 15 minutes a week contemplating the 80/20 rule.

EXPECTED VALUE

The weighted average expectation as to what an investment will be worth or what any other outcome (revenues, profits, etc.) will be. Usually calculated by constructing various scenarios and weighting them according to probability. For example, if I think there is a 10 per cent chance of selling an asset (usually at a specified future date) for £3m, a 50 per cent chance of selling it for £4m, and a 40 per cent chance of selling it for £5m, its expected value is £4.3m (0.1 × £3m + 0.5 × £4m + 0.4 × £5m). The expected value is not necessarily or even normally the most probable outcome (£4m in this case) but is the weighted average expectation. Expected value is sometimes guestimated without resorting to a formal calculation.

FASHIONISE

To pursue a 'fashionising' strategy, launching many new products and getting them to market quickly, segmenting the customer base repeat-edly, and moulding the organisation so that it can respond quickly to customers, by DELAYERING, using taskforces, partnering with outside firms, and pushing down decision-making to small, entrepreneurial units positioned as close to the customer as possible.

FIRST MOVER ADVANTAGE

The (usually correct) idea that the first into a market, the innovator, has an opportunity to stay ahead of competition, provided that the first mover builds in as much customer value as possible, lowers costs aggressively, and pursues a low-price policy rather than maximising short term profits. See price umbrella for an explanation of how the opposite often happens, and innovation.

FLAT ORGANISATION

One with relatively few levels, like the Roman Catholic Church (only five levels). Work by HAMPDEN-TURNER and TROMPENAARS has shown that managers from different countries describe their organisations with different degrees of flatness, as shown in Illustration 3.29.

This display should make one pause before asserting that flatter is better: it may be in many Western countries, but Japan, Hong Kong and Singapore has hierarchical structures that work well. Hampden-Turner and Trompenaars explain the paradox by these countries' having 'Organic Ordering' mechanisms: they are hierarchical, but they are also 'integrating', where knowledge flows *up* the hierarchy and where each level is harmonised effectively with the layer immediately above and immediately below. Western hierarchies operate in reverse, where orders and initiatives flow from top to bottom. Organic ordering allows the organisation to be close to the customer and may actually speed up the process of operating effectively in knowledge-intensive industries such as electronics. Flatter may only be better, therefore, in the Western paradigm, where knowledge has difficulty percolating up a steep structure. See *The Seven Cultures of Capitalism* by the two authors referred to: a brilliantly original and thought-provoking work.

FOCUS

One of the fundamental principles of strategy: preached with passion by Bruce HENDERSON since 1964, no less relevant today, and only a little less neglected. Smaller firms in particular must focus on a small number of BUSINESS SEGMENTS where they can be the largest. Even most large companies could raise their profits and market value by a

Illustration 3.29
Company triangles

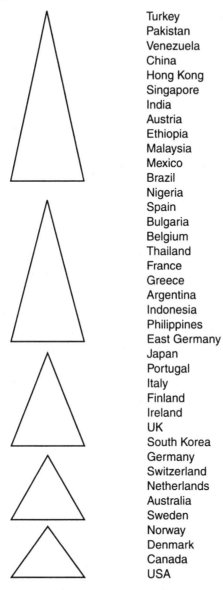

Turkey
Pakistan
Venezuela
China
Hong Kong
Singapore
India
Austria
Ethiopia
Malaysia
Mexico
Brazil
Nigeria
Spain
Bulgaria
Belgium
Thailand
France
Greece
Argentina
Indonesia
Philippines
East Germany
Japan
Portugal
Italy
Finland
Ireland
UK
South Korea
Germany
Switzerland
Netherlands
Australia
Sweden
Norway
Denmark
Canada
USA

tighter focus on the things they do best and most profitably. A good example of focus and tenacity is provided by Sharp, who stuck to exploiting liquid crystal technology in electronic calculators and concentrated all its efforts on making them as slim as possible. In 1975 there were 45 competitors; today Sharp is one of two dominant producers, largely as a result of superior focus.

GLOBALISATION, GLOBALIZATION

1. The process whereby global tastes and product offerings converge and are increasingly satisfied by global products rather than local ones. **2**. Also used to indicate something much more significant and far reaching. Few real global products exist, but globalisation is a reality for most of the world's largest companies, in the sense that they think and operate with a global perspective on customers, technology, costs, sourcing, strategic alliances and competitors. The market for these firms' products is wherever there are affluent consumers or significant industrial customers; the firms must appeal to their customers wherever they are, regardless of borders, the firm's nationality (an increasingly tenuous concept) or where its factories are. Globalisation is driven by hard economics: to compete effectively firms have to incur high fixed costs (for R&D, development of technology, sales and distribution networks, brand building and so on), forcing executives to spread these costs over higher volumes, which means trying to gain market share in all important world economies. New technologies also get dispersed globally very quickly, so that innovators must exploit their property on a global scale, if necessary by means of strategic alliances, or see it adopted and adapted by competitors. Global competition has accelerated sharply. Between 1987 and 1992, US direct investment outside the US rose 35 per cent to $776 billion, while the value of foreign direct investment into the US more than doubled, to $692 billion.

These trends do not require product universalism: product localisation is necessary for global success in most businesses. Some observers, such as Kenichi OHMAE, believe that the economic thrust of globalisation is irresistible and will cast aside conventional views of national politics, macro-economics, trade and citizenship. See also GLOBAL LOCALISATION, GLOCALISATION, multilocals, OHMAE and ILE **3**. Ability to carry out financial transactions on an international basis (in London, New York, Tokyo etc.) around the clock.

GLOBAL LOCALISATION

Sony catch-phrase where a GLOBAL PRODUCT is adapted to local tastes by low cost customisation. Has the advantages of low cost but somewhat differentiated product. May also involve use or creation of a local distribution network peculiar to one country or region. For example, Coca-Cola's success in Japan was due both to setting up its own route salesforces and to the rapid introduction of many products sold only in Japan. For most markets, the quest for the holy grail of a global product will fail; global localisation is a much surer route to success.

GLOCALISATION OF ORGANISATIONS

Contraction of 'global localisation' and a very useful word, describing an escalating process. Glocalisation aims at making the organisation everywhere responsive to customers, who may themselves be global, and insists that the organisation be structured in the way that makes it as easy as possible for the global customer to deal with. An important by-product of this approach is elimination of operational duplication and often dramatic reductions in management numbers and cost. The opportunity for organisational standardisation worldwide in large organisations is enormous. Standardisation alone usually reduces overhead by 20 per cent by eliminating administrative confusion on an international scale. Chief executives need to insist on the standardisation of organisations and roles worldwide in order to remove the heavy, hidden costs of complexity and confusion. European companies find this both harder to achieve, and more rewarding when accomplished, than US or Japanese companies, because the European firms are more likely to exhibit corporate federalism and feudalism and therefore huge local autonomy and diversity.

GODS OF MANAGEMENT

Four cultural types defined by Charles HANDY in the book of the same name. Strikingly original formulation of truths immediately recognisable by those who have worked in organisations. For a description of each god, see ATHENA (task culture), APOLLO (role culture), DIONYSUS (professional culture) and ZEUS (patron culture).

HARVESTING

Deliberate or unintentional running down of a business and its market share position in order to extract short term profit: 'selling' market share. Harvesting can result from a number of policies: holding or raising prices higher than competitors, not reinvesting in marketing and selling effort or in new equipment, or by stopping advertising. Such steps could result in a short term increase in profits but the competitive position of the business will be weakened and with loss of market share it will end up as a smaller business which may not even be viable in the medium term. Harvesting may happen without management being aware of it: reinvestment does not occur because it 'cannot be afforded', and market share is gradually lost without management realising, or, if they do realise, without them connecting it to the failure to invest as much as competitors.

Harvesting as a deliberate strategy is not much practised, and for good reason: you cannot tell how fast market share will be lost, and the business can disappear into an irreversible DOOM LOOP much faster than expected. Harvesting can be a very rewarding tactic, however, if it is intended to sell a business within a year or so. The final year's profits can be significantly boosted, and the buyer may apply a normal PE Ratio to buy the business without realising that it is losing market share and that the current profits are not sustainable.

Harvesting, like so many other concepts, was the invention of the Boston Consulting Group. See BCG MATRIX.

ILE, Inter-Linked Economy

Kenichi OHMAE's phrase for the 'borderless' economy comprising the US, Europe and Japan (the triad), and increasingly taking in aggressive, outward-looking economies such as Korea, Taiwan, Hong Kong and Singapore. The economy embraces much more than trade, being a complex network of corporate inter-dependencies led by the world's largest companies (which used to be called multinationals but are now more accurately described as multilocals). The ILE comprises a billion people, mainly affluent consumers, and most of the world's wealth is created and consumed in the ILE. See OHMAE, GLOBALISATION and GLOBAL LOCALISATION.

INSIDERISATION, INSIDERIZATION

1. Kenichi OHMAE's term for the process of replicating or re-creating a home-country business system in a new national market, adapting the

system to the new market's unique characteristics. The classic example is Coca-Cola's innovation in Japan when confronted with the multi-layered distribution system for soft drinks. Coke organised local bottlers to create a national network of Coke vans distributing bottles and collecting empties, driven by a new Coke national salesforce. The company thus became a fully paid-up 'insider', and was able to use its distribution network to sell a variety of soft drinks as well as Coke. Insiderisation means taking the trouble to understand and develop a local market rather than imposing a model based on 'home' market characteristics; it is an important method of GLOBAL LOCALISATION. **2.** The process of making outsiders to an organisation in some sense insiders, by sharing information with them and encouraging them to identify with the firm.

KEIRETSU

Literally, a 'headless combine', and one of the most important secret weapons of Japanese industry. An economic grouping of many firms organised around trading companies and/or banks. These groups originated from the Zaibatsu, the large and in many cases centuries-old groups of industrial and financial holding companies. Keiretsu are their descendants, and involve intricate cross-holdings of shares, where a bank will hold shares in all commercial companies, and the latter will own shares in each other. Examples include Dai Ichi Kangyo, Fuyo, Mitsui, Mitsubishi, Sanwa and the Sumitomo group.

Keiretsu are organised on the basis of common loyalty, reciprocity and complementarity. They collaborate to help members maximise their market shares, particular in the case of 'front line' companies competing on a global scale. They help procure cheap raw materials, share technology, raise and enforce quality standards, share market intelligence, and provide mutual financial support. They can pool resources to help the front line company win: Chrysler competes not with Mazda, but with the combined might of the Sumitomo group, which is willing to forego short term profit for market share gain. Technology sharing is perhaps the most important single benefit.

Not all Japanese firms belong to keiretsu: Canon, Sony and Toyota do not, for example. Even in these cases, however, the mentality of the keiretsu is evident: they collaborate with partners inside and outside Japan to develop new technologies and improve quality standards.

KEY FACTORS FOR SUCCESS (KFS)

The reasons why some firms are more successful than others in particular products or industries. Should be based on an in-depth understanding of why consumers buy the products concerned, as a spur to re-segmentation and/or innovation. See SEGMENTATION.

KNOWLEDGE MANAGEMENT STRUCTURE (KMS)

Concept put forward by Tom PETERS as a development of the LEARNING ORGANISATION. The 'new' firm must destroy bureaucracy but needs to nurture knowledge and skill, building expertise in ways that enhance the power of market-scale units, and that encourage those units to contribute knowledge for the benefit of the firm as a whole. This is a matter of shared values, feeling part of a family, and big travel budgets! McKinsey and Goldman Sachs are examples of firms operating KMSs, but the concept is applicable to all corporations, not just professional service firms.

LEADING INDICATOR

Early signal that something is about to happen. Noah's dove was a leading indicator that the flood was over. Market share gains can be a leading indicator of higher profits, even if these are currently depressed by the investments to gain market share.

LEAKAGES

Customers or customer segments that leak away from particular suppliers because the right product or service is not being provided; loss of revenue as a result. Very often a firm tries to find new customers without applying the same energy to the even more important task of retaining existing customers. See CUSTOMER RETENTION.

LEAN ENTERPRISE

Catch-phrase describing re-engineered companies that have five attributes: (1) they embrace a cluster of cross-functional processes; (2) they include close relationships with suppliers, distributors and customers to enhance value continually – the 'extended enterprise'; (3) they have a core of defined expertise; (4) functional areas like design, engineering, marketing, procurement, personnel and accounting should still exist, but be schools of learning and skill-bases that different teams in the firm can draw on; (5) careers should alternate between membership of multi-functional teams and time spent building up skill within particular functions or departments. Honda has used this alternating approach successfully both in Japan and the US.

LEARNING ORGANISATION

Term first used by Chris Argyris to mean a firm that learns as it goes along, adjusting its way of doing business very responsively. The organisation retains knowledge independently of its employees. All organisations are in fact learning organisations – they all have a CULTURE based in one way or another on their experience – but some are better than others in taking the rights lessons from experience and in changing accordingly. See also Tom PETERS' preferred concept of the KNOWLEDGE MANAGEMENT STRUCTURE.

MAKE OR BUY DECISION

1. The decision on whether to make components or any other part of the product or service in-house, or whether to use outside suppliers (the latter being called outsourcing). 'Make or buy' has long been a topic of debate, but it is becoming increasingly important. It can now determine relative profitability in an industry, as in computers. 2. Igor ANSOFF used 'make or buy' to mean organic expansion versus expansion by acquisition.

Charles Coates, an expert on manufacturing strategy, believes that a key condition of competitive advantage is that firms focus only on those activities that are critical to its proposition and where it has distinctive COMPETENCES, and outsource all other components and activities. In practice this means a great deal more outsourcing than most firms currently use. The reason outsourcing is so valuable is that the COSTS OF COMPLEXITY are crippling for a firm engaged in many activities. In some cases this complexity is not avoidable, but in most it is, via outsourcing.

Coates says that make/buy policy should follow three rules:

(1) Divide all components into 'critical' and 'non-critical'. Critical components are those that are key to the firm's competitive advantage, where it can undertake them to a quality standard and cost that is second to none. 'Critical components are those upon which delivery of the key attributes of the firm's proposition depend. They may include components which incur a high proportion of total cost, those that require specialised skills, high quality levels or quick response that outside suppliers could not match, or those that have proprietary technology that the firm must protect.' All critical components must be made in-house. It does not follow, however, that all non-critical components should be outsourced: a further rule is required.

(2) Outsource all non-critical components where suppliers have an advantage through greater focus and lower cost.

(3) For non-critical components where suppliers do not have an advantage, make them but manage the production of critical and non-critical components separately, and be ready to switch to outsourcing the latter if a low cost specialist emerges.

In the computer industry, make/buy decisions are now the most important in determining success. Coates showed that in 1991 there was a clear correlation between higher profits and higher outsourcing (Illustration 3.30).

Major established suppliers like IBM make many of their parts, including disk drives and processors. Recent entrants like Dell assemble products in leased factories and outsource all their parts. IBM's investment went into production, Dell's into an effective purchasing network and into sales and service training, focussing particularly on the quality and productivity of its telesales people.

MANAGERIALISM, THE MANAGEMENT THEORY OF THE FIRM, THE MANAGERIAL HERESY

Very important view that given absentee landlords in the form of institutional investors, power in corporations falls to the senior managers, who may advance their own interests rather than those of the owners. Evidence that the managerial theory has a strong element of truth can be seen in any or all of the following: valuing turnover growth even without profit growth; reluctance to sell non-core companies or

Illustration 3.30
Profitability in the Computer Industry (1991)

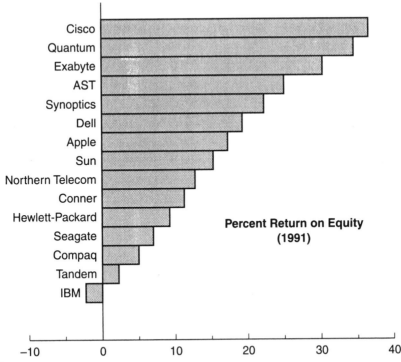

de-merge, leaving a smaller company; reluctance to outsource to the proper extent; a preference for acquisition rather than disposal, or than being acquired; large perquisites for executives, so that you would need a massive income to have an equivalent lifestyle if outside the firm and paying tax; executive jets, chartered planes, or, if times are hard and you have to slum it by flying on a commercial airline, first class travel, which almost nobody can afford if required to pay for oneself; retreats in expensive hotels; hospitality trips (at which the British excel) to Ascot, Wimbledon, Henley, Cheltenham, Glyndebourne, Covent Garden, and all the other delights of the season; paying top executives a very high multiple of average employee or lowest employee pay; increasing top executive pay above the rate of inflation, or when profits fall; granting oneself large share options, which give a free ride when the stock market goes up, regardless of the performance of the company itself; and generally ensuring that one has a pleasant lifestyle and interesting work, regardless of what the corporate priorities are. None of these activities advances the interest of shareholders, or of the firm as a whole. Who says that the managerial heresy is dead?

MARKET CHALLENGER

STRONG FOLLOWER in market share terms: companies that are not far behind the market leader in a particular product or service. The term is not wholly satisfactory, because it implies that the second or third player is gaining relative market share on the leader and challenging him. The term strong follower does not carry this implication, and is reserved for a RELATIVE MARKET SHARE of at least 0.7x, that is, at least 70 per cent the size of the leader. Neither term is widely used, hence the neglect of DOGS that may have potential. See DOGS.

MARKETISING

The process of turning cost centres into profit centres, making them respond to an internal or external market.

MAVERICK

An unconventional competitor, often a newcomer to the market, who does not respect the rules of the game, but writes his own rules. Excellent examples are Apple (revolutionising the computer business by developing very powerful PCs) and IKEA (the Swedish furniture retailer that made this a business susceptible to international scale and a new division of labour between customer and supplier: see DELIVERY SYSTEM for more on IKEA). It is very difficult for established competitors to cope with mavericks: all the familiar levers for dealing with competitors do no good. When considering market entry, a good question is: is there scope for being a maverick here? If not, enter another market, unless there is very high sharing of cost or know-how in the new market.

M-FORM ORGANISATION

Originally used by Oliver Williamson in *Markets and Hierarchies* (1975) to mean a multi-divisional enterprise. More recently a book by Bill

Ouchi called *The M-form Society* described Japanese corporations as forming multidivisional companies around a common central core of technology. M-form companies include Fujitsu, Honda, Hitachi, Matsushita, Mitsubishi, Nippon Electric, Toshiba, Sharp, and Sony. For example, Matsushita has a common technological 'learning core' that feeds into seven different divisions (consumer electronics, home appliances, lighting equipment, system/media products, business machines and electronic components). There are examples of M-forms in the West, including IBM, ICI, Apple, DEC and Philips, but in general there is a greater proportion of technology located in the divisions than in the Japanese M-form, and technological know-how tends to ooze around the divisions rather less luxuriantly. The West also has far more pure CONGLOMERATES, where there is common ownership but few or no operating links between the divisions or companies. The M-form is clearly superior at utilising technology.

MISSION

What a company is for; why it exists; its role in the world. This is an enormously important issue. A majority of US and UK companies now have formal mission statements; but a big distinction must be made between such documents and the company having a real mission, or 'sense of mission'. Most companies that have mission statements do not have a sense of mission: the document is propaganda, or at best well intended pabulum, but not what most people in the organisation believe. Yet some firms like Marks & Spencer that clearly have a sense of mission, do not have mission statements.

A sense of mission is essential if employees are to believe in their company. They have to think that the company is there to achieve something.

The concept of mission and 'sense of mission' covers all aspects of the firm's sense of direction and the way in which its members behave: there must be a consistent pattern that runs through all aspects of the firm's personality. The most useful way of thinking about this is the Ashridge Mission Model, which describes four parameters of mission: purpose, values, strategy and behaviour standards, as shown in Illustration 3.31.

The model can be illustrated by two examples of very different companies and mission. First Hanson, which is highly unusual in actually believing in shareholder value, rather than just making motherhood statements about it (Illustration 3.32).

The second example is Hewlett-Packard, a decentralised corporation with very different values to Hanson, but a similarly consistent sense of mission (Illustration 3.33).

Why does it matter that employees believe in their company? Well, most would rather work for a company they can believe in. A company that can be believed in will attract the best available recruits, and keep them. It will get the most out of its people, both as individuals and in teams. It will be respected by customers and investors. It will learn, renew itself, and become more powerful, while still having the ethic of service to others. It will gain market share, and have the best long term profitability, and the highest market rating.

All in all, it is quite important. Unfortunately, though most Western firms have mission statements, few have a sense of mission. Though precise data are not available, the best estimates are that 10 per cent of large UK firms, 20 per cent of US, but 50 per cent of Japanese, have a sense of mission. Clearly there is a great deal of need for TRANSFORMATION.

Illustration 3.31
The Ashridge Mission Model

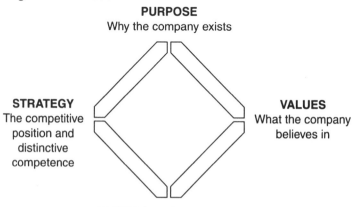

PURPOSE
Why the company exists

STRATEGY
The competitive
position and
distinctive
competence

VALUES
What the company
believes in

BEHAVIOUR STANDARDS
The policies and behaviour patterns that underpin the
distinctive competence and the value system

Illustration 3.32
A Summary of Hanson's Mission

PURPOSE
The shareholder is king.
Think of the pensioner living off
her investments

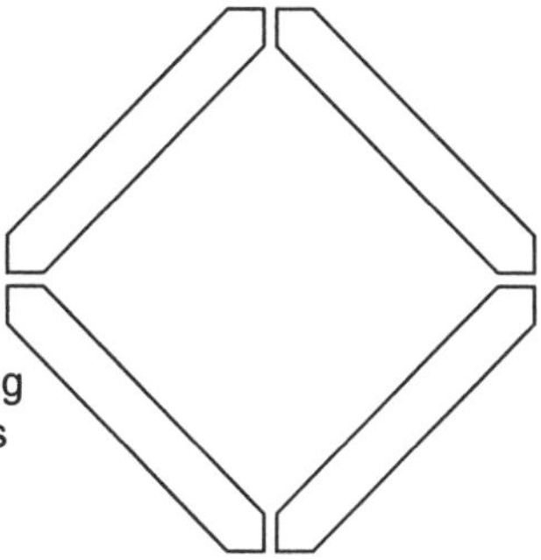

STRATEGY
- Better financial discipline
- Knowledge of cash cows
- Skill at buying and breaking
  up poor-performing groups
- Better operators

VALUES
- Individual responsibility
- Autonomy and
  accountability
- Efficiency is good
- Victorian work ethic

BEHAVIOUR STANDARDS
- Budgets must be met
- Managers work hard
- Keep businesses simple
- Decentralise
- Focus on short-term
  financial performance

Illustration 3.33
Hewlett-Packard's Mission

PURPOSE
Be respected by our customers,
our people and society

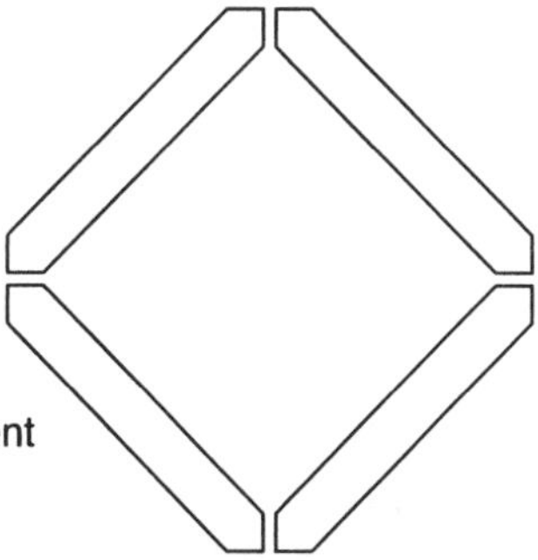

STRATEGY
- Better people, better
  motivated
- Engineering excellence
- New product development
- Best after-sales service

VALUES
- Good people need space
- Informality is good
- Creativity is a human
  being's ultimate purpose
- Caring is good
- Borrowing is weak

BEHAVIOUR STANDARDS
- Management by objectives
- MBWA
- Open door
- Team work
- Communication
- No borrowing

MOP UP STRATEGY

Consolidating an industry by gaining market share at the expense of smaller competitors and/or buying them up, usually in a so-called declining industry. Almost always a good strategy.

PIMS (PROFIT IMPACT OF MARKET STRATEGY)

A co-operative database originating from research by GE in the US that collects data from member firms about market share, profitability, and a variety of other variables (like R&D spend) that might be expected to influence profits. The data is confidential but aggregate results are fed back to members so that they can see how to raise profits. Some of the research has been published and demonstrated beyond reasonable doubt that high market share correlates with high profits, though there are significant industry variations. Two problems with the approach are that it accepts the firm's own segment definitions, which may not correctly describe business segmentation or be sufficiently disaggregated; and that it pays insufficient attention to relative market share. See RMS and OPPORTUNITY/VULNERABILITY MATRIX.

POSITIONING

Finding a marketing position for a product or a company that differentiates it from competitors and occupies a 'slot in the brain'. This may be entirely emotional and subjective rather than defined by product or verifiable criteria. For example, British Airways was repositioned as 'the world's favourite airline' to let travellers know that the cabin crew no longer bit their heads off or ignored them. An interesting positioning technique for a new entrant or a follower is to draw a veiled contrast with the market leader, as in Avis' successful slogan 'We're Number Two. We Try Harder', or 'Carlsberg, probably the best lager in the world', as opposed to the biggest or the strongest. Positioning is partly a matter of understanding the most appropriate battleground for a product, but it is also a highly creative process of identifying vacant ground and finding an emotionally warm pitch. Positioning is far more art than science.

PRICE UMBRELLA

Colourful term meaning a high general price level in an industry or product, held over all competitors to stop the rain of competition spoiling anyone's day. Although it leads to short term profits, it is usually a mistake for the market leader to hold out a price umbrella, as it prevents more marginal competitors exiting the business and makes it possible for them to build up experience and lower their costs, thus becoming more viable. See OPPORTUNITY/VULNERABILITY MATRIX.

PRICING STRATEGY

1. Setting prices in order to gain a long term competitive advantage, rather than to maximise short term profits. There are three main rules: (1) in introducing a product, price at or below cost in order to gain volume, cut costs, and deter competitors; (2) in fighting competition, especially when the market is still growing, consider sudden, startlingly short price cuts, so that the price is immediately perceived as low by the consumer, and as too low to be matched by competitors; and (3) ensure that the true costs of all products are known, including all overhead costs, and that the more complex, special products are not under-priced and the standard, high-volume products under-priced. See EXPERIENCE CURVE, AVERAGE COSTING, AVERAGE PRICING and BCG MATRIX. **2**. More broadly, the major decisions made on pricing.

QUESTION-MARK

A firm's position in a business segment where the market is growing fast (expected future volume growth of 10 per cent or more per annum) but the firm is a follower, that is, has a RELATIVE MARKET SHARE of less than 1.0x. One of the four positions on the BCG MATRIX. Unlike two of the others, very well named: there is a real question about such businesses that must be faced up to. Should the corporation invest a lot of cash and management talent to try to drive that business to a leading position, hence becoming a STAR (high market growth, high relative market share) and eventually a much bigger and highly positive CASH COW? Or should the business be sold for a high price earnings ratio, because people pay highly for 'growth' businesses without usually thinking too hard about the relative market share position? There is another option, which is usually taken, and usually wrong: putting *some* cash into the business but not enough to drive it to a leading position. The BCG theory and observation both lead to the conclusion that this will tend to give a poor return on the cash invested: the business will eventually become a dog, and though it may throw off rather more cash in this state than the original BCG theory, it is unlikely to show a very good return (IRR) on the cash invested.

So is it to be investment to drive to leadership, or a quick and lucrative sale? It depends, of course, on the sums of cash involved, but particularly on whether you think leadership is attainable at acceptable cost. And then it depends on the reaction of the current leader, who has the STAR position: he ought to defend it to the death, but may not. Getting into this kind of battle is unpredictable and like playing poker: once started, you have to keep upping the ante to persuade your opponent that you will win in the end; and if you are to cut your losses at any stage, you had better do it early. What is the size of your pot of cash compared to his? The strength of your hand versus his is also very important: do you have the knack of satisfying customers better or higher quality or better people or better technology or just greater will power and commitment, or preferably all of the above?

Star positions are enormously valuable once obtained and defended. But most attempts to back question-marks fail to turn them into stars. Unless you are determined to win and have a better than evens chance, sale is usually the option that will better enhance shareholder wealth. As a shareholder you had better hope that the latter consideration weighs more heavily with the management than wanting to stay in a glamorous growth business.

RCR, RELATIVE CUSTOMER RETENTION

How well a firm retains its customers relative to its competitors. A key influence on relative profitability. See CUSTOMER RETENTION.

RE-COMPETE

To change the basis of competition in an industry, to change the rules of the game, to find a new and more effective way of competing, to invent a whole new way of doing business that gives a new competitor a place in the sun and superior profitability.

One early example of re-competing was Georg Siemens' invention in 1870 of the first universal bank (Deutsche Bank) with a mission to unite and industrialise Germany. In the same decade, Mitsubishi was established as the first important Japanese multinational, on the principle we now know as the M-FORM ORGANISATION.

Another early example was Henry Ford's invention, at the start of the twentieth century, of the mass-produced automobile. After the First World War, Marks & Spencer changed the nature of clothes retailing by (1) intervening to design and commission clothes rather than just buy them and (2) creating a mass-market that spanned previously inviolate class barriers.

In the early 1950s, IBM replaced Univac as leader of the emergent computer industry by changing the rules of the game, manufacturing (rather than hand-crafting) multi-purpose machines. In the last 20 years, Apple 're-competed' by basing itself purely on Personal Computers, developing a symbiotic relationship with emergent software suppliers like Lotus and Microsoft.

Other recent examples include Direct Line insurance, First Direct banking (and other telephone- and computer-based banks without a branch network), Kwik-fit and Midas car service centres and IKEA (in furniture retailing).

Re-competing is discussed in detail on pages 67–8 above.

RIGHT FIRST TIME

The idea that goods should not need to be inspected for quality, because the objective should be to build quality in and ensure that all product is of high quality the first (and only) time round.

SBU (STRATEGIC BUSINESS UNIT)

A profit centre within a firm that is organised as an autonomous unit and that corresponds roughly to one particular market. SBUs originated in the 1970s and have proved popular since then. The story of how they came about is interesting. SBUs began in 1970 when Fred Borch, head of the American GE, decided to decentralise, abolish or curtail staff functions, and reorganise on the basis of stand-alone SBUs. GE set up the following criteria required for a group to be a pukka SBU:

- *An SBU must have an external, rather than an internal, market: must have a set of external customers.*
- *It should have a clear set of external competitors it is trying to beat.*

- *It should have control over its own destiny: decide what products to offer, how to obtain supplies, and whether or not to use shared corporate resources like R&D.*
- *It must be a profit centre, with performance measured by its profits.*

The move to SBUs in GE and other Western countries has on the whole been positive. The drawback with an SBU structure is that it does not encourage (though it does not prevent) full use of the common skill base and technology that a corporation may have. The SBU structure is not well equipped to deal with the challenge of Japanese companies who not only draw fully on common internal skills derived from and serving a variety of products, but also benefit from each others' skills in an interlocking way. See M-FORM ORGANISATION and KEIRETSU.

SEGMENT RETREAT

Policy of retiring from a particular market segment, conceding it to competitors, and focussing on other segments. Tends to be a continuous, sad process. One classic example is the UK motorcycle industry in the early 1970s which, faced with the onslaught of Japanese competition, retreated first of all from the small bikes segment, then the mid-bikes segment, so that it was left at the 'high end' of large and super-bikes. The problem was that the Japanese advanced just as the British retreated, and, given the high shared component cost between the segments, Japanese dominance in the lower end product eventually fed dominance in all segments. If pursuing a strategy of segment retreat, it is essential to build solid barriers against the advance, or the retreat will turn into a rout.

SHAMROCK, SHAMROCK ORGANISATION

A form of organisation described by Charles HANDY using the Irish national emblem, a three-leaved clover. According to Handy, today's organisation is increasingly like a shamrock, made up of three distinct but interlocking parts. The first leaf represents the CORE WORKERS or professional core, the people who hold the knowledge of the organisation and are essential to its success. The core must be looked after and treated as partners, but this is expensive, so the answer is to have a much more selective and smaller core, and rely increasingly for less essential input on the other two 'leaves' of the shamrock. The second leaf is the contractual fringe: specialists outside the organisation who are experts in a particular part of the work and have a close relationship with the firm, but who are not on its payroll. All work which need not be performed in-house should therefore be contracted out to lower cost specialists. The third leaf of the shamrock is the flexible labour force, part-time and temporary workers who come and go as required, and are an increasing proportion of the total. Many of this third group will not want full-time employment, and will be young, female or 'retired'. The organisation may invest in some elements of the flexible labour force, for example by giving training and some privileges, but this third tranche of labour will never have the commitment or ambition of the core. Handy believes that the shamrock organisation has increased, is increasing, and ought to be further increased, with a realisation that each part of the shamrock needs to be treated differently. Eventually the dominance of the shamrock organisation could change accepted patterns of behaviour, abolishing traditional views about work and career, leading many more people to take a portfolio of different sorts of work, significantly reducing the incidence of wasteful commuting, and making only a minority of people, the highly motivated professional core, really committed to their companies. This last group, however, must really believe in what the organisation does and be zealots for it.

There is no doubt that this is the wave of the future.

SHAREHOLDER VALUE, SHAREHOLDER WEALTH

Phrase often used to mean what is in shareholders' interests, as in 'create shareholder value'. Often means 'get the share price as high as sustainably possible', and includes a sense of medium and long term value creation rather than short term share price maximisation (or manipulation). Generally not a neutral term: the users tend to imply that the main or exclusive responsibility of top management is to maximise shareholder value rather than worry about other stakeholders' (e.g. customers' or employees') interests. Most US firms and many UK ones claim that shareholder value is their main objective; few mean it.

STAR

The most exciting of the four positions on the BCG MATRIX. A star is a business which is the market leader (has the highest relative market share) in a high growth business (generally over 10 per cent per annum anticipated future volume growth rate in the next 3–5 years). The star business is immensely valuable if it keeps its leadership position, because the market growth will make it much bigger and because it should be very profitable, having higher prices or lower costs than lower market share competitors. The star business may not yet be very cash positive, in fact the usual expectation is that it will be broadly cash neutral, since although it earns a lot of profits it will require reinvestment in new facilities and working capital to continue to grow. But when the market growth slows, if the leadership position has been successfully defended, the business will become a large CASH COW and provide a high proportion of cash for the whole business portfolio.

It is said that there are three policy rules for looking after stars: 'invest, invest and invest'. Almost no investment is too great; whatever the financial projections say, any investment is likely to show an excellent return. The worst possible thing to happen to stars is that they lose their leadership position to someone else's QUESTION-MARK (which then becomes the new star, relegating the erstwhile star to the position of a question-mark and eventually, as growth slows, a DOG). If leadership is lost, the cash previously invested in building up the (former) star may never be recovered, and for all the glamour the business would have proved a cash trap. Hence the necessity to invest to hold the star's leadership position, and if possible further extend it, so that competitors can never catch up. This may require very rapid growth, perhaps up to 40–50 per cent per annum, which requires skilful management and possibly large amounts of cash.

Star businesses are very rare. But star businesses that are well managed and that keep their leadership positions are even rarer. The model T Ford was once a star, but then lost its leadership position, became a question-mark and eventually a dog. The Xerox range of photocopiers, Kodak cameras, TI (US) semiconductor chips, Du Pont synthetic fibres, Gestetner office machines, and Hilton hotels are all examples of one-time stars that became dogs, and never yielded the anticipated returns to investors. On the other hand, McDonalds hamburger restaurants, the

Sony Walkman, and Coca-Cola are all examples of former stars that held their star status until the market growth slowed, and have since become enormous cash cows and given fantastic returns to shareholders. Filofax is an example of a business that lost its star position in personal organisers (outside the US), but then recovered it again. It is interesting that in all these cases the stock market fortunes of the companies reflected what BCG said would happen, with a time lag. All of these businesses were highly valued by the stock market when they were stars, often on PEs of 50 or over. Those businesses that lost share and ended up as dogs were over-valued and never fulfilled the implied promise; those that held on to leadership amply justified the confidence of investors.

The BCG theory really works, especially in relation to stars. What an irony that BCG almost never uses it these days!

STRATEGIC ALLIANCE

A mutual commitment by two or more independent companies to co-operate together for specific commercial objectives, usually because the cost of development is too high for a single company, and/or because the companies have complementary technologies or competences. A strategic alliance is different from a joint venture in that no legal entity is set up, and the scope of co-operation can be both broader and deeper, despite (or perhaps because of) the absence of tight contractual definitions of the partners' obligations. Strategic alliances can take place between competitors in the same business, as with that of Grundig and Philips to join their video and cordless phone businesses, or co-operation between Honda and Rover (but see below); between particular suppliers and their customers (Marks & Spencer has informal strategic alliances with many of its textile and food suppliers, which date from long before strategic alliances were fashionable, and supplier/customer links are hugely important in Japan: see KEIRETSU); or between different firms that are not competitors but can each use a particular technology in their respective markets, as in the case of the alliance between France Telecom and Deutsche Telecom.

Strategic alliances are already important; they will become one of the major global competitive weapons in the twenty-first century, and could conceivably lead to a new form of corporate organisation then too. But strategic alliances require a long term orientation and appropriate behaviour, the developing and cementing of trust, and above all the will from the top and middle of the partners to make them work. A recent example where a strategic alliance fell down was between Honda and Rover, where the alliance had been working extremely well and to enormous benefit for both parties. Then, in early 1994, British Aerospace, the owner of Rover, decided that it wanted to sell its majority stake in Rover (Honda held 20 per cent). Honda was not prepared to buy the whole of Rover, so British Aerospace sold its stake to give control to BMW. Honda executives were furious and could not believe that their trust would be violated in this way; the top brass at British Aerospace were surprised at the reaction, and believed that they had served their shareholders well. Two mutually uncomprehending cultures collided. Two things are clear: one, that Honda would never have behaved in a comparable way with a strategic partner; and two, that it will be much more difficult in the future for Japanese companies to trust British firms enough to enter strategic alliances with them. Strategic alliances are a passport to success, but the ability to receive passports may be restricted for British firms.

STRATEGIC DEGREES OF FREEDOM (SDF)

The dimensions along which a strategy can be radically re-worked. Kenichi OHMAE insists that the dimensions of product improvement, for example, should not be viewed too narrowly or imitatively. If General Electric has brought out a coffee percolator that makes coffee in ten minutes, its competitors should not aim to bring out one that takes seven minutes. People drink coffee for the taste, but the taste depends most of all on water quality. The strategic degree of freedom here is finding ways to improve the taste via the water quality: and this leads straight to the conclusion that the percolator had to have a de-chlorinating function. See also OHMAE and SEGMENTATION.

STRATEGIC INTENT

The overall medium to long term strategic objective of a company. Like a CAUSE, often expressed in a snappy form, like Henry Ford's aim in 1909 to 'democratise the automobile', Coke's objective of having its drink 'within arm's length of every consumer in the world', or Honda's desire to 'smash Yamaha'; but strategic intent usually has a timeframe of at least ten years, whereas a Cause should be attainable within 2–4 years.

STRONG FOLLOWER

Business that is between 70% and 99% the size of the segment leader. See MARKET CHALLENGER.

SYNERGY

2 + 2 = 5 (or more), rather than 4, or 3 (negative synergy). Usually used in the context of an acquisition: if there is no synergy expected, it is difficult to justify paying a premium for an acquisition; and even if it is a merger with no premium, why bother unless there is some synergy? There is often a great deal of cynicism about the reality of claimed synergies, and the word is certainly overused, but it is a key concept.

There are really two different types of synergy: structural synergy, where the synergy derives from combining resources to lower costs or raise revenues; and management synergy, where the improvement is due to better management, without structural change. Some people only use synergy in the structural sense. Examples are when two salesforces can be combined, saving costs; or when one company's products can be sold through the other's distribution network, both raising revenues and lowering the unit cost of sales. Structural synergy is clearly greatest where two firms are engaged in the same or adjacent products and markets, but where they have different in-going configurations. It is not unusual to see cost reductions of the order of 15–25 per cent or revenue gains of 20–30 per cent as a result of acquisitions pregnant with such structural synergy.

Management synergy exists when an acquiror runs a company better than the previous management, as when a new financial control system is put in to raise returns (as with BTR, Hanson, Tomkins or Williams Holdings), when managers are given greater responsibility and compulsion to meet budgets, when unnecessary costs are cut (without structural synergy), or when non-core businesses are sold to someone else who will pay more than their value to the seller. Management synergy can produce large cost reductions, though more rarely significant revenue increases.

Synergy can also exist independently of acquisitions: for example in joint ventures, in strategic alliances, in closer relationships with suppliers, from realising synergies within an existing group of companies, by getting managers to help each other. Such synergies could be called 'cheap synergies' because they do not involve paying an acquisition premium: they should be looked at before acquisitions. Synergy is any unrealised potential open to a group from mixing and matching resources better.

TRANSFORMATION

Changing an organisation's culture and behaviour, so that it ascends to a new level of financial and market performance. Not surprisingly, transformation is difficult: 75 per cent of all attempts fail. There do seem, however, to be six conditions of successful transformation, which are always present in successful transformations:

(1) They are driven by demanding and inspiring leaders, and one person embodies the transformation ethic.
(2) The top team (those who really run the company) are emotionally united; they are on the same side and want to help each other personally, as well as the firm.
(3) There is a slogan used as a rallying cry: either a medium term CAUSE or a longer term statement of STRATEGIC INTENT.
(4) Baronies are absent or destroyed.
(5) The change process focusses on real business issues, changing attitudes on the back of commercial success. There are simple performance measures so that everyone knows what is expected.
(6) The firm has or builds at least one world class COMPETENCE: a skill where it is as good as or better than any competitor.

TYPE 1, TYPE ONE EXECUTIVE

A very useful typology of people into three types (1, 2 and 3), invented by Harold Leavitt. Type ones are Visionaries: bold, charismatic, original, often eccentric, brilliant and uncompromising, someone who offers a clean break with the past and a new heaven and earth. Historical examples include Jesus Christ, Churchill, Garibaldi, Ghandi, Gladstone, Hitler, John F. Kennedy, the Ayatollah Khomeni, Martin Luther King, and Margaret Thatcher. Type ones have insights and inspire followers, they follow their instincts, led by heart more than head, and they can see the destination so clearly that they are often impractical about the obstacles *en route*. They can be extremely impractical and bad at getting things done.

Understanding whether you (or close colleagues) are type 1, 2 or 3 can be of practical value, for two reasons. First, you should aim to move your job in the direction where the skills of your particular type can be deployed most fully and effectively. Second, you should aim to team up with and rely on close colleagues who exemplify the two types different from your own, to provide a balanced ticket and the skills you lack. See also TYPE 2 and TYPE 3.

TYPE 2, TYPE TWO EXECUTIVE

See TYPE 1. Type 2 executives are Analysts. They deal with numbers and facts, not opinions; they are rationalists, calculators and controllers. They deal in black and white, not grey: there is always a right answer. The analyst par excellence uses numbers and accounting to control a vast empire: to run a financial control company. Examples include Clement Atlee and Sir Owen Green, Robert Macnamara, [Lord] Arnold Weinstock, Harold Geneen, and from further back in history, Pitt the Younger, Sir Robert Peel and Jimmy Carter. Type 2 are great systematisers and control system users. See also TYPE 3.

TYPE 3, TYPE THREE EXECUTIVE

See TYPE 1 and TYPE 2. Type 3 are Doers, successful men of action, implementers, fixers, pragmatists. Generally unencumbered by either vision or analysis, the type 3 leader revels in arm-twisting, lining people up to do his will, leading troops into battle, and all the hurly-burly of business. Historical type threes include Noah, Attila the Hun, Alexander the Great, Julius Caesar, Louis XIV, Napoleon, Bismarck, Lloyd George, Lenin, Stalin, Eisenhower, James Callaghan and Lyndon Johnson. Type 3 need a programme or vision from a type 1 and the calculation of a type 2 as supplements to increase their own effectiveness.

UNBUNDLING

1. When a firm (especially after a takeover) decides to sell off non-core businesses and focus on just one or two core businesses. Sometimes less politely called asset stripping. 2. Process of segmentation whereby customers are offered the chance to buy individual parts or modules of a product, rather than having to buy everything together. For example,

investors used to buy a bundled service from stockbrokers, comprising advice and execution; now, execution-only services exist for those who do not need advice. Every supplier should ask whether there is an opportunity or threat from unbundling. See BUSINESS SEGMENT.

UNIVERSAL PRODUCT

One that is sold in the same form throughout the world, like the original model-T Ford, or Coca-Cola, the Mars bar or the Big Mac, or indeed, the Macintosh computer. In many ways this is the American dream: a standard product, made up of defined and highly controlled parts (thus the servant of analysis), high quality and low cost, capable of being rolled out around the world for ever. The two keys are the widest possible product appeal, based on the insight that people around the world may be different, but consumers are the same; and standardised manufacture, so that the product can be produced cheaply and to the same standards anywhere around the world. In a way the whole concept of business strategy à la BCG or PORTER is a vision of a Universal Product, battling against the cultural peculiarities of different nations. Note that the idea of a Universal Product could never have originated in France or Germany, and these countries have a poor record in producing Universal Products.

VALUE CHAIN

A firm's co-ordinated set of activities to satisfy customer needs, starting with relationships with suppliers and procurement, going through production, selling and marketing, and delivery to the customer. Each stage of the value chain is linked with the next stage, and looks forward to the customer's needs, and backwards from the customer too. Each link in the value chain must seek COMPETITIVE ADVANTAGE: it must either be lower cost than the corresponding link in competing firms, or add more value by superior quality or differentiated features. The basic idea behind the value chain has been around ever since the concept of value added and COST STRUCTURES, but was first made explicit by Michael PORTER in 1980. See also COMPETITIVE ADVANTAGE and PORTER.

VIRTUOUS CIRCLE

The opposite of a DOOM LOOP: when a firm is able to continuously reinforce a strong position. Illustration 3.34 shows how a virtuous circle can operate:

Illustration 3.34
Do you have a good strategy?

1. Who are your five most important competitiors?

2. Are you more or less profitable than these firms?.

3. Do you generally have higher or lower prices than these firms, for equivalent product/service offering? Is this difference due mainly to the mix of customers, to different costs, or to different requirements for profit?

4. Do you have higher or lower relative costs than your main competitors? Where in the COST STRUCTURE (for example, cost of raw materials, cost of production, cost of selling, cost of distributing, cost of advertising and marketing) are the differences most pronounced?

5. Define the different BUSINESS SEGMENTS which account for 80% of your profits. Be careful to apply the segmentation criteria given in the entry for SEGMENTATION above. You will probably find that you are in many more segments than you thought, and that their profit variability is much greater. If you cannot define the segments that constitute 80% of your total profits, you need to conduct a detailed PRODUCT LINE PROFITABILITY review.

6. In each of the business segments defined above, how large are you relative to the largest of your competitors? Position each of the businesses on the BCG MATRIX and the OPPORTUNITY/VULNERABILITY MATRIX. Are you gaining or losing relative market share? Why?

7. In each of your important business segments what are your customers' and potential customers' most important purchase criteria?

8. How do you and your main competitors in each segement rate on these market purchase criteria? (See COMB ANALYSIS.)

9. What are the main strengths of the company as a whole, based on aggregating customers' views of your firm in the segments that comprise most of your profits? What other COMPETENCES do you believe the firm has, and why do they not seem to be appreciated by the market?

10. Which are your priority segments, where it is most important to the firm as a whole that you gain market share? How confident are you that you will achieve this, given that other firms may have targeted the same segments for share gain? What is your competitive advantage in these segments and how sure are you that this advantage is real rather than imagined (if you are not gaining relative market share the advantage is probably illusory)?

Vision, an inspiring view of what a company could become, a dream about its future shape and success, a picture of a potential future for a firm, a glimpse into its Promised Land. A vision is the long term aspiration of a leader for his or her firm, that can be described to colleagues and that will urge them on through the desert.

The word vision is often used as a synonym for MISSION, particularly in non-English speaking countries, where 'mission' is difficult to translate. But the two concepts are different. Mission is why a firm exists, its role in life. Vision is a view of what the firm could become, imagining a desired future.

Vision may be thought of as reaching a future goal. A good example of a vision that was fulfilled was President Kennedy's preposterous pledge in 1961 of 'achieving the goal, before this decade is out, of landing a man on the moon and returning him safely to earth'. An industrial equivalent may be the number 26 in the world league table of drug companies aiming to reach the top five by the year 2000. Another popular vision is for a regional (say, European) company to become 'truly global', where this is defined as having at least 25 per cent of sales and profits in each TRIAD of the world (North America, Asia and Europe). Another vision is for a small company to become larger than its largest competitor, or for a derided airline to become 'the world's favourite'. It was a vision of Marvin Bower in the 1940s to think that McKinsey, a small, regional US consultancy, could become a huge firm with offices all around the world and with a reputation for developing professional management. Likewise, it was Henry Ford's vision in 1909 to 'democratise the automobile'. Steve Jobs' vision at Apple was to change work habits by making PCs user friendly to normal executives. The vision at IKEA was to change for ever the structure of the furniture market, become the first and leading global competitor in an industry previously dominated by separate national leaders. And so on.

Many writers imply that a new leader should have a ready-made vision from the start or in the early stages of the TRANSFORMATION process. This is wrong. The best visions evolve from experience during the first five years of a transformation process. In the early stages it is best to concentrate on making a break with the past, developing a cadre of supporters of the change process, modifying values, and obtaining early commercial successes with the new approach. Once real progress has been made, the leader should lift up his or her eyes, and identify the vision.

See also TYPE 1, MISSION and VALUES.

VULNERABILITY

The extent to which a firm faces threats; the degree to which sales and profits may come under attack. Vulnerability is not the opposite of profitability; rather, it is its soft underbelly. Many very profitable firms are highly vulnerable.

Vulnerability exists when any of the following conditions apply:

- *when high profitability (measured by ROS or ROCE) co-exists with a poor relative market share (RMS) position*
- *when a firm is more profitable than competitors yet has lower productivity per employee*
- *when RMS is being lost to at least one more aggressive competitor*
- *when depreciation exceeds new capital investment over a sustained period*
- *when the rate of investment in new capacity is lower than that of one or more competitors*
- *when expense investment in R&D, marketing and management development is lower than that of competitors*
- *when competitors have access to greater cost sharing, shared technological development, a superior supplier network, or better distribution*
- *when some of the best people have been leaving, for whatever reasons*
- *when it is difficult to recruit the best people in the industry into the firm*
- *when the firm is locked into SEGMENT RETREAT, conceding more and more markets and focussing on a narrower customer base*
- *when competitors can bring out new products faster*
- *when competitors have owners that will accept a lower rate of investment return or lower dividends.*

Vulnerability exists, in short, when a business has been HARVESTING its position, preferring short term profits to long term reinvestment, or, conversely, when a competitor has been doing the reverse, investing for the future, to a greater extent. Systematic identification of when companies are vulnerable, or the opposite (what we may perhaps call latent opportunity), is the key to identifying shifts in relative market share and is a leading indicator of future swings in shareholder value. See OPPORTUNITY/VULNERABILITY MATRIX.

ZEUS

One of Charles HANDY's four GODS OF MANAGEMENT. A Zeus culture is a club based around one leader, so that the organisation can best be depicted not as a normal hierarchy (as on a pyramid-like organisation chart) but as a series of lines running into the centre, where the leader (Zeus) sits; or as a web radiating out from this centre. The concentric lines closest to the centre represent the greatest power (apart from Zeus himself); power and influence are measured by the amount of time that Zeus spends with each executive and the regard in which Zeus holds him or her.

The culture is the norm in young, entrepreneurial firms, and also in investment banks, boutiques of all sorts, small and medium-sized brokers, any small professional service firms, in politics, sport and the performing arts.

The great advantages of the Zeus culture are (1) speed of decision taking; (2) empathy, trust and emotional commitment ('what would Zeus do in this circumstance?'); and (3) lean and economical structure and absence of bureaucracy (no memos, committees or corporate politics).

Zeus organisations can be amateur, blinkered, inequitable, cruel, and riddled with courtiers rather than good professional managers. But equally, with high quality people, Zeus organisations can exhibit great flair, unleash enormous energy and commitment, and change the world. Microsoft is a Zeus organisation; so too are (or were) The Body Shop (with the more dominant Zeus being female), Egon Zehnder, GEC, Filofax, Hanson, LL Bean, Mars, Maxwell Communications Corporation, McKinsey, Polly Peck and Virgin. Lonrho was a Zeus organisation before Tiny Rowland ceded power to Dieter Beck. Succession is always a major issue.

Zeus organisations flout all the laws of scientific management and most of the classic management principles that we still implicitly believe in. Zeus organisations are the wave of the past but also the wave of the future. See also ATHENA, APOLLO, and DIONYSUS.

INDEX

Dear Pitman Publishing Customer

IMPORTANT – Please Read This Now!

We are delighted to announce a special free service for all of our customers.

Simply complete this form and return it to the FREEPOST address overleaf to receive:

A Free Customer Newsletter

B Free Information Service

C Exclusive Customer Offers – which have included free software, videos and relevant products

D Opportunity to take part in product development sessions

E The chance for you to write about your own business experience and become one of our respected authors

Fill this in now and return it to us (no stamp needed in the UK) to join our customer information service.

Name: _____ Position: _____

Company/Organisation: _____

Address (including postcode): _____

Country: _____

Telephone: _____ Fax: _____

Nature of business: _____

Title of book purchased: _____

ISBN (printed on back cover): `0` `2` `7` `3` ☐ ☐ ☐ ☐ ☐

Comments: _____

-------------------------------- | Fold Here Then Staple Once | --------------------------------

We would be very grateful if you could answer these questions to help us with market research.

1 Where/How did you hear of this book?

☐ in a bookshop

☐ in a magazine/newspaper (please state which): _____

☐ information through the post

☐ recommendation from a colleague

☐ other (please state which): _____

2 Where did you buy this book

☐ Direct from Pitman Publishing

☐ From a bookclub

☐ From a bookshop (state which)

3 Which newspaper(s)/magazine(s) do you read regularly?:

4 When buying a business book which factors influence you most?

(Please rank in order)

☐ recommendation from a colleague

☐ price

☐ content

☐ recommendation in a bookshop

☐ author

☐ publisher

☐ title

☐ other(s):

5 Is this book a

☐ personal purchase?

☐ company purchase?

6 Would you be prepared to spend a few minutes talking to our customer services staff to help with product development? YES/NO

We occasionally make our customer lists available to companies whose products or services we feel may be of interest. If you do not want this service write 'exclude from other mailings' on this card. The Customer Information Service is liable to change without notice.

The Business Publisher

Written for managers competing in today's tough business world, our books will give you a competitive edge by showing you how to:

● increase quality, efficiency and productivity throughout your organisation
● use both proven and innovative management techniques
● improve your management skills and those of your staff
● implement winning customer strategies

In short they provide concise, practical information that you can use every

Free Information Service
Pitman Professional Publishing
FREEPOST
128 Long Acre
LONDON
WC2E 9BR, UK

No stamp
necessary
in the UK